OUTDOOR PURSUITS PROGRAMMING

OUTDOOR PURSUITS PROGRAMMING
Legal Liability and Risk Management

Glenda Hanna

THE UNIVERSITY OF ALBERTA PRESS

First published by
The University of Alberta Press
Athabasca Hall
Edmonton, Alberta
Canada T6G 2E8

Copyright © 1991 The University of Alberta Press

ISBN 0-88864-205-9 cloth
0-88864-206-7 paper

Canadian Cataloguing in Publication Data
Hanna, Glenda, 1957-

Outdoor Pursuits Programming

Includes bibliographical references.
ISBN 0-88864-205-9 (bound).—ISBN 0-88864-206-7 (pbk.)

1. Outdoor recreation - Law and legislation
- Canada. 2. Liability for sports accidents
- Canada. I. Title.
KE3792.H36 1991   346.7103'2   C90-019015-1

DISCLAIMER

The reader is cautioned that the information provided in this book is not intended as an absolute legal reference, but merely as a guide for outdoor education/recreation practitioners, based on statutory, common and case law as they exist at this time. The writer is an outdoor educator and not a member of the legal profession. She does not assume any responsiblity for the conduct of individuals acting on the content of this text.

Typesetting by The Typeworks, Vancouver, British Columbia.
Printed by John Deyell Company, Lindsay, Ontario, Canada

Printed on acid free paper. ∞

This book is dedicated to my husband
Michael Timothy William Hanna

CONTENTS

ACKNOWLEDGEMENTS

I would like to thank a number of people who generously gave their time and energy to this book.

Warmest heartfelt appreciation is extended to Dr. Harvey Scott, my mentor and friend, whose constant encouragement made this research a pleasure to pursue. Very special thanks also go to Dr. Gerry Glassford and Professor Ellen Picard, whose energy, time, and informed advice were much appreciated.

I would also like to gratefully acknowledge assistance, feedback, and enthusiasm for this work received from Dr. Richard Moriarty, Dr. Robert Wilkinson, Mr. Bill March, Ms. Donna Hawley, and Professor Lewis Klar.

The Alberta Foundation for the Literary Arts provided funds toward publication.

Last, but certainly not least, to my dear husband Michael, who for weeks tiptoed around the house wearing his Walkman so I could write and edit in peace, thank you.

1 IS THE RISK WORTH TAKING?

HUMANS HAVE ALWAYS been risk takers. It was some fifteen million years ago that our arboreal prehuman ancestors took their first tentative steps out of the trees and onto the grasslands and plains. Here they confronted wild animals, droughts, floods and other perils. They quickly learned to adapt their primitive skills to survive in this new and challenging element.

Over the millennia, humans developed along with their technologies. It was a vastly advanced species who first set sail from the Old World to face the risks involved in uncharted open sea exploration and the search for new lands. The neoclassical Viking adventurers, who first landed in Newfoundland almost two thousand years ago, began exploring this New World. They soon discovered aboriginal North Americans whose more primitive lifestyle must have appeared fraught with risk and hardship.

Almost as fast as the land was mapped, charted by daring scientific explorers like David Thompson and Sir Alexander Mackenzie, so it was exploited by merchant adventurers, fur traders and voyageurs. All of these brave venturers faced not only those hazards created by the harsh environment, but also those frequently related to the inhospitable natives they encountered.

When the land had been duly conquered and settled, romantic adventurers turned their philosophical minds to notions of the inherent value of exploring wild areas en route to discovering self. The ideals of Henry David Thoreau and John Muir and their successors have been reflected in the growth and development of the existing outdoor movement.

I

Contemporary urban society has learned to protect itself from most of the natural risks faced by our ancestors and has replaced them with risks inherent to many of today's technologically complex "necessities": motorized transportation, electrical and nuclear energy, and the development and utilization of an ever increasing number of largely synthetic and often toxic substances. Although every member of Canadian society is affected in one way or another by these factors, actual risk of injury or premature death has been increasingly minimized through improved production standards, government regulations and medical technology. As a direct result of living in this somewhat sterilized society, the lives of most Canadians, while longer, have become relatively routine and mundane.

Over the past two decades, the increased popularity of recreational pursuits involving inherent elements of challenge, adventure and risk has been a largely unintended reaction designed to combat urbanization and associated boredom. Numerous factors such as increased population and urbanization, increased mobility, advances in clothing and equipment and media coverage have all been influential in this trend.[1] However, the need to see and experience the land, to confront different risks and challenges, and to be temporarily relieved from "city stress" has been the common denominator promoting all outdoor pursuits (such as backpacking, canoeing, cross-country skiing) currently in vogue.[2]

Leaders in Canadian school systems, as well as a wide variety of public and private education and recreation agencies have seen first-hand the physical, intellectual and social benefits derivable from participation in these types of leisure activities and have hence become directly involved as programmers and facilitators of these types of experiences, especially for youth. The late Bill March, leader of the 1984 Canadian Everest Expedition and Outdoor Pursuits Co-ordinator at The University of Calgary, believed:

> [The teaching of] ... outdoor pursuits has attracted the educationalists as an extremely potent tool in the development of the fully actualized person. The element of interpersonal competition, an all-pervasive and not always healthy aspect of modern living, is subordinated to an inner growth of self, others and the environment.[3]

Adventure education/recreation can also be viewed as a complement to our increasingly technological orientation, helping bring balance to our information-rich and experience-poor lives. John Naisbitt, in his best selling book, *Megatrends*, noted that "whenever new technology is introduced into society, there must be a counterbalancing human response—that is, high touch."[4] The wilderness environment is the most natural high touch environment imaginable. Wilderness experiences can help us appreciate our creative potential and promote a more holistic view of intelligence. They can help us distinguish between the excessive "I want" in favor of an attitude of voluntary simplicity; the "I need." The power of outdoor education as a means of improving the participant's perceived competence and feelings of self-determination, in short, an enhanced self-concept, has been well substantiated and documented by a number of researchers.[5] Finally, outdoor experiences can foster a willingness to take real risks with real consequences and to understand that personal action or inaction can and does make a difference.[6]

Given these powerful testimonials to the potential benefits of outdoor programs, it is disturbing to think that liability and insurance concerns are affecting their vitality and in fact, their very viability. However, because of the inevitability of accidents (a statement of fact), the subsequent potential for resulting legal litigation and the ever increasing problem of finding affordable insurance coverage, many school boards and recreation delivery agencies and associations are questioning the validity of offering such activities as part of their curricula or program. In their efforts to avoid legal reprisal, many potential lifetime leisure activities have been either completely avoided, discontinued or taught in a manner which has rendered them so safe that they no longer contain the essential ingredients of risk and excitement. The "watered down" remnants have often been labelled "too soft, too dull, and too ordinary."[7]

Even by understanding the basis of legal liability in outdoor education and recreation and how accidents, which may result in unfavorable litigation, can be avoided, it must be realized that the practitioners' fears of litigation are not completely unfounded. The last decade has seen a tremendous increase in the number of civil suits brought against the professions in general (for example, law, medicine, education), and a concomitant increase in the standard of care expected by these people has not made the situation any easier. "Nowhere are these trends more noticeable or causing more concern, than in our educational system" says Donald Rogers, a lawyer and solicitor for the North York Board of Education in Ontario.[8] He attributes these trends to society's decreased individualism and increased reliance on government. He also sees an ever increasing association with large corporate entities and smaller, but well insured private enterprises, which allow us to become emotionally distanced from them.

Betty van der Smissen, an American lawyer and a prolific writer in the area of legal liability in the physical education/recreation professions, believes that today's suits against the individual "indicate a lack of the old sense of community feeling."[9] She thinks that it has been replaced with the somewhat questionable attitude that regardless of fault, society "owes" the individual in the event of an injury. As Rogers notes, "The public of today is less and less likely to accept misfortune as a fact of life and is more inclined to look to the courts for compensation."[10]

Although most school boards and recreation delivery agencies have been well insured against negligence, the international insurance crisis of the mid-eighties has reduced, and in some cases eliminated, this protective cushion. Those instructors and leaders teaching or guiding so-called "high-risk" activities (and insurance companies consider most outdoor pursuits as high-risk activities) are quite justly concerned and anxious to know and understand what standards of performance the courts expect of them.

THE OUTDOOR LEADER—A CONCEPTUAL DEFINITION

There are probably as many definitions of the terms "outdoor education," "outdoor recreation" and "outdoor leader" as there are individuals working in this area. Outdoor education is an umbrella term which includes all activities and processes which rely, at least in part, on the natural environment and which are oriented to enhancing the individual's achievement of a variety of educational objectives.[11] Educational objectives are typically outcome oriented (utilitarian), are of long-term interest and are time/situation independent (that is, a variety of processes, usually experiential, may be used to achieve these same outcomes). Outdoor education includes adventure education and environmental education. Outdoor pursuits are activities, such as camping, backpacking, canoeing, rock climbing and skiing, which may be used to achieve a variety of adventure education, environmental education, and/or recreation ends.

Adventure education emphasizes engagement in outdoor pursuit activities and utilizes progressive stress/challenge situations and uncertainty of outcome to enhance the individual's intrapersonal (self-knowledge) and interpersonal (social) skills. Environmental education involves educational activities oriented toward the enhancement of ecological knowledge and awareness of our relationship with the natural environment. Its ultimate objective is the development of an environmentally conscious and active citizenry.[12]

Outdoor recreation includes all activities and processes undertaken in, or relying in large part on, the natural environment, during nonobligatory time, for recreational as opposed to educational purposes. Outcomes are typically nonwork related, short-term and time/situation specific.[13] One component of outdoor recreation is adventure recreation, referring to explorations in wildland environments with some physical risk, challenge and uncertainty of outcome present. In true adventure situations, outcomes are influenced by the actions of the individual and circumstances.[14] The recreational adventurer progressively seeks higher levels of risk in order to test skills and strategies and to improve them as necessary.[15] Adventure recreation often involves pursuits carried out at higher objective risk levels than adventure education programs can educationally defend.

However, there is, to date, no universally accepted definition of "outdoor education" or "outdoor recreation" in Canada, Britain, Australia, the United States or any other country. For example, Backiel[16] did a replicative thesis, comparing American Association for Health, Physical Education and Recreation (AAHPER)(now AAHPERD) Outdoor Education Council members' attitudes toward the term "outdoor education." Even with a 71 percent return rate on her questionnaire, she found that the responses were so variable that it was impossible to distinguish what the population discerned as the meaning of the term.

A number of reasons exist for this lack of agreement concerning the content of the discipline of "outdoor education," and even more exist regarding the qualifications and certifications which are commensurate to the recognition of individuals as outdoor educators. First, outdoor education is a relatively young field. Doctors, lawyers and most other professionals and paraprofessionals have been recognized by function and by their organization for centuries, whereas a resurgence in broad interest outdoor programs and development of outdoor clubs and organizations has only really begun to grow within the last 20 to 30 years.

A second crucial factor in the slow growth of this area is the lack of a unifying organizational or administrative governing body or association. Although a number of activity-specific governing bodies and professional associations exist in Canada (such as the Canadian Association of Nordic

Ski Instructors, Canadian Ski Association, Canadian Recreational Canoeing Association, Canadian Orienteering Federation, and the Association of Canadian Mountain Guides), the closest these groups have come to a nationally representative organization is the Canadian Association for Health, Physical Education and Recreation (CAHPER) Outdoor Committee, with about 150 members who are primarily involved in outdoor education as school teachers, physical education consultants and university professors.

This committee, like its American counterpart, has been unsuccessful in its previous attempts at arriving at unanimously acceptable definitions of the terms "outdoor education" and "outdoor educator." The list of the activities, teaching and leadership methodologies and environmental components the members of this group have pursued in the guise of outdoor education in this country is extensive. In a 1980-81 study by the author and others,[17] a nationwide survey of CAHPER Outdoor Committee members and other known outdoor education practitioners indicated that the most commonly held certifications, perceived as vital for leaders involved in the delivery of these programs and curricula, were:

1. A St. John's Ambulance First Aid certificate (33 percent)
2. A Royal Life Saving Society Lifesaving Award (Bronze Medallion assumed) (28 percent)
3. A Red Cross Water Safety Award (23 percent)
4. A teaching certificate from the province of the individual's employ (23 percent)

About 56 percent of the agencies responding to the questionnaire either provided one or more certification programs or required their leaders to hold one or more certifications. However, other than the first aid, aquatic and teaching awards mentioned, most organizations appear to be selecting their leaders' certifications on an ad hoc basis; little or no consistency existed among the provinces.

The vast majority (78 percent of respondents) appeared to see some value in the promotion of certifications to facilitate the development and selection of outdoor leaders, as long as they do not provide the sole criterion. However, a small but vociferous group (22 percent) indicated strong opposition to the use or promotion of certifications for these purposes. These individuals and the agencies and boards they represent advocated practical experience and apprenticeship as the best means to developing in leaders the judgment, empathy, initiative and other desirable leadership characteristics not perceived to be nurtured in existing technical skill oriented certification programs. This same attitude was reinforced by a nationally representative panel[18] and by a presentation by March on "The Pros and Cons of Outdoor Education Certification," both heard at the 1981 CAHPER conference in Victoria.

Overall, it appears that strong leadership experiential qualifications are valued somewhat more than certifications and that leaders are by and large selected on the basis of their experience and perceived judgmental abilities, commensurate with the risk perceived in the activity to be pursued. These results were again supported in a 1981 Alberta Law Foundation Study, carried out by The University of Calgary, and coordinated in part by the author.[19] In a section entitled "A Survey of Population, Program Standards and Liability Factors in Outdoor Risk Activities in Alberta," Grav noted that personal and job related outdoor experience were deemed the most important criteria assessed by Alberta employers (65 and 62 percent, respectively).[20] The 49 respondents ranked federal (55 percent) and provincial (45 percent) certifications as the next most desirable factors. However, he also noted that a number of the agencies participating were bound by statute to hiring individuals with certain prescribed certifications (for example, teaching certification, national park guiding certification, a university degree).[21]

The study done for the Alberta Law Foundation focused on a wide variety of Alberta public and private agencies and camps. Alberta has been nationally regarded as one of the most certification/regulation oriented provinces in the country with respect to the outdoor programming area, undoubtedly due in large part to national park regulations requiring National Park guiding or Association of Canadian Mountain Guides certification for high country entrepreneurial leaders.

Since no single source may be drawn upon in presenting a satisfactory definition of who qualifies as an outdoor leader in the Canadian context, a fairly broad operational definition of the outdoor leader includes the following parameters:

1. An outdoor leader may work as an outdoor education or recreation program instructor/leader or facilitator and/or as an agency administrator where the latter's responsibilities may pertain to agency liability or to vicarious liability for subordinates in the field.
2. An outdoor leader may be responsible for any number of program participants, from as few as one or two in the case of a guide to as many as 15 or 20 in the case of some agencies and camps.
3. No definite age delineations can be made for leaders. Although for

most leaders it is assumed that they are over the age of 16, a large number of adolescent leaders or counsellors-in-training open to liability would not meet the standard expected of their elders.

4. An outdoor leader can either be paid or working as a volunteer. Although the majority of people working in the field are paid for their services, there are a tremendous number of volunteers involved as well (such as Boy Scouts/Girl Guides, YMCA/YWCA leaders and leaders-in-training).

5. An outdoor leader may operate programs in any environment from municipal parkland to true wilderness setting. The emphasis here, however, is placed on the wildland environment in which most agencies and camps function (such as private lands, national, provincial and municipal parks and crown lands).

Outdoor participants come in all ages and ranges of abilities and disabilities. However, for three reasons children from the ages of 6 to 18 are most often involved in accidents resulting in legal actions. First, this group accounts for the largest number of participants in outdoor programs. Second, due to inexperience and impulsiveness, youths in this age range appear to have the greatest propensity for accidents. Finally, case law indicates that adults are most often held personally accountable for exposing themselves to risks common in the out-of-doors and therefore are less successful in bringing actions against others.

There are a wide variety of activities currently being taught in outdoor education/recreation programs. Although for this study an emphasis was placed on nonmotorized activities, there are few limits to the types of activities that can be included in outdoor education/recreation programs today.

2 AN OVERVIEW OF THE CANADIAN LEGAL SYSTEM

SOURCES OF CANADIAN LAW

IN ORDER TO INTERPRET and apply the law, the courts must rely upon a number of "sources" which establish what the law is. These sources have traditionally been divided into two categories: (1) *legal* sources, which are in essence "the authority of any proposition of law," and (2) *literary* sources, which serve primarily in the recording of legal sources.[1]

The two most commonly used legal sources of Canadian law are: (1) legislated statutory enactments and (2) the rationale behind decisions in adjudicated cases, commonly referred to as "case law." Other legal sources include subordinate legislation which may take the form of by-laws, ordinances, statutory instruments, orders-in-council and rules and regulations "enacted by a person, body or tribunal subordinate to a sovereign legislative body."[2] Two other factors in Canadian law which, although used rather infrequently, may be of particular relevance to outdoor and recreation programs include custom or convention and judicial morality.[3] Literary sources include books of authority written by notable scholars and various aids used in locating legal source material.[4]

Statute Law and Its Interpretation

Legislatively enacted statutes are the most important source of law. The consistency and precision of the statutes created by Canada's elected parliament and provincial legislatures make them the first course the courts

9

take in attempting to settle a dispute. In fact, a judge must apply relevant statutes even if not personally in agreement with them.

Fortunately, statute law is alterable through a repeal by the legislative body which created it or through the creation of a new statute to replace an outdated one. This may be done to determine the law where none previously existed or to affirm or reverse a standing judicial decision.

Examples of statutory acts which outdoor leaders should be familiar with may include education oriented acts such as *Teaching Profession Acts, Education and School Acts* and others such as *National* and *Provincial Parks Acts, Occupiers' Liability Acts, Emergency Medical Aid Acts* and the *Highway Acts.*

Although, due to the imprecision of our language, the interpretation of statutes is occasionally a problem, it should normally be soluble by attempting to determine the intention of the legislator in relation to a given set of facts, and then applying the statute accordingly.[5] This means that the wording of a statute should be interpreted as literally as possible, but where ambiguity exists, the words must be considered in their context.

In 1982, Canada patriated its constitution through the enactment of its own *Constitution Act*, R.S.C. 1982. Many relevant cases have already been heard, but the scope and implications of the new constitution on negligence law will not be discussed here. Current texts on this subject may be consulted if this topic is of interest.

Case Law and the Rule of Precedent

Case law is the second major legal source of law in Canada with the exception of Quebec. The distinction between English speaking Canada's "common law" provinces and Quebec's "civil law" system is an important one. The fundamental difference between the common law and civil law approaches lies in the relationship between case situations and accepted principles of law. Quebec's civil law system begins with the civil code: a set of accepted legal principles. Individual cases are then decided on the basis of the judge's interpretation of these pre-established tenets.

The common law approach is to study the judgments of previous cases and extract general principles which are then applied to specific problems at hand.[6] The common law's case law grew out of "the principles enunciated through the decisions of courts over the past six hundred years... initially in Great Britain and subsequently in Canada."[7] While not purposely avoiding Quebec, the vast majority of cases relevant to the topic of this book have been decided in common law provinces and this system will subsequently receive much more attention.

The case law source of law continues to develop and expand its principles and content as new fact situations arise and are decided upon by judges. With each new case, the judge in making a decision identifies the reason(s) for that decision (called the *ratio decidendi*) and the legal principle laid down must be followed (subject to certain reservations) by other judges dealing with subsequent similar situations.

This compulsory adherence to previous decisions is known as the rule of precedent. The courts are bound to abide by this rule of precedent in accordance with the doctrine of *stare decisis*, which literally means "to stand by decided matters," and which states that once a court has laid down a principle of law as applicable to a certain state of facts, it will abide by or adhere to that principle and apply it to all future cases in which the facts are essentially the same.[8]

The purposes of the rule of precedent are probably twofold. First, it removes some of the responsibility and accompanying psychological pressure from judges by allowing them to justify their decisions through reference to previous findings. Second, it helps ensure order and consistency and hence, fairness and credibility in the common law system.[9]

In Canada, this rule of precedent is manifested in the country's hierarchical court structure. This means that the law in each court is binding on any and all courts subordinate to that court. Therefore:

1. Supreme Court of Canada decisions are binding on all other courts in the land.
2. Provincial Supreme Court (Appellate Division) decisions are binding on all courts of that particular province.
3. Provincial Supreme Court (Trial Division) decisions are binding on all District and Provincial Judges' Courts.
4. District Court decisions are binding on Provincial Judges' Court decisions.

Decisions of all provincial level courts, from Judges' Court to the Provincial Court of Appeal, will only be of persuasive value in the decision making which occurs in the courts of the other provinces and territories. The degree of their persuasive influence is directly related to their relative position in the hierarchy in relation to the particular out of province court attempting to settle the case at hand.[10]

To look at the process in another light, a decision made in any court, save the Supreme Court of Canada, may be appealed in a higher court and the higher court will have the authority to affirm or overturn the decision of the lower court. Supreme Court of Canada decisions can only be altered or reversed by a subsequent Supreme Court of Canada decision, or by an act of legislature.

In addition to the appeal process, a number of other judicially recognized procedures have been adopted by the courts in order to mitigate the rigidity and inflexibility inherent in a system which operates under the doctrines of precedent and *stare decisis* and to satisfy the dictates of justice and fairness. The best example of these processes is called "distinguishing" where a case is decided on its own merit and not according to persuasive or binding precedents. To distinguish a case, the court must demonstrate significant differences between either the societal situation or the specific facts of the case at hand in comparison with the earlier ones.[11]

As with statute law, the existence of various mechanisms which permit modification of the common law (for example, appeals, distinguishing) facilitate its dynamic growth with the society it is intended to serve. Unfortunately, its constant state of flux also results in a certain degree of instability and uncertainty, not only for the layperson, but also for the legal practitioner who must interpret it.

Custom or Convention

While not a legal source of law, custom or convention is often drawn upon in education/recreation cases in the provision of expert evidence which may lead to decisions in these cases. Custom refers to a practice or application of methods, which by common oft-repeated use by the people of a society, comes to acquire the force of law with respect to the place and subject matter to which it relates. Where no statutes or case law exists to set a precedent, a court will often assess existing conventions to determine their validity.

The validity of a custom has been traditionally evaluated according to Gladstone's six criteria: (1) antiquity, (2) continuance, (3) peaceable enjoyment, (4) obligatory force, (5) certainty, (6) consistency.[12] Technically, the criteria of antiquity means that the custom must be traceable back to at least 1189. Fortunately, in actual practice the courts are normally willing to accept as law, customs which meet the remaining criteria and which can be shown to have been in existence for a significantly long period of time. However, the problem of ascertaining what constitutes a "significantly long period of time" remains; when does an "oft-repeated practice" acquire the power of law?

Morality

Again, while perhaps not a source of law in the technical intent of the term, an important factor in the development of common law remedies lies in the concept of morality. In cases where no statutes or adjudicated precedents are applicable and where custom and convention are either nonexistent or extremely conflicting and variable, the judge "must find out for himself; he must determine what the law ought to be; he must have recourse to the principle of morality."[13] Although situations such as these are typically rare, the relative infancy of the field of outdoor education/recreation may lead to more than one decision being made through this final recourse.

A judge assessing such a case is likely to weigh on his or her imaginary judicial scales, the social utility of the activity (in this case, benefits accrued through participation in the outdoor activity) on the one side and the probability of loss (injury or death) on the other side. The fulcrum of the scale represents the relative cost of increasing the safeness of the activity, without sacrificing its supposed benefits to the participant.

DIVISIONS OF CANADIAN LAW

The various sources of law manifest themselves in a number of categories or divisions of law. Although each division is intimately related to all other divisions, only a simple description of the entire structure is included here. The differences between public and private law and also among a few of the subdivisions of private law, one of which is the tort law on which this book will focus, will be illustrated.

I. Substantive Law
  A. Public Law
     1. Constitutional Law
     2. Criminal Law
     3. Administrative Law

B. Private Law
   1. Contract Law
   2. Tort Law
   3. Property Law
   4. Others

In this divisional summary, the positive domestic or "substantive" legal principles identified in the legal sources of Canadian law are reviewed. This division of law as opposed to public international law is oriented toward governing the people of Canada. Substantive law is delineated into two divisions, public and private law.

Public Law

Public law includes constitutional, administrative, criminal, and taxation law; the four areas of the law where the public interest is involved. Of these four subdivisions, criminal law can be identified as an example of public law and used to differentiate it from private law.

Criminal law involves the judgment of offences committed "against the state, against the people and against the public interest,"[14] as opposed to wrongs done to specific individuals. It serves to punish individual criminals, to protect society from them and to deter others from following similar courses of action; restitution of wrongs is not one of its objectives.

In a criminal proceeding, the crown prosecutes the accused individual for violating one of its criminal statutes, for criminal law is almost entirely statute law. If the accused is found guilty of intentionally committing a crime, then he or she is convicted and sentenced, usually to a fine or term of incarceration in a federal or provincial government operated rehabilitation institution.

Private Law

Private law, or civil law as it is more commonly known, involves the attempts of one individual to claim restitution from another individual believed to have wronged him or her. As illustrated in the divisional summary, there are a great many subdivisions of private law, far too many to consider here.

The only type of private law this book will deal with is tort or negligence law, where one individual is attempting to receive compensation (usually financial), for an injury(ies) received due to the perceived negligence of the person being sued. Tort law has the compensation of victims as its primary aim and usually not the punishment or rehabilitation of the defendant (person/organization being sued).

In a civil tort action, the plaintiff (person seeking remuneration) sues the defendant and if the plaintiff wins, the court orders the defendant to pay the assessed damages to the plaintiff.

Although the objectives, procedures and results of public versus private law cases appear to differ quite dramatically, the distinction lies more in the legal consequences of the action than in the actual nature of the act or omission itself. As is frequently seen, the same set of facts may constitute both a crime and a civil wrong, and therefore be tried in both courts.[15] For example, an impaired driver involved in a motor vehicle accident may face criminal charges for impaired driving as well as a civil suit brought by one injured through a driver's recklessness.

THE CANADIAN COURT SYSTEM

In 1867, the *British North America Act* granted the Parliament of Canada the right to establish a Supreme Court of Canada[16] and the provinces of Canada, the right to create the necessary courts in each province[17] to enforce the laws of the land. Although minor variations exist, especially at the lower court levels, the courts present in any province include the following:

The Supreme Court of Canada
The Supreme Court of a Province
    Appellate Division
    Trial Division
County or District Courts
Surrogate Courts
Provincial Court
    Juvenile Court
    Family Court
    Provincial Court (Criminal Division)
    Small Claims Court[18]

The functions of each given court may be found in the enabling statutes establishing that particular court (such as *The Supreme Court Act, The District Courts Act, The Provincial Courts Act*). In addition, *The Judicature Act* and the rules of court are examples of other types of statute law distinct from the enabling court legislation, which must be considered in defining the jurisdiction of a Provincial Supreme Court. It becomes readily apparent that the sources which identify the functions of any particular court are numerous and complex.

The Supreme Court of Canada

According to the *Supreme Court Act*:

> The Supreme Court shall have, hold and exercise exclusive ultimate appellate civil and criminal jurisdiction within and for Canada; and the judgment of the Court is, and for all cases, final and conclusive.[19]

This general court of appeal is presided over by one Chief Justice, who is also the acting Chief Justice of Canada and eight Prusine Justices.[20] At least five of these Justices must be present to hold court.[21]

In terms of civil case authority, the Supreme Court hears all appeals under the 1975 amendment to the *Supreme Court Act*, but only if the issue is of public or legal import or of mixed law and fact. In addition, there is no stipulation as to the quantum of money involved in the case; the legal principle evolving from the case is more crucial than the settlement in the particular case.[22]

The Supreme Court of a Province

This court is the highest level court with criminal and civil jurisdiction in the province.[23] The majority of cases and appeals from lower courts are heard within the Trial division of this court.[24] All civil matters over a set monetary amount also are heard here.

The Appellate division of this court will hear, among other duties, all civil matter appeals from District or County Court and Supreme Court, Trial Division.

County or District Courts

Most provinces have two or more County or District Courts and again their function in civil cases will be to hear those disputes within a predetermined geographical and monetary jurisdiction.[25]

The Surrogate Court

Surrogate Court cases are adjudicated by County or District Court judges and normally deal with issues such as testamentary matters and wills and the guardianship of children.[26]

Provincial Courts

This court is subdivided into Juvenile Court, Family Court, the Provincial Court (Criminal Division) and Small Claims Court, none of which is likely to be relevant to the topic at hand.

The courts with which people should be familiar are the County or District Courts in their area, both divisions of the Supreme Court of their province and of course, the Supreme Court of Canada. A tort case may be initiated in either the County or District Court in an area, or the Trial Division of the Supreme Court of the province in which the incident occurred if the claim for damages exceeds the stipulated minimum for that province's County/District Court. The unsuccessful party, if it so chooses, may appeal the trial decision to the Appellate Division of the Province's Supreme Court and the defeated party of this appeal may make a final appeal to the Supreme Court of Canada.

STEPS INVOLVED IN A CIVIL COURT PROCEEDING

Although this process can be quite complex and drawn out, often over a period of years, a quick review of the critical path these proceedings typically follow may be of interest.

After an accident occurs, the injured party obtains legal advice from his or her lawyer concerning the advisability of proceeding with a lawsuit. If deciding to sue, the plaintiff's lawyer is informed of this fact and the wheels are set in motion.

The Rules of Court of each province lay out the complex, but consistent procedure which begins with the initiation of a suit and terminates with its settlement or a judgment and assessment of damages by the courts. Briefly, the following steps are, or may be, involved:

1. *The Serving of a Writ*—This involves the issuance of a writ by the plaintiff to the defendant, outlining the case as he or she perceives it,

the restitution sought and summonsing the defendant to enter an appearance within the prescribed time period.[27]

2. *Pleadings*—If the two parties fail to settle out of court and if there is some dispute of the facts, then both parties begin pleadings. The plaintiff's pleadings are called Statements of Claims and the defendant's Statements of Defense and once completed (which may involve more than one amendment by each party), they are both filed away in a record for the trial judge's use later.[28] Frequently, the defendant's Statements of Defense will involve one or more "counterclaims" (for example, contributory negligence) and/or the implicating of additional parties to accept at least a share of the liability.

3. *Discovery Period*—During this interlocutory period between pleadings and trial, each lawyer is permitted to ask the opponent party to answer under oath, a number of written questions[29] regarding the material facts of the accident and injury. These inquiries and replies are recorded and may be transcribed for use at the trial."[30]

4. *Summary Judgment or Trial*—If the two parties have still failed to settle the matter out of court, the pursuance of one of two alternate courses of action is likely. If the facts of the case are not in dispute and if the results of the case depend solely on the application of the selected law, then a "summary judgment" may be made by the judge.[31] If the facts are in dispute and/or if the law is uncertain, then the case may proceed to trial.

5. *Trial Brief*—If the parties have still not buckled under the pressure to settle out of court, then a trial date and place are set. During the period before the trial date (which may be up to and even over a year away in some jurisdictions), both parties' lawyers prepare to present their client's position to the best of their abilities.

6. *Trial*—If a jury is to be used they will be selected before the trial date. Fortunately, most cases are resolved by judge and not judge and jury, as the time and costs are much reduced.

Following opening statements by both counsels, the plaintiff's lawyer presents the plaintiff's case and examines selected witnesses. These witnesses are then cross-examined by the defense lawyer and they may be subsequently re-examined by the plaintiff's lawyer before the entire procedure is repeated in reverse with the defense's witnesses. If the plaintiff can provide sufficient evidence to establish at least a *prima facie* case (a case established by sufficient evidence by the plaintiff which can be overturned only by equal or greater rebutting evidence produced by the defense), then the defendant will be obliged to present evidence which proves there is no legal liability, that some other defendant is liable, and/or that even if there is liability, the plaintiff has overestimated the damages.[32]

Following these presentations and closing addresses by both counsels, the judge has the option of entering a directed verdict (judgment) for one party or the other, or if uncertain, maintaining the right to reserve judgment to consider the decision. If a jury has been involved, the judge may either enter a directed verdict or send the case to the jury for their decision, "instructing them on the law to be applied to the facts as they were presented during the trial."[33]

Once the jury's verdict is reported to the court, "it is reduced to a judgment directing disposition of the case."[34] The losing party is usually held responsible for paying their own court costs and legal fees. The actual amounts involved will vary significantly depending on the difficulty and duration of the case. Anyone interested in estimating these costs is advised to refer to their province's Court Schedule of Rules. It should also be remembered that lawyers' fees (both the plaintiff's and the defendant's), or parts thereof, are often over and above those cited in the schedule and the combined costs and fees for both parties may easily rise into the thousands of dollars.

ASSESSMENT OF DAMAGES

At the conclusion of the case, if the plaintiff has been successful in convincing the judge (or jury) that the defendant was liable for the plaintiff's injuries, then the defendant will be required to pay at least a portion of the assessed damages. If a third party has been shown to be liable as well, and/or if the plaintiff was careless in some way which contributed to his or her injury(ies), then the assessed damages may be apportioned among the negligent parties as the court decides.

Damages are assessed and awarded an injured plaintiff according to the principle of *restitutio in integrum*: money is awarded in an attempt to restore to the victim what was lost as a result of the accident.[35] As restoration is impossible for many victims (no amount of financial remuneration is going to allow a quadriplegic to enjoy a walk in the park again), the damages usually attempt to compensate the plaintiff for the unique loss suffered. The compensability of the plaintiff does not depend solely on the "severity of the injury, but rather on the consequences to the individual affected by the tortious act."[36]

In order to make the task of assessing damages easier, the courts have categorized the types of consequences which may warrant compensation. These categories include:

1. The physical injury itself and the pain and suffering associated with it up to the time of trial;
2. Disability and loss of amenities before trial;
3. Loss of earnings before trial;
4. Expenses incurred before trial;
5. Pain and suffering expected to be suffered in the future, either temporarily or permanently;
6. Loss of amenities after trial;
7. Loss of life expectancy;
8. Loss of earnings to be suffered after the trial and into the foreseeable future;
9. Cost of future care and other expenses.[37]

In the case of a fatal accident, the dependants of the deceased and/or their estate may have a right of action. This "statutory right of action, granted only for the limited claim of specified dependents, rests upon their loss of dependency: the loss of security they derived from the continued existence of the deceased."[38]

Damages sought by the injured plaintiff will all fall under one of two larger categories, special and general damages. Special damages pleaded will include all of those expenses which can be reasonably precisely calculated, such as medical expenses, loss of earnings and/or business profits.[39] General damages, which are more arbitrary in nature and less given to precise calculation, include things like loss of future income, future medical costs, compensation for "pain, suffering, loss of amenities and inconvenience."[40]

The amount of damages will vary tremendously with the specific consequences the court is attempting to compensate the victim for. The greatest amount of damages has in recent years been awarded to victims rendered quadriplegics and paraplegics, due to the extremely high cost of the hospital and home care they require for the rest of their lives. For example, over the past two decades, there have been three Supreme Court of Canada case decisions made concerning youths (15 and 16 years of age) rendered quadriplegics as a result of school gymnastics accidents. In the first, *Mckay* v. *Govan School Unit No. 29 of Saskatchewan,*[41] a student who was injured when he fell from the parallel bars was awarded $183,000. A decade later, in *Thornton* v. *Board of School Trustees of Dictrict No. 57 (Prince George) et al.,*[42] a 15-year-old boy injured when he vaulted over his protective landing mats received $1,534,059.

Most recently, the Ontario Supreme Court awarded a 14-year-old youth, left a quadriplegic following a trail bike accident, an unprecedented $7,023,150. In this, the well-publicized case of *McErlean* v. *Sarel and the City of Brampton,*[43] the defendant municipal corporation was ordered to pay 75 percent of the damages assessed. While this case was reversed upon appeal[44] and the damages reduced significantly (to $3,689,435), it still has the potential to affect future assessments.

The assessments for victims losing only half of their limb functions is significantly less, but may easily exceed the half-million-dollar mark. In a 1981 British Columbia Supreme Court decision, a young woman received $600,000 in compensatory damages when she was rendered a paraplegic by reason of injuries suffered in a parachute jump she attempted during an instructional course offered by the defendant.[45]

By contrast, if the victim dies as a result of the accident, damages seem less likely to exceed half a million dollars. In a recent avalanche accident in British Columbia, the estates of the two deceased heli-skiers were only able to obtain assessments of $200,000 and $500,000 respectively. The latter assessment was significantly higher only because this victim had been a surgeon with a large family to support.[46]

Interestingly, the assessment of damages for a deceased child is very low, rarely exceeding $10,000 dollars in Canada. Due to the low pecuniary damages allowed, and the time, money and trauma involved in pursuing a lawsuit, most parents settle their claims out of court. While this certainly is preferable for the parties concerned, it leaves the legal case books rather lean on adjudicated precedent involving this sector of the population, which represents the largest participation in outdoor education/recreation programs.

Because of the tremendous variety in the types of expenses an accident victim may incur, and the range of amounts the courts may award for each type, the quantum of damages to be awarded in any accident where liability is found is difficult, if not impossible, for the layperson to estimate. This fact has had substantial bearing not only on outdoor program practitioners, but on the insurance industry which covers such financial risks.

3 THE BASIS OF TORT LIABILITY

THE FUNCTIONS OF TORT LAW

THE WORD TORT DERIVES from the Latin *tortus* (twisted) and is also directly connected with the French word *tort* (wrong).[1] Tort has been defined as "a civil wrong for which the remedy is a common law action for unliquidated damages, and which is not exclusively the breach of a contract or the breach of a trust or other merely equitable obligation."[2] In simpler terms, this body of law is primarily concerned with compensating victims who have sustained injury as a result of the conduct (or misconduct) of others.

In addition to its aims of justice, compensation and appeasement of accident victims, tort law has a number of other functions. One such function is the assessment of the relative abilities of the respective parties to bear the financial loss which must be accepted by one or the other. As defendants in tort cases are often publicly funded or highly insured agencies, they have the capacity to bear an economic loss by increasing their rates and thereby distributing the cost among all other purchasers of their goods or services. The doctrine of strict liability ("without fault") for inherently dangerous activities and/or conditions and that of vicarious liability both developed out of this philosophical basis.[3]

Punishment of wrongs committed and discouragement of repetition of the wrongful act by the original wrongdoer as well as all other members of society are two other subsidiary functions of tort law.

GENERAL PRINCIPLES OF LIABILITY IN TORT LAW

A tort is not a specific wrong. Rather, tort law refers to the identification of a variety of wrongs including, among others: assault, battery, false imprisonment, defamation and negligence. Negligence leads to the most litigation and is the tort upon which this book focuses.

The tort of negligence is not concerned with any particular activity, but rather the manner in which all "activities are carried out."[4] A negligent act or statement is one which is viewed as reckless, careless and/or involving judgmental error. The allegation in a negligence action is basically that the defendant paid insufficient attention to the interests of others, and has pursued personal objectives, at the risk of the safety of other persons' lives and property; and this is perhaps the foundation for the view that negligence is a moral fault.[5]

Unlike a criminal action, the plaintiff involved in a negligence case need not prove any intention of committing a wrong on the part of the defendant; proof of negligent conduct alone is deemed sufficient.

NEGLIGENCE AS A BASIS OF TORT LIABILITY

The following five criteria must be proven by the claimant before a cause for action in negligence will be recognized:
1. A duty of care owed by the defendant to the plaintiff, requiring that the defendant meet a certain standard of care.
2. A breach of the established standard of care or a failure to conform to it.
3. Actual injury(ies) suffered by the plaintiff.
4. A proximate connection between the defendant's conduct and the plaintiff's injury(ies).
5. No conduct by the plaintiff that would prejudice his or her case. (voluntary assumption of risk).[6]

Duty of Care

The concept of a duty of care implies a relationship between the defendant and the plaintiff or the class of people to which the plaintiff belonged (for example, driver-pedestrian, instructor-student, guide-client.)

Duty of care is normally not a questionable issue in establishing a cause of action, except perhaps in two types of situations. The first of these are "common adventure" types of situations where no formal leader/participant relationship exists. These situations arise when, for example, two friends go hiking or skiing together. While one will almost always have more relevant knowledge and experience than the other, it is difficult to determine if one actually has a duty to care for the other. The second situation where duty of care may be in question arises when an agency divorces itself from the actions of the staff whose conduct is in question. This may occur when the staff person(s) are operating outside the scope of their employment.

Standard of Care

Determining the appropriate standard of care for an individual relating to a given group in a specified environmental setting and participating in a particular activity becomes much more difficult. However, once the standard is established, proving whether it was breached or not becomes a somewhat easier matter.

THE REASONABLE PERSON   The courts have created an objectively employable fictitious entity, the "reasonable person," to help define the standard of care required in any risk situation. This reasonable person was first introduced in 1856 by Baron Alderson when he defined negligence as:

> ... the omission to so something which a reasonable man, guided upon those considerations which ordinarily regulate the conduct of human affairs, would do, or doing something which a prudent and reasonable man would not do.[7]

If the defendant can show that a reasonably prudent person placed in the same circumstances would have acted similarly, then the standard of care required in that situation will have been met and the defendant will not be liable.

In addition to being granted average skill, intelligence, memory and judgmental capacities, the reasonable person is perceived to be one who takes the time to use foresight to seriously consider the potential risk present in the situation. Negligence, recalled, consists of conduct involving an unreasonable risk of harm. Almost any activity is fraught with some degree of danger to others, but if the remotest chance of mishap were sufficient to attract the stigma of negligence, most human action would be inhibited. Inevitably, therefore, one is only required to guard against those risks which society recognizes as sufficiently great to demand precaution. The risk must be great before the reasonable person can be expected to subordinate his or her own interests to those of others. Whether the act or omission in question is one which a reasonable person would recognize as posing an unreasonable risk must be determined by balancing the magnitude of the risk, in the light of the likelihood of an accident happening and the possible seriousness of its consequences, against the difficulty, expense or any other disadvantage of desisting from the venture or taking a particular precaution.[8]

Therefore, an accident must be a foreseeable possibility before the defendant will have breached the standard of care; "there must be a recognizable risk of injury sufficient to cause the reasonable man to pause."[9] In addition to the consideration of the likelihood of injury occurring, an evaluation of the potential severity of such injury is also an important aspect of a risk assessment.

The reasonable person will also consider the appropriateness of the activity and the potential risk for each individual involved. For example, in Saskatoon, an obese 13-year-old boy fractured a leg while performing a 7-foot vertical jump off some bleachers as part of a required physical education class. The instructor was found negligent and the school board held liable because this activity was perceived by the courts to be very dangerous for a youth in the plaintiff's physical condition and the instructor should have foreseen the risk of harm to this individual.[10]

Finally, the reasonable person will consider the degree of risk in relation to the utility of the conduct or activity being pursued. The following equation is useful in weighing the aforementioned factors in relation to the purpose of the act and the cost of reducing the hazard. The equation states that:

$$P \times L = O \times C \text{ where:}$$

P is the severity of the potential harm which is likely to ensue if the accident transpires,
L is the likelihood that the harm will occur,
O is the object or purpose of the conduct in question and
C is the cost of eliminating the hazard which the defendant must bear.[11]

Therefore:

> If the probability times the loss is greater than the object times the cost, liability ensues; conversely, if the probability times the loss is less than the object times the cost, the conduct is blameless.[12]

Unfortunately, this equation fails to account for the degree to which the individual can establish that the victim has voluntarily assumed responsibility for his or her own safety.

The following case demonstrates how this combination of factors has been historically considered. In *Bolton et al. v. Stone,*[13] a cricket ball was struck over a 7-foot fence and injured the plaintiff, travelling on a roadway 100 feet from the fence. Although the ball had been hit over the fence half a dozen times in the preceding 30 years, no one had been injured in this manner in the entire 90 years the pitch had been in use. The House of Lords held that the likelihood of injury and the potential for it to be severe should it occur were minimal in relation to the utility of the game and the cost of eliminating the hazard (such as building a higher fence or finding another place to play). Lord Reid summarized the test:

> In the crowded conditions of modern life even the most careful person cannot avoid creating some risks and accepting others. What a man must not do, and what I think a careful man tries not to do is to create a risk which is substantial. . . . In my judgment, the test to be applied here is whether the risk of damage to a person on the road was so small that a reasonable man in the position of the appellants, considering the matter from the point of view of safety, would have thought it right to refrain from taking steps to prevent the danger. In considering that matter I think that it would be right to take into account, not only how remote is the chance that a person might be struck, but also how serious the consequences are likely to be if a person is struck. . .[14]

THE PRUDENT PROFESSIONAL The standard of care will be higher than that of the reasonable person for individuals presenting themselves as professionals in a field of endeavor. Although the particular standard will vary from one profession to another, commensurate with the type and degree of knowledge and technical skill required of its practitioners, all professional people are expected to measure up to the standard of competence of the ordinary person professing such special skill.[15]

A highly trained specialist will normally be expected to conform to a higher standard than the average professional in the same field (for example, an orthopedic surgeon must conform to higher standards than a general practitioner). However, those who hold themselves up as professionals will be expected to conduct their practice at the level they advertise themselves. For example, a chiropractor who failed to properly diagnose the condition of a patient because he had not been trained to do so, who did not request assistance in making the diagnosis and who, as a result, gave an improper treatment to the patient, was found liable for negligence. In deciding the case, the learned judge stated:

> ... the defendant held himself out to be, at least, a reasonably prudent and skillful man. . . . His falling short of the knowledge and skill which he should have possessed to diagnose the case, and working in the dark, presuming to deal with it, in effect regardless of the results, constituted negligence. . . . [16]

Neither does the law make any special concessions for the beginner.[17] Just as a new driver must abide by all traffic laws and be held liable for any accidents he or she may cause, so must the newly trained professional who accepts the position be prepared to deal with its many contingencies.

THE CAREFUL PARENT Another standard is that of the careful parent, which is adhered to by members of the teaching profession and most others charged with responsibility for the supervision and care of children. This doctrine first evolved out of Justice Cave's late nineteenth century definition of a schoolmaster's duty. In his words, "The schoolmaster is bound to take such care of his boys as a careful father would take of his boys."[18]

Although the standard of the reasonable and careful parent has come under much criticism of late due to the special training teachers have and the class sizes they must contend with, even the most recent Supreme Court decisions in Canada dealing with teachers have employed this doctrine in determining the appropriateness of the standard of care rendered.[19]

Proximate Cause—The Foreseeability Test

Assuming that a plaintiff can demonstrate proof that the defendant breached a duty to care and that he or she was injured (physically and/or psychologically), there remains the often onerous task of proving that the defendant's failure to conform to established standards was the proximate cause of the injury(ies). That is, it must be shown conclusively that it was in fact the defendant's error or omission and not some other independent act or cause (by nature or another party, including the plaintiff), that precipitated the accident resulting in the plaintiff's injury(ies).[20]

Today the courts commonly apply the foreseeability test to establish causation. The reasonable person is held to possess an average capacity to foresee harm coming to individuals to whom a duty is owed, and should this standard of foresight not be met, then liability will be found for any injuries which ensue.

In advocating a shift from the earlier used directness rule to this foreseeability test, Viscount Simonds argued that:

> It is a principle of civil liability that a man must be considered to be responsible for the probable consequences of his act. To demand more of him is too harsh a rule, to demand less is to ignore that civilized order requires the observance of a minimum standard of behavior,[21]

and later:

> After the event even a fool is wise. But it is not the hindsight of a fool; it is the foresight of the reasonable man which alone can determine responsibility.[22]

TYPE OF FORESEEABLE DAMAGE DETERMINES LIABILITY   In later applications of this test of foreseeability, it was established that the injury(ies) resulting from an accident need not occur in the exact manner which was foreseeable. For example, in *Hughes* v. *Lord Advocate*[23] an 8-year-old boy tripped over a paraffin lamp left near an open manhole, causing it to fall into the hole. The fallen lamp set off an explosion, the force of which caused the boy to fall into the hole and be burned. The House of Lords held the defendant post office liable because although the exact nature of the accident may not have been foreseeable (paraffin lamps were not expected to fall into manholes and set off explosions), the type of injury which was sustained by the youth (burning) was reasonably foreseeable. In citing his reasons for supporting this appeal, Lord Reid stated:

> No doubt it was not to be suspected that the injuries would be as serious as those which the appellant in fact sustained. But a defender is liable, although the damage may be a good deal greater in extent than

was foreseeable. He can only escape liability if the damage can be regarded as differing in kind from what was foreseeable.[24]

This rule has been upheld in Canadian courts from the early 1970s on. In *School Division of Assiniboine South No. 3 v. Hoffer et al.*[25] a 14-year-old youth, his father and the Greater Winnipeg Gas Company were apportioned damages when the youth negligently allowed his father's snowmobile to escape from his control and hit an unprotected gas riser pipe. Some gas escaped, entered a nearby school building and exploded. Justice Dickson set out the Canadian test while discussing the liability of the boy.

> It is enough to fix liability if one could foresee in a general way the sort of thing that happened. The extent of the damage and its manner of incidence need not be foreseeable if physical damage of the kind which in fact ensues is foreseeable.[26]

THE THIN-SKULL RULE When discussing the awarding of damages to injured victims, Lord Parker stated that, "it has always been the law of this country that a tortfeasor takes his victim as he finds him."[27] He referred to the rationale of an earlier decision by Justice Kennedy, where the latter stated:

> If a man is negligently run over or otherwise negligently injured in his body, it is no answer to the sufferer's claim for damages that he would have suffered less injury, or no injury at all, if he had not had an unusually thin skull or an unusually weak heart.[28]

Therefore, it is only necessary for the defendant to have been capable of foreseeing the type of injury which may occur. If the particular victim injured happens to have some predisposing weakness or condition which makes him or her more susceptible to injury and/or to a more severe form of the foreseeable harm, this is unfortunate for the defendant, but he or she will still be held fully liable for the plaintiff's injuries.

INTERVENING FORCES It should be apparent at this point that tort law is oriented toward the compensation of hapless victims and that defendants in negligence actions must be prepared to justify their every action and demonstrate that they evaluated the risk of harm to those they owed a duty before engaging in the questionable conduct.

The courts also recognize that any number of extenuating variables and circumstances must be assessed in each case brought to them. Over time, these intervening forces have been categorically identified and a brief review of these factors may help clarify causation and liability in any incident in question. These intervening forces will act to reduce or even eliminate the liability of the original defendant.

The most obvious type of intervening force which acts in favor of the defendant is the potentially negligent conduct of the plaintiff. Because of the frequency of occurrence of accidents where the victim's own actions have contributed to the injury(ies) sustained, especially in physical education/recreation/sport situations, this factor will be dealt with separately later in this chapter.

Secondly, it is possible that a third party may be wholly or partially liable for negligence resulting in damage to a plaintiff. In the evidence cited earlier in the case of *School Division of Assiniboine* v. *Hoffer et al.*[29] it was shown that although the boy's negligent driving of the snowmobile actually caused the explosion, the gas company was negligent to an even greater extent for leaving the pipe in a hazardous state and position. The boy and his father were each found 25 percent liable for damages; the gas company was forced to pay the remaining half of the damages.

RECURRING SITUATIONS A variety of recurring situations can increase the number of actions or damages claimed by the plaintiff(s) against the defendant. For example, rescue situations where a third party is injured or killed while attempting to rescue a victim at harm because of the defendant's negligence, can result in a suit.

Another category includes second accidents where a plaintiff injured due to the defendant's negligence is left in a state or condition which predisposes him or her to subsequent accidents.[30] Unless another tortfeasor (including the plaintiff) is present to accept liability for the additional damage, the original defendant may be liable for injuries sustained or worsened in the second accident.[31]

A final category of recurring situations to be considered is medical mishaps which complicate the plaintiff's condition and result in additional damages. Unless the defendant can prove that the medical or surgical treatment rendered was "so negligent as to be actionable"[32] (therefore an intervening act in itself), the plaintiff has the right to claim from the defendant, damages which result from errors in treatment made by qualified, reputable medical practitioners.[33]

Breach of Statute

Another factor which may lead to litigation is the failure of a defendant to perform to standard, a statutory duty. Fortunately, while long the sub-, ject of much confusion and misinterpretation, the effect a breach of statute has on a tort action has been substantially clarified in recent years. In the case of *R. in Right of Canada* v. *Saskatchewan Wheat Pool*,[34] the Federal Court of Appeal decided that where a breach of statute has an effect upon civil liability, this effect should be considered within the context of the general law of negligence and not outside it.[35] Rather than allowing a suit to succeed simply on the basis that the defendant violated a statute, it was determined that the other elements of tortious responsibility apply equally to situations involving statutory breach. Justice Heald provided a set of summary conclusions which have been adopted widely for their succinct clarification of the law in this area. These conclusions included the following:

1. Civil consequences of breach of statute should be subsumed in the law of negligence.
2. The notion of a nominate tort of statutory breach giving a right to recovery merely on proof of breach and damages should be rejected, as should the view that unexcused breach constitutes negligence *per se* giving rise to absolute liability.
3. Proof of statutory breach, causative of damages, may be evidence of negligence.
4. The statutory formulation of the duty may afford a specific, and useful, standard of reasonable conduct.[36]

Therefore, one cannot be sued for violation of a statute independent of causation of damages. The identification of a duty and/or standards of care in statutory legislation may help clarify expectations the courts hold of individuals in various roles. The court assumes that persons of ordinary prudence will reasonably endeavor to obey the law and will do so unless causes not of their own intended making induce them, without moral fault to do otherwise.[37]

Breach of statute does not appear to be a commonly pleaded cause of action in physical education/recreation cases.

CONDUCT OF THE PLAINTIFF

The most commonly seen intervening factor in any negligence action is the conduct of the plaintiff at the time of the accident. Hence, this fifth and final criterion of the test for negligence has been included, supported by the philosophic rationale that the law should compensate only those individuals felt deserving of its protection. The courts believe that "anyone who is negligent with regard to his own safety is denied the protection of the law in whole or in part."[38] In addition, one who knowingly agrees to accept the risk of harm will be considered to have effectively waived his or her right to legal action.[39]

Contributory Negligence

Contributory negligence has been defined as "conduct on the part of the plaintiff, contributing as a legal cause to the harm he has suffered, which falls below the standard to which he is required to conform for his own protection."[40] Therefore, the standard of care which a plaintiff must exercise is the same as that expected of a defendant; "he must exercise such care for his own safety as a reasonable person would in like circumstances."[41] A plaintiff being accused of contributory negligence by a defendant will be evaluated according to the same guiding principles and the same criteria (duty to care, standard of care, proximate cause) as that defendant. The onus is on the defendant in such cases to prove that "the injured party did not in his own interest take reasonable care of himself and contributed by this want of care to his own injury."[42]

Historically in common law, a plaintiff found contributorily negligent was barred from any potential recovery from the defendant.[43] Provinces in Canada, along with a number of other commonwealth countries, have enacted apportionment legislation which allows a plaintiff to recover a portion of damages from the tortfeasor in proportion to his or her negligence.[44] This statute assures a fair and equitable accountability for negligence not seen with the earlier system. Contributory negligence is viewed as a defense in Canada and only after negligence on the part of the defendant has been established will it be considered by the courts.

The test for contributory negligence of a child plaintiff is much more subjective than the one employed with adult victims. Children under the age of six are generally immune from charges of contributory negligence and other children are only expected to conform to the standard of a "reasonable person of like age, intelligence and experience under like circumstances."[45]

In the gymnastics case of *Meyers et al.* v. *Peel County Board of Education*, it was found that the 15-year-old plaintiff Meyers was of sufficient age, intelligence and experience to know that the stunt he was attempting when he fell "was a difficult maneuver, fraught with some danger. He knew he was not to attempt anything on the rings without the presence of a spotter in position."[46] As a result of his intentional contravention of the rules laid out by his teacher, Meyers was found 20 percent contributorily negligent for damages resulting from his quadriplegia.[47]

Voluntary Assumption of Risk

The Latin maxim *volenti non fit injuria,* which translates into "no injury is done to one who consents,"[48] is a complete defense, barring the plaintiff from recovering any damages whatsoever from the defendant. In sport and recreation cases, arguing volenti (voluntary assumption of risk) may mean claiming that either: (a) no duty was owed the plaintiff by the defendant, or (b) the plaintiff knew and appreciated the consequences of the risks and purposely waived his or her right of legal action.[49]

As the existence of a duty to care is normally fairly easy to establish, most volenti cases are argued on the grounds that the plaintiff voluntarily assumed the consequences of risks which he or she understood and appreciated.[50] It is crucial to understand and appreciate the difference between assuming the *physical risks* involved in an outdoor activity (for example, breaking a leg while downhill skiing, drowning while whitewater kayaking) and assuming the *legal risks* involved (personal, financial responsibility for all losses and damages, howsoever incurred). An individual who voluntarily assumes the legal risks involved will necessarily have assumed the inherent physical risks present as well, but one who agrees to assume the physical risks will not necessarily have agreed to assume the legal risks involved in participation. This implies that although the plaintiff may consent to the assumption of particular physical risks, there is no barment from recovery if he or she is injured as a result of some other risk which was not assumed, one, for example, that was incurred through the negligence of another.[51] Hence, a snowmobile passenger who assumes the risk of falling off the machine does not necessarily waive the right to action should they be run over by another snowmobile.[52] And a water skier who voluntarily assumes the risk of running into an obstruction does not necessarily waive the right to sue the boat driver for negligently failing to warn of such an obstruction.[53]

A natural extension of this study of volenti is the legal power of responsibility release statements or waivers. In order to have any chance of receiving legal recognition, such exemption clauses must be expressed and not implied. Only an express disclaimer may function as an absolute waiver of rights and the courts are reluctant to accept even such explicit releases as they circumvent perceived legal rights and accountabilities.[54] In addition, it should be known that parents may not waive their child's legal rights by signing a consent form or a waiver.

Because proving voluntary assumption of risk on the part of the plaintiff is extremely difficult, such counters are rarely successful. However, this defense has been recognized as valid in a number of outdoor recreation/sport related cases and it will therefore be discussed in much detail as it relates to participation in many of the inherently dangerous outdoor activities pursued in this country.

NEGLIGENT STATEMENTS

Another relevant area of negligence law pertains to the legal accountability one has, not for negligent acts, but for verbal or written statements made which are found to be the proximate cause of another's injuries.

In the classic case in this area, *Hedley Byrne and Co. Ltd.* v. *Heller and Partners Ltd,*[55] the defendant's bank was found negligent for making statements which led to the plaintiff's financial loss when a business the bank endorsed liquidated. Of the principle enunciated in this case, Justice Holland later stated:

> In order for there to be liability for negligent misrepresentation there must be first a duty of care; second, a negligent misrepresentation; third, reliance on the misrepresentation by the plaintiff and fourth, loss resulting from this reliance.[56]

Such a situation could arise when, for example, a student or client acts on an outdoor adventure instructor's or guide's verbal assurance that a particular rapid was safe to run or a particular slope was safe from avalanche hazards. Should an accident ensue directly as a result of the specific failure of an environmental feature represented as safe, the instructor or guide could be found negligent for misrepresentation of the risk.

4 THE CHILD PLAINTIFF

THE VAST MAJORITY of individuals participating in outdoor education/recreation programs and pursuits are between the ages of 6 and 25, with the largest portion falling under the recognized age of majority, 18 years. The inexperience and lack of skill most of these young people possess has resulted in their relatively high propensity for accidents and subsequent injury. Consequently, it is vital for the outdoor leader who may be supervising, instructing and/or leading children to understand the special position they hold in tort law. This includes both their rights to action and the responsibility the courts deem they must have for their own accidents.

THE STANDARD OF CARE OWED THE YOUNG

Although an infant will not technically be granted special status in tort law, children are generally owed a higher standard of care in negligence law than are adults.[1] It is common knowledge that as risk increases, so does the expectation that the standard of care exercised by the reasonable person will also rise to meet the situation. The accepted unpredictability of children makes their presence or reasonably anticipative presence sufficient reason for the taking of greater care. Harris, Chief Justice in *Seamone v. Fancy*, stated that:

Children, wherever they go, must be expected to act upon childish instincts and impulses, and those who are charged with a duty and caution towards them, must calculate upon this and take precaution accordingly.[2]

The degree to which the standard of care must be raised for children depends not only on the relatively objective "reasonable person" test, but also on a rather subjective evaluation of the age, intellect and experience of the particular child acting in the particular circumstances.[3]

Of these three factors, the youth's age will normally have the strongest effect in establishing negligence or absence thereof. In *Williams* v. *Eady*,[4] Justice Cave stated that, "to leave a knife about where a child of four could get at it would amount to negligence, but it would not if boys of 18 had access to it."[5] This opinion was rearticulated in *Smerkinich* v. *Newport Corporation*, where a 19-year-old youth injured while using an unguarded circular saw, sued the education authority for negligently failing to provide a guard for the saw. In finding for the defendant education authority, Justice Lush said, "If he had been a child, the case might have been different but, so far from being a child, he was a lad of 19 years of age. . . . "[6]

The test for the standard of care has been defined by inquiring, "Is the thing one of a class which children of that age, are in the ordinary course of things, not allowed without supervision?"[7]

THE CAPACITY OF A CHILD TO ENTER LITIGATION

Children or youth under the age of 18 years, injured due to another's negligence, have the right to claim damages through the legal process. However, plaintiff minors may not represent themselves in court; they must have an adult "next friend" accept this responsibility.[8] One of the juvenile's parents or guardians will usually perform this role.[9]

Children are well protected through this system. For example, Canadian courts have held that the next friend of a child plaintiff "may not settle or compromise or release the infant's claim without the approval of the court."[10] Child plaintiffs are doubly favored in this process as approval will not be granted by the court for a "settlement or compromise of the claim of an infant plaintiff unless the proposed settlement or compromise is one which is beneficial to the plaintiff."[11]

An interesting fact is that although married spouses may not sue each other in tort for personal injuries, children have the right to sue one or both of their parents in tort. Although the incentive for such claims would historically have been difficult to ascertain, the "modern prevalence of indemnity insurance has raised the question to practical importance."[12] Although most of the case law involving parties with this relationship has involved torts such as assault or negligent driving, there is one particularly relevant Canadian case of note. In *Deziel et al. v. Deziel*,[13] an 11-year-old youth sued his father for injuries he received while riding on the latter's carnival ride. In allowing the case, Justice Lebel stated:

> ... a situation such as this could only arise where insurance is involved... I know of no case in our courts dealing with the point, but I have no doubt that the law as it has been decided in *Young v. Rankin* [1937] S.C. 499, a Scottish case, is also the law of Ontario. I subscribe to the view of Lord Fleming in that case, where he said at the end of his remarks at p. 520: "I do not think that a wrongdoer should be relieved from responsibility for the consequences of his negligence merely because the injured party happens to be his own child."[14]

Therefore children, while being owed a higher duty of care than adults, also have the right to seek legal restitution from wrongdoers whose negligence causes them harm, regardless of their relationship with the tortfeasor.

THE DUTY OWED CHILDREN BY THEIR PARENTS

In Canada, statutory requirements stipulate that parents must provide for their children and ensure that they receive appropriate education until they are of school leaving age, now 16 years.[15] Parents also have a common law duty to supervise their children in order to protect them from harm and to protect others who may be foreseeably injured by the childrens' negligence. The standard of care pertinent to meeting this duty will involve the exercise of reasonable care in the circumstances, as established by community custom and a subjective evaluation of the child's particular attributes and subsequent requirements for care. As Professor Fleming states:

> Without going so far as to attach vicarious liability, the common law insists that parents at least exercise reasonable care, commensurate

with their peculiar ability to keep their offspring under discipline and supervise their activities for the sake of the public safety.[16]

The large subjective element in cases dealing with children, be they plaintiffs or tortfeasors, means that each case will be assessed according to the particular fact situation and characters involved. Although this makes prediction of the outcomes of such cases difficult, a number of duties and the subsequent standards of care they imply have become reasonably established through precedent. Some of the factors parents and anyone who accepts a supervisory role in place of parents should be aware to include:

1. "The practices and usages prevailing in the community and the common understanding of what is practicable."[17]
2. Knowledge of foreseeable propensities, peculiar to the particular child, of which parental awareness is known.[18]
3. General well-known propensities common to all or most children at a given stage of development, of which parental knowledge may be assumed.[19]
4. The provision of adequate instruction and supervision to children working or playing with potentially dangerous apparatus, the design and delivery of such training appropriate to the comprehension level of the youth.[20]
5. Parental knowledge of the child's physical capacities and physical ability to follow instructions given by the parent.[21]

A case in point which illustrates a number of these duty elements is the situation and findings outlined in *Ryan et al.* v. *Hickson et al.*[22] In this case, the 12-year-old defendant was giving a ride to the 9-year-old plaintiff on the back of the former's snowmobile. The plaintiff released his hold and turned to wave at the second defendant, a 14-year-old boy driving a second snowmobile behind him, just as the machine the plaintiff was a passenger on hit a snowbank. The impact threw the plaintiff from his snowmobile and directly into the path of the oncoming machine which injured him. Both drivers were found negligent and the plaintiff was found 33.3 percent contributorily negligent. But perhaps more importantly here, the courts found the fathers of both defending youths to be jointly and equally responsible with their respective sons, with the apportionment of responsibility being equal between both defendant boys at 33.3 percent. The reason was cited as follows:

It is an act of negligence to give a young boy care and control of a snowmobile which is a thing known to be dangerous or capable of causing danger to others, unless it is proved a) that he was properly trained in its use, with particular regard to using it safely and carefully, and b) that the boy was of an age, character and intelligence such that the father might safely assume the boy would apprehend and obey the instructions given to him... [T]he parent must, in addition to the above requirements, prove not only that he could safely assume that the child would apprehend and obey the instructions given him, but that he was physically capable of safely following those instructions and also of safely operating the vehicle.[23]

In this case, the courts found the defendant boys' fathers negligent in both their instruction of their sons in the safe operation of snowmobiles and in their supervision of the boys using these inherently dangerous machines. This same duty would fall upon the shoulders of a responsible teacher or leader standing *in loco parentis*—in the place of the parent.

THE LIABILITY OF THOSE TAKING THE PLACE OF PARENTS

Individuals who stand *in loco parentis*, as teachers, coaches, recreation programmers or outdoor educators, will be handed full responsibility for the youngsters in their care and will also be granted the concomitant authority required to fulfill this responsibility. The duty is to act as a reasonably prudent parent, including the often onerous task of protecting the child from participating in any activity in a manner which is likely to lead to harm to the child and/or others. Again, to generalize Lord Esher's words to other professionals working with children:

The school master was bound to take such care of his boys as a careful father would take care of his boys and there could not be a better definition of the duty of a schoolmaster. Then he was bound to take notice of the ordinary nature of young boys, their tendency to do mischievous acts and their propensity to meddle with anything that came in their way.[24]

Although this standard does exhibit a certain appealing simplicity and is still respected in Canadian courts,[25] in other ways it is a somewhat antiquated British anomaly requiring more serious reflection[26] and perhaps replacement with the more appropriate standard of the careful professional. Two reasons for a move to this alternative exist.

First, the careful parent test fails to account for the size of group in a professional educator/leader's care. What is deemed reasonable care for young members in a family of 4 or 5 (a large family by today's standards), may be totally unfeasible for a teacher[27] or recreation programmer with 20 or more students/participants to supervise.

Second, most of these professionals have had specialized training which should indicate a duty to perform to a higher standard than those who lack this supplementary education. "Teachers are expected to know more of the vagaries of children than most people do"[28] and the writer would hazard to add that well-seasoned teachers probably know more of the characteristics and propensities of children in the age group they teach, than most parents of like-aged children. With the small families prevalent today, the parents are most likely still engaged in intensive "in-service training" in child rearing. The same superior knowledge and training could probably be granted many recreation leaders, minor sport coaches and outdoor education practitioners.

Fortunately, the courts have taken the first step toward changing the standard. In the 1981 *Meyers*[29] Supreme Court of Canada decision, acceptance was given of the earlier trial judge's application of the tests articulated by Justice Carrothers in *Thornton et al. v. Board of School Trustees of District No. 57 (Prince George) et al.*[30] He refers to this part of Carrothers's judgment:

> This is not to say that... the school authorities were relieved of their common law duty to take care of this pupil during this activity in the manner of a reasonable and careful parent, taking into account the judicial modification of the reasonable-and-careful-parent test to allow for the larger-than-family size of the physical education class and the supraparental expertise commanded of a gymnastics instructor.[31]

Justice McIntyre, who gave the Supreme Court reasons for judgment in the *Meyers* case, added this in his discussion of the standard of care in physical education situations:

> It (the standard) has, no doubt become qualified in modern times because of the greater variety of activities conducted in schools, with

probably larger groups of students using more complicated and more dangerous equipment than formerly: see *McKay* v. *The Board of Govan School Unit No. 29 of Saskatchewan et al.* [1968] S.C.R. 589, but with the qualification expressed in the *McKay* case and noted by Carrothers in *Thornton*, supra, it remains the appropriate standard for such cases. It is not, however, a standard which can be applied in the same manner and to the same extent in every case. Its application will vary from case to case and will depend upon the number of students being supervised at any given time, the nature of the exercise or activity in progress, the age and degree of skill and training which the students may have received in connection with such activity, the nature and condition of the equipment in use at the time, the competency and capacity of the students involved, and a host of other matters which may be widely varied but which, in a given case, may affect the application of the prudent parent standard to the conduct of the school authority in the circumstances.[32]

This statement quite explicitly explains the inadequacy of the reasonable parent test used without supplementary qualification. Perhaps as education/recreation related disciplines earn professional status and credibility, the need for its application will pass. In order to attain this professional credibility, universities and professional education/recreation organizations and associations must devote much time and energy to the development of sound guidelines and standards for physical education, recreation and their associated disciplines. Individuals cannot be judged according to the criteria of the reasonably careful professional until the standards of performance to which that fictitious entity must conform have been established.[33]

CONTRIBUTORY NEGLIGENCE OF THE YOUNG

The judicial system has often been accused of exhibiting an unacceptable partiality to child plaintiffs. This sympathetic response was discussed in a British decision:

Our law reports show how fatally attractive childrens' cases have been to those who have to try them. Judges are human beings and their feelings are easily aroused in favor of the child, especially children of tender years. When they meet with an accident, any court is liable to strain the law in favor of the child, but an infant plaintiff has exactly the same burden of proving his case as any other plaintiff.[34]

Although this unwritten policy of reduced accountability of the young for injuries resulting from their immaturity has been widely accepted historically,[35] the current trend in apportionment of damages makes the finding that a child plaintiff has failed to exercise reasonable personal care is a more likely outcome than previously. The determination of "reasonable care" when dealing with a child plaintiff involves the same test as that used to establish negligence on the part of a child tortfeasor. Although the entire test is rather subjective when compared with the adult evaluation, it is deemed to be a two-part test, with one part being quite objective and the second, more subjective in nature.

The first half of the test of child contributory negligence was established in the Supreme Court of Canada decision in *McEllistrum* v. *Etches*.[36] Although the facts of the case are not particularly relevant, what was of interest was the court's finding that:

> ...where the age is not such as to make a discussion of contributory negligence absurd, it is a question for the jury in each case whether the infant exercised the care to be expected from a child of like age, intelligence and experience.[37]

Although no definite age has been determined for whether a child may be found contributorily negligent, it appears that children in Canada have enjoyed total immunity from this charge while they have remained below 5 years of age. However, this complete exemption most likely does not extend through a child's sixth year.[38]

For example, the Supreme Court of Nova Scotia found a child of five years and nine months 65 percent responsible for the injuries she incurred when she darted from behind a parked car onto the busy street in front of her home.[39] The Supreme Court of Canada believes that a child of six may be found guilty of contributory negligence.[40] However, this high court has clarified its position by stating that although the objective test involves a comparison with the reasonably "prudent child of given years,"[41] "... age is not to be taken too literally" because, "as with the adult, the standard takes into account any clearly shown special knowledge"[42] or experience on the part of the plaintiff. This comment extends not only to those children at or around the lower limit of potential liability, but indeed throughout the time juveniles spend between their tender years and the time they reach the age of majority, when they must meet adult standards of maturity.

Therefore, although a youth falling in the 5 to 18 year age range, of average intelligence and little experience in the injury-producing activity, may easily be absolved of a defendant's claims of contributory negligence, one who is perceived as displaying above average intelligence or "shrewdness" and who has had some experience in the activity may not enjoy the same exonerations.[43]

The subjective aspect of the test of infantile contributory negligence involves more detailed evaluation of the particular child's intelligence and experience to ascertain whether that child was capable of the foresight necessary to understand and appreciate the potential consequences of the conduct.[44] This test involves an assessment of such criteria as: (a) the child's ability to rationalize in the situation and to perceive, understand and appreciate any hazards present;[45] (b) the type and extent of instruction and supervision the child previously received in the activity;[46] and (c) knowledge of essential safety precautions in the activity, learned through experience in the activity under question or in related activities.[47]

Thus, in the *Messenger et al. v. Sears and Murray Knowles Ltd.*[48] case, the courts felt that the 5-year, 9-month-old girl defendant was contributorily negligent for her own injuries because it was

... highly probable that the child would have learned from her brothers and sisters, if not from her parents, as well as from her own experience, to appreciate the risks involved in running into a vehicular traffic pathway on this street in the circumstances disclosed in this case. ... [49]

In *Ryan et al. v. Hickson et al.*,[50] the child plaintiff, a passenger on a snowmobile, was found one third contributorily liable for injuries sustained when he fell off the machine he was riding only to be struck by a trailing snow machine. The Ontario High Court decided that Ryan was "of normal intelligence for his age" and that he had had "considerable experience in riding as a passenger on snowmobiles."[51] He was therefore deemed to know and appreciate the importance of hanging on to the driver and watching where they were going and to take these precautions whenever he was riding on the back of a snowmobile.

Similarly, in *Meyers*,[52] the Supreme Court of Canada restored the trial judge's finding that the 15-year-old Meyers was 20 percent contributorily negligent for the temporary quadriplegia he suffered as a result of his gymnastics accident. In this precedent setting case, the plaintiff was found negligent in attempting a straddle dismount from the rings "without proper experience and precautions."[53] Factors which operated against Meyers were the fact that the accident occurred very near the end of a 5-week unit in gymnastics throughout which the function and importance of the use of spotters had been stressed by Meyers' teacher.[54] At the time of the accident, the plaintiff was attempting a risky maneuver for the first time in his life, without practising any progressions and without making sure that his spotter knew what he was going to do and was prepared to catch him should he miss on his attempt. The Supreme Court reiterated the trial judge's finding that Meyers was intelligent enough and had had sufficient experience to know that what he was doing was wrong. In the trial judge's words,

> I find that Gregory Meyers knew that it was a difficult manoeuver, fraught with some danger. He knew that he was not to attempt anything on the rings without the presence of a spotter in position.[55]

In both of these cases, the plaintiffs were believed to be of sufficient age, intelligence and experience to be capable of foreseeing the consequences of their careless acts. Additional Canadian case examples where children have been found contributorily negligent include incidents where 11- and 12-year-old juveniles tampered with explosives left at a worksite,[56] where an 8-year-old boy was injured while playing street hockey on a slippery road[57] and where a 15-year-old weak swimmer disobeyed instructions to stay with the boat and subsequently drowned.[58]

The judicial protection of child plaintiffs ceases to be exercised when the child, regardless of age, is "engaged in an adult activity which is normally insured."[59] As society permits youths of 15 and 16 years the opportunity to drive automobiles,[60] to say nothing of the 12- and 13-year-olds that it allows to operate motorboats, trail bikes and snowmobiles, it must hold them to the standard of the reasonable adult while they are engaged in these activities.

In summary, as a general guiding principle, the younger the child plaintiff (usually under seven years), the more subjective will be the evaluation of the standard of care owed and whether or not the child contrib-uted to his or her own injuries; thus more emphasis is placed on the child's intellectual and experiential development. Concomitantly, the older the youth, the greater the emphasis placed on more objective cri-teria such as age.

5 STATUTE LAW AND THE OUTDOOR LEADER

IN REVIEWING AN ACTION based on the alleged negligence of an outdoor leader, before looking at the common law for precedential assistance, the courts must first check for any acts containing statutes relevant to the situation. Because of the great range of activity pursuits and environmental settings utilized in the delivery of outdoor education/recreation programs in Canada, there are numerous federal and provincial acts and municipal by-laws which may be relevant to the outdoor programmer in each region of the country. But, in all the legislation there are statutory elements fairly common to the majority of these professionals.

THE STATUTORY DUTIES OF TEACHERS

A large sector of outdoor educators in Canada are employed as teachers by school boards in various urban and rural municipalities. In addition to the common law which dictates many of these individuals' duties, most provinces have enacted statutory legislation to help standardize these duties for legal purposes.[1]

While some provinces have placed all primary and secondary education related statutes in one act (for example, Saskatchewan), others have a number of acts directed at individuals involved in the education system (for example, Alberta). These may be intended for persons involved as policy writers,[2] administrators[3] and teachers.[4] Usually, however, only one act will provide regulations regarding the legislated duties of teachers. In very few provinces these duties have not been laid out in statutes. Ac-

47

cording to a cross-national sample of some of the statutes relevant to teachers, particularly those involved in teaching physical education curricula, teachers have a duty to:

1. "perform the teaching and other educational services required or assigned by a board or the ministry."[5]

2. "inculcate by precept and example respect for religion and the principles of Judaeo-Christian morality and the highest regard for truth, justice, loyalty, love of country, humanity, benevolence, sobriety, industry, frugality, purity, temperance and all other virtues."[6]

3. "maintain proper order and discipline in the school or room in his charge."[7]

4. "plan and organize the learning activities of the class with due regard for individual differences and needs of the pupils."[8]

5. "conduct and manage assigned functions in the instructional program in accordance with the educational policies of the board of education and the applicable regulations."[9]

6. "report regularly... to the parent or guardian of each pupil with respect to his progress and any circumstances or conditions which may be of mutual interest and concern to the teacher and the parent or guardian."[10]

7. "report immediately to the board and the inspector the existence of any infectious or contagious disease in the school or the existence of any unsanitary condition in the school building or surroundings."[11]

8. "give constant attention to the health and comfort of the pupils... "[12]

9. "see that the premises and other property of the school are, as far as possible, preserved from damage... "[13]

10. "report to the school board any necessary repairs to the school building or furniture and any required... furniture or equipment."[14]

In addition to these rather generic statutory duties, common to most provinces, some provinces have enacted legislation specifically designed to protect their teachers and school boards from legal actions arising from accidents, except where negligence can be proven. For example, the *Public School Act* of Manitoba contains a number of liability specific statutory provisions. Following are a few examples of this legislation:

Where injury or death is caused to a pupil enrolled in or attending a public school... during, or as a result of, physical training, physical culture, gymnastic exercises, or drill, carried on in connection with the school activities... no cause of action accrues to the pupil or to any other person for loss for damage suffered by reason of the bodily injury or death, against the school district or any servant or agent thereof or any trustee of the district unless it is shown that the injury or death was caused by the negligence of the school district or misconduct of any of its servants or agents or of any one or more of the trustees.[15]

This rather wordy statute does little more than state the necessity for a student plaintiff to prove the breach of an owed duty by the defendant school board and/or teacher as the proximate cause of injury(ies) sustained.

Manitoba's *Public School Act* also alludes to the duty owed by the school board as an occupier.

Where the bodily injury or death of a pupil... is caused by defective or dangerous apparatus supplied by the school district for the use of the pupil, the district and its servants and agents and the trustees shall be deemed not to have been guilty of negligence or misconduct unless it is shown that the district or one or more of the servants or agents thereof or the trustees had actual knowledge of the defect in, or the dangerous nature of, the apparatus and failed to remedy or replace the apparatus within a reasonable time after acquiring the knowledge.[16]

The Manitoba school statutes also address the voluntary assumption of inherent risks accepted by those involved in technical or vocational training.

Any pupil attending any course in technical or vocational training... shall be deemed to have accepted the risks incidental to the business, trade, or industry in which he is being instructed or trained; and if bodily injury or death is caused to any such pupil during or as a result of the course, no cause of action for loss or damage suffered by reason of the bodily injury or death accrues to the pupil or to any other person,

(a) against the school district or any of the trustees, if it is shown that, after making investigations, the board of trustees believed, upon reasonable grounds, that the person with whom the pupil was placed was competent to give the instruction, and that his plant and equipment were such as to provide reasonable safeguards against injury; or (b) against the person giving the instruction or his servants or agents, unless the bodily injury or death of the pupil was caused or contributed to by the negligence or the misconduct of the person giving the instruction or his servants or agents.[17]

Although not directed at students participating in outdoor education curricula, this statute would very likely receive analogous attention in Manitoba in the event of a school outdoor education accident where the defendant school board wished to claim volenti on the part of the student plaintiff.

Alberta statutes are unique in that they do not include a section setting out the statutory duties of teachers, but they do require school boards in the province to carry accident and liability insurance policies for the express purpose of indemnifying any board and/or teacher sued in tort law.

In addition, many school boards have developed written guidelines regulating the manner in which outdoor education programs are conducted within their system. Nationally, perhaps the most comprehensive of these guidelines are the *Safety Oriented Guidelines For Outdoor Education Leadership and Programming*, published in 1986 by the Canadian Association for Health, Physical Education, and Recreation (CAHPER). CAHPER's guidelines were based upon both legal principle and custom. Dozens of board and agency standards were reviewed and synthesized into their lowest common denominators, allowing teachers/leaders to raise the standards as dictated by their unique situation. Although not presented as a legal source of law, the general and specific guidelines such professional associations have written for their members running outdoor education field trips may set useful examples not only for their own members, but for other boards, agencies or associations interested in developing similar standards.

In sum, the existence of legislated teacher/school board duties provides educators in most provinces with a set of relatively general guidelines upon which to conduct their curricula and premises. However, it should be noted that the vast majority of actions which may arise in physical education programs have been settled on the basis of adjudicated precedents in case law, only rarely drawing on a breach of statute as the cause of action.

THE STATUTORY DUTIES OF OCCUPIERS

Although occupiers' liability issues may be dealt with through common law processes, most provinces have taken the initiative in enacting legislation[18] and have done much to help clear up the haze surrounding this issue in their respective regions. As Professor Fleming so aptly described the problem:

> Indeed, nowhere else in the law of torts has confusion been as prevalent and injustice as rampant as it has been in disputes arising out of injuries sustained on the land of another.[19]

In addition, the power of occupiers' liability legislation, in those provinces adopting it, supersedes the common law duty of care.

> ...the provisions of the Act apply in place of the rules of the common law that determine the care that the occupier of premises at common law is required to show for the purpose of determining his liability in law in respect of dangers to persons entering the premises.... [20]

While adopting occupier's liability legislation, courts in most Canadian provinces still adhere to the belief that an occupier's liability is largely dependent on the duty owed to the plaintiff visitor and that this duty depends upon the visitor's category. A number of provinces have held to the traditional three category system, where visitors have been treated as either (a) trespassers, (b) licensees, or (c) invitees.[21]

A trespasser typically enters the occupier's land without the former's permission and to the trespasser, the occupier owes only the duty not to intentionally lay traps likely to injure.[22] The licensee is generally viewed as a social guest entering the occupier's land with the latter's consent, but not to conduct any business. To a licensee, the occupier owes a duty to give warnings or otherwise prevent injury resulting "from concealed dangers or traps of which (the occupier) has actual knowledge."[23] And the invitee, who is a "lawful visitor from whose visit the occupier stands to derive an economic advantage,"[24] can expect the occupier to "use reasonable care to prevent damage from unusual dangers, of which he knows or ought to know...."[25] Participants paying for outdoor programs would fall into the category of invitees as they have a contractual right to be on the premises and protected from hidden dangers.

Recently, there has been a strong movement toward the reduction of the licensee and invitee categories to one, due in large part to the tremendous inconsistency with which plaintiffs are typically assigned these categories. In case law this inconsistency has been evidenced in situations where, for example, school students[26] and library patrons,[27] whose presence is not usually economically advantageous to the occupier, were nevertheless termed invitees. In statute law, Alberta, British Columbia, Ontario, and others have eliminated the distinction between licensees and invitees. For example, The Alberta *Occupiers' Liability Act* of 1973[28] states that:

> An occupier of premises owes a duty to every visitor on his premises to take such care as in all the circumstances of the case is reasonable to see that the visitor will be reasonably safe in using the premises

> where "visitor" means:
> ... a person who is lawfully present on premises by virtue of an express or implied term of contract, or
> ... any other person whose presence on the premises is lawful.[29]

> The common law duty of care which has been accepted in this statute applies to
>   (a) the condition of the premises,
>   (b) activities on the premises, and
>   (c) the conduct of third parties on the premises.[30]

However, these reform acts clarify the occupier's position further by granting the authority to "restrict, modify or exclude his duty"[31] "by express agreement or by express stipulation or notice. . . . "[32] In addition, the common duty of care owed to a group of individuals who voluntarily assume certain inherent risks when entering the occupier's premises may only be that described as owed a trespasser, i.e., the duty not to willfully or recklessly create unnecessary dangers for that visitor.[33] A visitor will be subject to this lower duty of care because of voluntary assumption of risk,

> ... where the entry is for the purpose of a recreational activity and, no fee is paid for the entry or activity of the person, other than a bene-

fit or payment received from a government or government agency or a non-profit recreational club or association, and the person is not being provided with living accommodation by the occupier.[34]

Some of the premises applicable to this subsection include:

    (a) a rural premises that is
        (i) used for agricultural purposes
        (ii) vacant or undeveloped premises
        (iii) forested or wilderness premises
    (b) golf courses when not open for playing...
    (h) recreational trails reasonably marked by notice as such.[35]

These sections concerning the occupier's right of exclusion of duty and the responsibilities of those willingly accepting risks have quite obvious implications for outdoor agencies and/or programmers operating on property other than their own. This personal responsibility may extend to the running of programs on public as well as private land.

The inevitable dissipation of the licensee-invitee dichotomy is indicated by the reduction in the power of warnings, previously held as adequate protection for the occupier in his dealings with licensees on his property.

A warning, without more, shall not be treated as absolving an occupier from discharging the common duty of care to his visitor unless in all the circumstances the warning is enough to enable the visitor to be reasonably safe.[36]

In Alberta, agencies operating programs on their own property must be aware of the special duty they owe children whether they technically be licensee-invitees or trespassers.[37] A child trespasser is owed a higher duty of care than an adult trespasser. In an entire section devoted to this relationship, the Alberta Act says:

(1) When an occupier knows or has reason to know
    (a) that a child trespasser is on his premises, and
    (b) that the condition of, or activities on, the premises create a danger of death or serious bodily harm to that child, the occupier

owes a duty to that child to take such care as in all the circumstances of the case is reasonable to see that the child will be reasonably safe from that danger.

(2) In determining whether the duty of care under subsection (1) has been discharged consideration shall be given to

(a) the age of the child,

(b) the ability of the child to appreciate danger, and

(c) the burden on the occupier of eliminating the danger or protecting the child from the danger as compared to the risk of the danger to the child.

(3) For the purposes of subsection (1), the occupier has reason to know that a child trespasser is on his premises if he has knowledge of facts from which a reasonable man would infer that a child is present or that the presence of a child is so probable that the occupier should conduct himself on the assumption that a child is present.[38]

Although this section of the Alberta Act is the only one of its sort in Canada, British statutes have long recognized that an occupier must be prepared for children to be less careful than adults. The most common cause for the raising of the standard of care owed a child trespasser is the existence of some allurement or "attractive nuisance" on the occupier's property which while fascinating the child is also "inherently dangerous in ways which [the child] cannot be expected to appreciate."[39] In order to apply the doctrine of attractive nuisance, the child must be of sufficient age to be drawn by the object, yet still too immature to appreciate the hazards associated with it.[40]

In the classic case in this area of law, *Glasgow Corporation v. Taylor*,[41] a 7-year-old boy died after eating some poisonous berries he picked in the defendant's public botanical garden park. It was held that the defendant municipal occupier was liable by virtue of the fact that although they were aware of the poisonous nature of the berries and the constant presence of children in the park, they did not take measures to fence off the shrub or to give adequate warning intelligible to younger patrons. The big, black berries were considered an allurement and a trap to the plaintiff as he could not be expected to know their contents.[42]

Therefore, in order to constitute an "attractive nuisance" in law, the location or item must have some hidden danger. According to some, open water, whether naturally or artificially occurring, is an obvious hazard which has no dangers that are not apparent and as such cannot be considered a trap.[43] The author contends that this is not necessarily so as unexpected drop-offs,[44] undercurrents and dangerous objects concealed in murky water have caused many injuries and deaths.

In *Latham v. R. Johnson and Nephew Ltd.*[45] it was established that an occupier could not be liable unless the item could be shown to be a dangerous allurement.

> ...A trap is a figure of speech, not a formula. It involves the idea of concealment and surprise, of an appearance of safety under the circumstances cloaking a reality of danger.[46]

The Alberta *Occupiers' Liability Act* takes the allurement doctrine one step further by considering not only the probability of harm coming to a child because of an attractive nuisance, but also the feasibility of the occupier removing the hazard or otherwise "protecting the child from the danger."[47] In the 1949 Alberta case of *Ware's Taxi Ltd. v. Gilliham,*[48] the defendant taxi company was contracted by a school to drive children to and from its kindergarten. The children it served were from ages three to eight and the vehicle used was a regular four-door sedan with handles and push button locks on all the doors, which the taxi driver made sure were down before starting the car. The 5-year-old plaintiff was injured when she fell out of the vehicle after tampering with the button and handle on her side of the car. The Supreme Court of Canada upheld the trial decision which found the defendant taxi company liable for not installing inexpensive safety devices readily available on the market which made it impossible for children to open the car doors. The push buttons were deemed an attractive nuisance. Justice Estay discussed the allurement of the door lock mechanism.

> This push button was within easy reach of every child in the rear seat of the automobile. Moreover, that it could be raised up and pushed down was made evident to each child every time the driver of the automobile opened or closed that door.[49]

Although this particular case is not concerned with the liability of an "occupier" of land, it serves to provide an excellent illustration of the concept of allurement, which may be readily applied to many items and situations including those involving land.

The statutes and cases presented here should help clarify the legal position of outdoor leaders, whether they be visitors or occupiers. Many questions still exist in this area of law, in Canada and indeed throughout the commonwealth. Rather subjective questions often raised in these cases include: (a) whether a given hazardous condition actually constituted a concealed danger, (b) whether the occupier, acting as a reasonable person, should have realized the hazard held a concealed danger, and (c) whether in the cost-benefit analysis, it was feasible to eliminate the hazard or at least warn of its presence. The agency operating facilities and/or programs on its own land must take time to regularly inspect the site for potential hazards and take steps to remove, isolate (for example, fence off) or at least warn of any hazards which hold concealed dangers.

In a highly publicized 1985 case, the City of Brampton, Ontario, was sued by a youth injured in a trail bike collision on some municipally owned property. In this, the case of *McErlean* v. *Sarel and the City of Brampton*,[50] the 14-year-old plaintiff was riding his trail bike on some undeveloped vacant land which contained a gravel pit. Around the water filled pit was a good quality gravel road which narrowed considerably as it passed around the only curve. In addition to its tightness, this curve was also sharp (almost 90°), and blind because of the presence of rocks, trees, and shrubs.

On the day of the accident, the defendant Neil Sarel, then 13, was attempting to drive a borrowed trail bike. His inexperience resulted in erratic driving along the road, with much weaving from one side of the road to the other. Unfortunately, he was on the left hand side of the road as he entered the sharp curve. At the same time, the unsuspecting McErlean entered the curve from the opposite direction, on his own side of the road, at the moderate speed of about 55 kilometers per hour. The collision which ensued left Michael McErlean conscious but a quadriplegic, incontinent and unable to speak.[51]

At trial, the Ontario Supreme Court apportioned the extremely high $7,023,150 damages between both defendants and the plaintiff. In finding the defendant City of Brampton 75 percent obliged, this court relied upon admissions by the municipal official responsible for the site. He testified that he was aware

1. of the presence of children on the property;
2. of the condition of the road and curve;
3. that the area was an allurement to children;

4. that children drove trail bikes on other gravel pit properties of the city.
5. that there were problems with respect to the safety of trail bikes.

In finding liability, the court decided that due to the aforementioned knowledge, the case of access, and the absence of "no trespassing" signs, the site was "in fact and law, a park and the plaintiff a licensee of the city."[52]

Neil Sarel was found 15 percent responsible for his negligent operation of a trail bike on a road frequented by other young trail bike riders. Michael McErlean was found 10 percent contributorily negligent because of his prior knowledge of the dangerous curve and the hazards presented by other young riders. In the court's words "to have used that curve, even at a moderate rate of speed and entirely on his own side, in all the circumstances, was a failure to take reasonable care for his own safety."[53]

The unprecedented damage award resulted in a prompt appeal of this case by the defendant City of Brampton, and as noted earlier, the city won its appeal, the finding was reversed and the damage award reduced by almost half. In stating the rationale for overturning the trial decision, Chief Justice Howland discussed the licensee status of the plaintiff. He noted that the city had not endeavored to exclude people such as the plaintiff from the land in question. The common law duty owed by an occupier to a licensee was again reiterated, recognizing the higher standard of care recently identified in the *Occupiers' Liability Act.*

However, the learned judge also clearly noted that under the law, a licensor's duty does not extend to usual or common dangers which ordinary reasonable persons can be expected to know and appreciate.[54] He believed, based on the evidence presented at trial, that both of the trail bike riders involved in the accident were very familiar with the road and curve in question and the obvious hazard created by the partially blind corner. The danger present was not construed as an unusual one for youths of their age, experience, and intelligence and the condition was not such that the occupier could be expected to know more than the users of the property. The judge also dismissed the doctrine of allurement alluded to at trial, stating that these were teenagers who were fully aware of the risks they were taking and who were not owed warnings of such self evident dangers. In addition, Sarel's liability was conceded based on the fact that both youths had been involved in an "adult activity" and "no allowance should be made for their immaturity, whether in policy or in law."[55] McErlean was found to have been contributorily negligent due to his recklessness in failing to slow down while negotiating the sharp, narrow and partially blind curve.

While Brampton was alleviated of most of its responsibility for this accident which occurred on its property, a raft moored in shallow water in a lake or ocean, especially where murky water would reduce visibility and subsequent examination of the depth by a diver, could be found to constitute an unwarranted municipal hazard. In 1980, the British Columbia Court of Appeal found the Town of Powell River 80 percent responsible for the quadriplegia suffered by a 22-year-old swimming instructor/examiner, injured when he dove off a five-meter diving board on an ocean raft into only two meters of water.[56] Although the plaintiff was 20 percent contributorily negligent due to his specialized training and lack of care for himself in the situation, the defendant municipality was held primarily responsible for his damages as they induced him into a false sense of security by failing to post warning signs on the raft.[57]

In this example, the hazardous condition contained a concealed trap (shallow water); the town recreation department ought to have foreseen the danger present and the cost of erecting a sign was in no way prohibitory or unreasonable in light of the potential harm which a patron could, and did, incur. This same opinion was asserted in the Saskatchewan case of *Bundas* v. *Oyma Regional Park Authority*,[58] where the plaintiff dove off a raft in the defendant's park lake into water he knew was of irregular depth. In this case the defendant park authority was held 25 percent liable for the plaintiff Bundas' spinal injury (which left him unable to lift heavy objects), because it failed to post warning signs. However, Bundas was held 75 percent liable for his injury, because it was believed that he failed in his duty to protect himself from hazards of which he should have been aware. Regardless, it is incumbent on each outdoor agency to evaluate such hazards and protect or at least warn its participants accordingly.

RELEVANT LEGISLATION FOR USE OF PUBLIC AND PRIVATE WILDLANDS FOR OUTDOOR PROGRAMMING

The outdoor leaders operating on lands other than their or their agency's own, whether publicly or privately maintained, must be prepared to accept this same responsibility for surveying the site and protecting participants from any hazards identified. Although a good leader will do this re-gardless of legal duty, this evaluation is especially crucial in situations where the occupier has graciously allowed the use of the land while ex-pressly restricting or excluding himself or herself from liability for inju-ries incurred by the outdoor leader and program participants. It almost goes without saying that an outdoor leader will always check with the owner of private land before using it for a program, to avoid any poten-tial classification as a trespasser.

In Alberta, the *Petty Trespass Act*[59] deems it an offence subject to cer-tain conditions, to trespass on "privately owned land" or posted "Crown land subject to any disposition except a grazing lease or grazing permit."[60] Therefore, this Alberta Act identifies all privately owned and occupied Crown land as off limits to uninvited entrants, with the exception of grazing leases or permits, as long as the visitor has been notified by writ-ten or verbal communication or by signage which states that trespassing is not permitted.[61]

Again using the Alberta example, the *Public Lands Act*[62] serves to limit access to vacant public lands. All public lands are open for use except those receiving special disposition (for example, under Mineral Surface Lease, Homesteading Lease, Grazing Lease) and here access may be re-stricted to those with a lease or licence of occupation.[63] Similarly, the *Forests Act*[64] permits access to all public lands containing timber berths.[65]

Although some variation in the names and scope of these and similar acts exists interprovincially, all provinces do have legislation addressing public and private land access and usage (camping, hunting, etcetera). Outdoor leaders intent on utilizing any land of which they are not the primary occupiers should familiarize themselves with the statutes and regulations pertinent to that particular area's use. The law is there to pre-vent user group conflicts from arising as well as to protect various types of wildlands from indiscriminate use.

Environmental Legal and Ethical Considerations

One of the primary justifications for outdoor education/recreation pro-gramming today is found in its value in teaching people how to use and enjoy the natural environment in a manner which facilitates its preserva-tion for future generations. An essential part of such programming is the inculcation of an understanding and appreciation of that environment, hopefully leading to each participant internalizing a sense of stewardship

for the land in its natural state. In order to achieve this obviously meritorious objective, outdoor educators must act as strong role models, designing their programs in ways which impart minimal impact upon the sites used.

Not only is this an important consideration ethically, but all provinces have statutory laws regulating destructive activities on public lands. In Alberta for example, the Environment Council (formerly the Environment Conservation Authority) deals with matters pertaining to environment conservation, including:

(a) the conservation, management and utilization of natural resources;

(b) the prevention and control of pollution of natural resources;

(c) any operations or activities, whether carried on for commercial or industrial purposes or otherwise,

    (i) that adversely affect or are likely to adversely affect the quality or quantity of any natural resource, or

    (ii) that destroy, disturb, pollute, alter or make use of a natural resource or are likely to do so; . . .

(f) the preservation of natural resources for their aesthetic value;

(g) laws in force in Alberta that relate to or directly or indirectly affect natural resources.[66]

The outdoor leader and/or agency should readily see the implications for environmentally conscious resource utilization in terms of sanitation, woodcutting, trail development and so on. Often outdoor programming clubs and agencies actively oppose various commercial and industrial operations polluting or otherwise degrading the environment, especially in areas with outdoor education/recreation potential. Although not a strong lobby group to date in any province, outdoor educators have a definite vested interest in the conservation of wildlands, both within and outside designated park areas. They should therefore strive to be heard, both collectively and severally in integrated management plans and processes and/or in voicing opposition to ecologically unsound proposals affecting natural areas.

Relevant Legislation for Use of Public Parklands for Outdoor Programming

NATIONAL PARKS LEGISLATION The *National Parks Act*[67] stipulates that:

The National Parks of Canada are hereby dedicated to the people of Canada for their benefit, education and enjoyment, subject to this Act and the regulations, and the National Parks shall be maintained and made use of so as to leave them unimpaired for the enjoyment of future generations.[68]

In order to achieve this goal, the Minister retains the power of controlling:

... amusements, sports, occupations and other activities or undertakings, and prescribing the places where any such activities or undertakings may be carried on; and the levying of licence fees in respect thereof.[69]

When assessing the statutory basis of a litigation against a National Park in Canada, the courts will refer to the *Crown Liability Act*,[70] which allows actions against the Crown based on either (a) injury(ies) resulting from the negligence of an employee of the Crown[71] or (b) injury(ies) resulting from a breach of Crown duty related to its occupation or control of land.[72]

Due to the inconsistencies in the law related to occupiers' liability, it becomes rather difficult to predict Crown liability under the second subsection. Although the Crown is free to submit to evaluation under the provincial occupiers' liability reform legislation currently enacted in most provinces, it is not legally bound to do so.[73] In provinces without such legislation, cases will be decided solely upon common law principles.

Part of the problem in predicting federal Crown liability lies in the paucity of cases actually adjudicated against it. This may be due in part to the exceptionally short (seven day) limitation period within which the plaintiff must make a claim to the appropriate property administrator and the Deputy Attorney-General of Canada.[74] As most park visitors are unaware of this statute, their claims have occasionally been extinguished prematurely. Outdoor leaders taking people into Federal parks should definitely keep this statute in mind and begin proceedings immediately if The Canadian Parks Service or another Crown agency's negligence is the suspected proximate cause of an injury to oneself or one's participants.

A number of other Acts may become relevant in cases related to the management of provincial lands and resources. For example, provincial Wildlife Acts hold legislation of import in the event of personal or property damage caused by wildlife. In a recent wildlife damage related case, the effect of one provincial Wildlife Act was raised in question. In this, the case of *Diversified Holdings Ltd. v. The Queen in Right of B.C.*,[75] a landowner sued the Wildlife Branch of the Provincial Ministry of the Environment for damage done to his alfalfa fields and stacks by elk which had been conditioned to this type of feed through the winter feeding programs of the Ministry. In finding the Crown agency and its staff not negligent, the Supreme Court of B.C. relied upon various aspects of the provincial *Wildlife Act*. For example, this Act states unequivocally that:

> 80(3) Notwithstanding anything in this Act, no right of action lies and no right of compensation exists against the Crown in right of the Province for death, personal injury or property damage caused by any wildlife declared by this Act or the regulations to be the property of the Crown.

This same Act would undoubtedly be applied today in the event of a grizzly bear attack resulting in personal injury in B.C. Most other provinces' Wildlife Acts contain a similar or identical exclusion clause.[76]

In addition, provincial Wildlife Acts may specify the rights and responsibilities of Crown land managers to close areas to the public when wildlife creates a hazard to that public. The Alberta *Wildlife Act* for example, states that:

> 81(1) If a wildlife officer or wildlife guardian believes that the health or safety of the public is in jeopardy in any area owing to the presence of a wildlife or exotic animal, he may make a written or oral order that the area be closed to public access for the period specified in the order.

Such legislation is certainly relevant in the event of problem bears or other animal hazards and those leading or recreating in and around such areas should be aware of the physical and legal risks they would assume in ignoring such closures. Most park visitors are viewed as invitees and the responsible Parks department has the duty to exercise "reasonable care to prevent damage from unusual danger, of which it knows or ought to know."[77] In *Sturdy et al. v. R.*,[78] a female grizzly bear and her cubs were held not to constitute an unusual danger to the plaintiff, injured by the she-bear while walking near a garbage dump in Jasper National Park. The Federal Court of Canada believed that there was no breach of The

Canadian Parks Service's duty to warn the plaintiff invitee about the inherent dangers presented by the natural occurrence of bears in the park. Although no signs had been posted at the particular site of the mauling, pamphlets distributed at the park gates and highway signs warning of potential hazards posed by bears were held to provide reasonable warning.[79] However, the courts clarified their finding of volenti on the part of the plaintiff, stating that even if Sturdy implicitly agreed to assume physical risks by walking near the dump "there was no consent or agreement, implied or expressed, that he waived any right of action in case of injury by a bear."[80]

In a recent case against The Canadian Parks Service, a middle-aged couple became lost on a series of cross country ski trails at Lake Louise in Banff National Park. The pair, equipped for only a day trip, ended up spending the night out and as a result the wife died of hypothermia. The husband suffered frostbite which necessitated amputation of some toes in addition to severe emotional distress. In this, the case of *Rudko et al. v. R.*[81] the statutes contained in the *Crown Liability Act*, the *National Parks Act*, and the *Occupiers' Liability Act* were all considered in finding the defendant Parks department not liable.[82] Some of the relevant legislation raised included the fact that the seven day statute of limitations on cases against the Crown was waived. While the plaintiffs did not bring their case forward until nearly two years after the incident, it was believed that enforcement of statute would be an injustice where one of the plaintiffs had died as a result of the accident.[83]

In addition, the plaintiffs' case was based on the *Crown Liability Act*, the Park's personal liability, and the vicarious liability for the acts of its agents or servants, especially the latter. Rudko's reason for attributing much of the blame on this basis was due to his perception that erroneous directions had been given him and his wife by information personnel working in the Lake Louise warden's office. The young lady they consulted suggested they take a connecting trail between two well used loops to extend their proposed afternoon ski trip.

After accepting this woman's advice, the couple set off. They were well dressed in multiple layers and carrying food, drink, maps, matches, and lighters. The plaintiffs' testimony indicated that the couple were frequent skiers and were very experienced and conscientious with regard to travel in the mountain parks. However, unfortunately on this day, they took the wrong trail cut-off and this error was compounded by at least three subsequent route decision errors. As it was a warm March day, the couple became wet from the snow, chilled, exhausted, and eventually unable to help themselves.

Mr. Rudko contends that if the woman in the information office had not misled them into believing they could not miss the cut-off trail, the other errors would not have occurred. Although the judge noted that this was persuasive, he was not prepared to hold that her assistance was the cause of accident, nor that a personal action against her would have held up.[84]

In Rudko's claim of personal fault by The Canadian Parks Service, the defendant objected to the court's requiring it to produce as evidence information exhibits indicating modifications made to the ski trails since the accident. The Canadian Parks Service made significant changes to the trail system and their signage subsequent to the Rudko's accident, but claimed that layouts for the proposed changes had been begun prior to the accident. The defense counsel added that:

> Improving or eliminating a situation which has given rise to an accident (if indeed that is what was done) after an accident has taken place is not equivalent to an admission of liability for the accident. It is merely a matter of common sense.[85]

He continued by drawing parallels to building owners/managers filling cracks or wiping up slippery portions on floors to avoid additional accidents once one has occurred, stating that neither situation necessarily implied negligence. To prove liability, the plaintiffs must show that the defendant knew of the dangerous conditions prior to the accident.

Using the fourth section of the *National Parks Act* in its defense, The Parks Service noted that its responsibility is to maintain the parks in a manner which leaves them unimpaired for the enjoyment of future generations. This, it believed, implies a different standard of care than is required for owners of private property frequented by the public.[86]

In the Rudko case, the judge dismissed the action based on the absence of fault under the *Crown Liability Act* or the *Occupiers' Liability Act* of Alberta. He stated that it was not reasonably foreseeable that a skier on these short, novice level ski trails "would become so lost as to lead to a fatal result."[87] He believed that "Parks Canada was not the insurer of persons using its wilderness trails" and while he agreed that better signage and a more detailed map would have been helpful, their absence was not sufficient under the circumstances to constitute actionable negligence on the part of the National Parks.[88]

The Crown may employ a number of techniques to restrict or exclude its liability as an occupier. As the *Sturdy* case demonstrated, general warnings of an inherent hazard, such as pamphlets or road signs may be sufficient. However, where a definable danger exists at a particular site, say an avalanche danger on a designated cross-country ski trail, then a more specific warning may be required. Other expressly stated disclaimers, either on posted signs[89] or on entry tickets[90] may be sufficient to relieve the Crown of liability as long as these waivers are brought to the attention of the visitor.

A final method of exclusion practised by The Canadian Parks Service is their requirement that concessionaires such as ski lift operators and mountain guides carry adequate liability insurance and indemnify the park from any personal injury actions resulting from accidents. This reliance upon other agencies and groups operating in the parks to be insured has led to an increase in regulations regarding who has the privilege of operating profit oriented backcountry programs, especially in the mountain parks where activity risk levels are highest. For example, no one is allowed to lead technical ascents in the mountain parks for money without certification as a member of the Association of Canadian Mountain Guides. Although such regulations are perceived as unnecessarily restrictive by many outdoor leaders, they have probably been instrumental in keeping the standard of leadership very high and the rate of injuries concomitantly low in high country travel.

Although little litigation has been successful against The Canadian Parks Service to date, the greatly increased use of backcountry trails for hiking, skiing and trail riding and the equally significant growth of wildwater paddling in the parks have opened up a tremendous potential for legal actions. In cases where a sanctioned outdoor instructor/guide is leading a group within Federal Park boundaries, the specific facts of the case will undoubtedly need to be scrutinized in order to determine whether (a) the Crown was negligent under its duty as an occupier, (b) whether the agency and/or leaders were negligent in their duty to supervise and lead the group, and/or (c) whether the personal conduct of the participant contributed to the injury(ies). For example, some years ago, in an unlitigated incident in Alberta, a 12-year-old boy disappeared (his body was recovered the following spring) while he and the grade six class to which he belonged were viewing the Maligne Canyon in Jasper National Park. Who would have been liable had a suit been brought? (a) Parks Canada, for failing to take reasonable care in erecting fences to keep invited visitors back from the lip of the canyon, and/or posting signs to warn patrons to stay back; (b) the youth's teacher, who failed to supervise the child and keep him on the designated walkway; (c) the school board, who perhaps allowed a teacher to take the group without sufficient supervisory assistance; or (d) the boy himself, who at twelve years of age should have had sufficient intelligence and experience to appreciate the hazards associated with going too close to the edge? Unfortunately, there are still many more questions than answers regarding the law in this area.

For outdoor leaders, the chance of attributing liability to, or at least sharing liability with, the Crown will be highest when leaders are running programs in highly human-influenced environments such as ski hills and designated interpretive trails, and lowest when venturing into the backcountry, off specified trails. Here, leaders must have the judgment, skill and insurance to cover themselves and their participants (especially if these are children), as their level of specialized training and knowledge would very likely leave them liable for damages resulting from risks which the participants themselves could not or did not assume.

PROVINCIAL PARKS AND RECREATION AREA LEGISLATION The principles regarding provincial parks management and liability are the same as those concerning liability in national parks. No provincial park statute reviewed shed any new light on the position of the provincial parks department or of outdoor programmers running programs within provincial parks boundaries. Thus, it must be recognized that this constitutes a difficult area of public tort liability. The courts must repeatedly distinguish between issues of policy and operationalization, and many grey areas exist.

In terms of Crown liability in tort law, the principles adhered to are virtually the same as those outlined in the *Crown Liability Act*.[91] In Alberta, since the eradication of Section 24 of the *Judicature Act*,[92] Alberta's *Proceedings Against the Crown Act*[93] has held the province liable for its torts.

> . . . the Crown is subject to all those liabilities in tort to which, if it were a person of full age and capacity, it would be subject,

(a) in respect of a tort committed by any of its officers or agents,
(b) in respect of any breach of those duties that a person owes to his servants or agents by reason of being their employer,
(c) in respect of any breach of the duties attaching to the ownership, occupation, possession or control of property, and
(d) under any statute or under any regulation or by-law made or passed under the authority of any statute.[94]

None of the provinces in Canada has retained governmental immunity and all may now be tried in tort law for any of the four aforementioned causes of action.

According to the *Provincial Parks Act* of Alberta:[95]

3. Parks shall be developed and maintained...
   (c) to facilitate their use and enjoyment for outdoor recreation,

and,

4. Recreation areas shall be developed and maintained to facilitate their use and enjoyment for outdoor recreation.[96]

The recreation values of parks have been largely tempered with natural history conservation and preservation values, whereas the primary orientation of provincially designated recreation areas is outdoor recreation. Although a number of residence camps and more transitory outdoor programs operate sites in provincial parks and recreation areas, this may not be practised without written authorization from the Minister. The Minister also has the authority to prescribe standards for the operation of camps and other commercial ventures operated within parks or recreation areas.[97]

MUNICIPAL PARKS AND RECREATION BY-LAWS Although the majority of outdoor educators are school teachers at the primary and secondary levels, a substantial number are also scout leaders, YMCA/YWCA programmers, and municipal recreation program leaders (such as, outdoor program instructors, playground and daycamp leaders). Therefore, it stands to reason that a significant portion, in fact most, outdoor education/recreation will occur within urban and rural municipal boundaries—in public parks, along river valleys, and ravines. Individuals and/or agencies utilizing municipal property and/or facilities for outdoor education/recreation purposes should be aware of the municipal statutes, by-laws, ordinances and regulations governing the use of those areas or sites.

In Alberta, for example, the only statutes of any particular relevance to the outdoor programmer working in a municipal setting are found in the *Municipal Government Act*.[98] This act contains a section on legal proceedings, including statutes pertinent to the raising of an action against a municipality, based on negligence or occupiers' liability.

Most municipal law is contained in by-laws, passed by the urban or rural municipal council. Although some of these by-laws will be relevant to only some outdoor leaders, others are generic enough to apply to anyone operating in this role. For example, a school teacher wishing to begin a canoeing unit with a few basic sessions in a municipal swimming pool may be bound by the rights and conditions of use of such facilities cited in the municipality's *Parks/School Joint Use Agreement*,[99] if such a contract exists. Such agreements will also be relevant to teachers working in municipal districts, but would not apply to those teaching in county run schools where county council administers all public services including the public school system coterminous with its boundaries. This by-law will likely not apply to any outdoor educators except teachers, unless they represent a community group seeking an indoor school facility (for example, a crafts room), through the Parks and Recreation Department.

All outdoor program leaders, regardless of the agency or organization they are employed by, should be fully aware of the enacted duties and powers of the Parks and/or Recreation Department of the municipality, municipal district or county. In Edmonton, for example, By-law No. 2202 concerns the city's Parks and Recreation Departmental structure, responsibilities and authority.[100] The duties of this and like departments includes a general duty:

...To be responsible for the planning, design, construction, operation, maintenance and administration of all Public Park and Recreation and other lands under the control of the Department...,

To develop sound and comprehensive recreation programs...[and]

To act as a recreational co-ordinating body... and to ensure that all maximum and most efficient and economic use is made of all available recreational opportunities and facilities.... [101]

Such departments are also responsible for developing by-laws, ordinances and regulations for the use and preservation of the parklands within their jurisdiction. In Edmonton, for example, general park regulations state that:

10. No person while within the confines of a park shall:
    ...(4) Cut, break, bend or in any way injure or deface any turf, tree, shrub, hedge, plant, flower or park ornament...
    (8) Start any fire or permit any person under his control to start any fire except in fireplaces provided therein for that purpose...
    (13) Tease, molest or injure any mammal, bird or fish...
    (14) ... erect, build or locate nor permit the erection, building or locating in any park of any trailer, shelter or other building or any tent or other shelter without first obtaining the written permission of the City Commissioners.[102]

The outdoor leader will quickly recognize the implications of these selected regulations for environmental studies, campfire and shelter building programs and/or overnights. In addition, like most large cities, Edmonton also has a by-law which prevents overnighting by closing all parks to the public from 11 o'clock in the evening until 8 o'clock in the morning.[103] However, it may be possible to receive special dispensation by justifying the outdoor program to the Parks Department and receiving a permit from the Commissioner. Outdoor leaders should remember that it is their responsibility to receive clearance before initiating a program which may violate one or more regulations.

The outdoor instructor/guide has a duty to know and adhere to the enacted rules and regulations governing any and all public or private wildlands utilized as the setting for programs, at least as far as program use of the area is concerned. While operating outdoor education and adventure programs in designated park environments has certain attractions to the outdoor programmer, including relatively easy access to wildland areas, no direct costs for area operations and maintenance and the presence of backcountry search and rescue services (usually at no charge to registered groups), numerous responsibilities accompany these benefits.

One of these duties is the learning of the statutes, by-laws and/or regulations which establish parameters for the outdoor programmers' use of the area. A discussion with Parks Department representatives concerning these guidelines as well as the department's policies and legal position regarding use of the area for outdoor education/recreation purposes may be valuable time spent by the outdoor programming agency. Finally, as many such departments will attempt to restrict or exclude themselves from personal injury liability in such situations, the onus of checking for hazards inherent to use of or travel in a given area and of subsequently protecting program participants from unreasonable risks, will often remain largely on the shoulders of the outdoor leader.

6 THE LEGAL LIABILITY OF
THE OUTDOOR LEADER

THE TEST FOR OUTDOOR LEADER LIABILITY

THE TEST USED to determine the negligence of an outdoor leader is the same as that used for any other defendant. This test involves an evaluation of five factors:

1. Determination of a duty owed by the leader to the participant.
2. A breach of that established duty; the failure to meet a prescribed standard of care.
3. Actual physical and/or mental injury to the participant.
4. Proof that the defendant leader's negligence was the proximate cause of the participant's injury(ies).
5. Evidence showing that the participant did not voluntarily assume the particular physical and legal risks associated with the injury(ies) sustained.

If the defendant can show that the plaintiff was injured by a risk inherent to participation in the activity, or that the plaintiff willingly accepted a legal risk which was understood and appreciated, then the injured party will have no recourse to legal action against the defendant. If, however, the participant did not assume the risk in either of these ways, but somehow otherwise contributed to the injury(ies) through his or her own negligence, then the courts will likely apportion damages between the two parties according to their relative degrees of negligence.

The relationship between outdoor leaders and participants can be paralleled with that of teacher-student[1] or coach-player, where through some express agreement, contractual or not, the outdoor programming agency has agreed to supervise, instruct and train the participant in one or more of the potentially "high risk" outdoor activity pursuit areas (such as hiking and backpacking, cross-country ski instruction and touring, canoe and kayak instruction and touring, etcetera). In determining whether the standard of care demonstrated by the outdoor leader was adequate for an adult participant, the courts would apply the "reasonable person" test. Because of the scarcity of established standards in outdoor activity pursuits, the judiciary would probably rely on one or more professed "experts" in the field to convince them that the leader did (or did not) conduct the activity as a reasonably prudent person with the defendant's knowledge and training would have. The court would strive to establish whether the leader properly evaluated the likelihood of injury and its potential gravity against the utility of the activity being pursued and the cost of eliminating the risk.[2]

First of all, tremendous judgmental capacities must be attributed to any leader who can take a group of heterogeneously skilled people, realistically evaluate the magnitude of risk for *each* individual participant performing the activity in the selected environment, and plan a program accordingly. The tendency, all too often, is for leaders to gear their program to the average participant, leaving the risk level higher for the less experienced or weaker members of the group. Achieving the ultimate objective of having everyone in the group learning and practicing their skills while at an optimal level of arousal (challenged, but not to the point of being too anxious to learn or perform) is the mark of a sensitive and usually a seasoned leader.

Secondly, outdoor education/recreation is also unique in that it relies upon the presence of perceived risk and danger for its success. People register for outdoor adventure programs involving physical, mental and social challenges in order that through the facing of a number of "controlled" risks, they may overcome them on their way to achieving feelings of perceived competence and self-determination in the world. However, in weighing the magnitude of risk warranted by the utility of the activity being pursued, the courts will not recognize this rationale as justification for exposing participants to unreasonable risks. In fact,

... in practice the activity being pursued is irrelevant in the great majority of cases of personal injury or property damages. The courts are not prepared to acquit someone of negligence because he was doing something very useful, nor conversely are they prepared to convict someone of negligence because he is doing something useless or even anti-social.[3]

Therefore, regardless of program goals and objectives, placing participants, either individually or in groups, in situations where the real or "objective" risk in the situation makes their injury a likely occurrence, especially if such injury is likely to be serious, is completely unjustifiable in a court of law.

This concept is clearly enunciated in the recent Nova Scotia case of *Michalak* v. *Dalhousie College and University, Governors of.*[4] In this case, an 18-year-old student was seriously injured when she lost her grip on the "Tarzan-Swing" rope, which she was using as part of a high ropes course. It was the final element of the course, set up as part of a 5-day Base Camp challenge program designed for recreation students at Dalhousie University. At the camp, the students were divided into groups of eight, under the leadership of a senior student experienced in the program. Activities included a 24-hour hike, swimming, canoeing, high ropes course, and a number of other pursuits.[5]

While participating in the high ropes course, students were kept on a safety belay. Upon reaching the Tarzan-Swing, the student sat upon a beam about 3.7 to 4.6 meters above the ground while disconnecting the belay wire from his/her waist safety harness to reattach it to a nylon rope attached to the main swinging rope. The primary rope was tied to an overhead beam supported by two large trees. After resetting the safety system, the student placed one foot in a loop at the bottom of the swinging rope, grasped the rope with both hands, and then eased himself or herself off the beam. The student would fall a short distance before the rope would become taut, and then would swing down to the ground.[6]

In this particular case, the plaintiff, Michalak, accidently let go of the rope as she was swinging down. Although she was still attached to the main rope by her safety harness, the inverted position she assumed caused her to hit the ground with her back. This resulted in a compression fracture of her fourth thoracic vertabra. Fortunately, she suffered no permanent loss of function. However, she was forced to give up some physical activities she previously enjoyed and to modify her preferred course of study at university from the physically demanding recreation program she had enrolled in.

She sued the defendant, Dalhousie University, for failing in its duty to care for her, and while the appeal court lowered her damages from

$200,000 to $30,000 (due to her substantial recovery between trials), both courts agreed that she was justified in her claim on four grounds:

1. The course was too advanced for beginners;
2. A full body harness should have been used;
3. The ropes should have been checked before each swing;
4. Inadequate instruction was given to the students.[7]

In defending the program, the professor who designed the ropes course stated that the Base Camp program was designed to promote "personal growth, a standard of excellence, and group learning opportunities." In the old Outward Bound tradition, he stated that he purposely attempted to

> take the students beyond the "comfort" zone of their lives by placing them in situations of fear, danger and confusion from which they could only escape by convincing themselves to take the risks confronting them.[8]

Surely, few outdoor leaders would argue that these have long been considered valid objectives for programs for young adult students. It is important for program delivery agencies to determine their aims, objectives, and methodologies, based on common customs in this field or on other sound rationale. However, it must be recognized that this will not necessarily protect an agency or board from lawsuits.

Finally, there is the concept surrounding the feasibility of instituting "precautions or alternatives which might eliminate or minimize the danger."[9] This concept is also interesting to outdoor leaders in that while they are (or should be) taking precautions to reduce or eliminate the real risk of injury present in the situation, the safety procedures employed are not necessarily intended to simultaneously decrease the participant's perceived risk, the apparent or "subjective" risk present in that same situation. Thus, the use of lifejackets for canoeing or kayaking does not eliminate the chance of dumping in an intermediate whitewater river, but they do greatly reduce the chance of any traumatic physical injury resulting from an unexpected swim. They also allow the leader to keep the group challenged and improving quickly. If a leader could only take the group on rivers in which they would be highly unlikely to tip their rate of skill progress and their enthusiasm for the activity would suffer.

Fortunately, what the courts may recognize as an unreasonable risk without such safety equipment as lifejackets, would probably not be deemed unreasonable with the use of such highly accepted safety devices. Therefore, it is the outdoor leader's duty to be familiar with the equipment and procedures employed by other individuals and agencies in the field and to either use these in adopting custom, or be able to justify why they are not being employed. To use another canoeing example, most outdoor agencies have adopted the carriage of throw bags by their staff. A throw bag is a brightly colored nylon stuff sack full of rope. The rescuer holds or loosely loops the free end of the rope around his or her hand and throws the bag toward the victim, allowing the loose rope to play out as the bag travels through the air. The sack is believed to be easier to see and grab in the water and also reduces the potential of paddlers entwining their feet in coils of rescue throw lines stored in the craft. At a current purchase cost of about $40 (less if homemade), some agencies and/or individuals may not believe the additional safety they offer to be worth their cost. However, if an accident occurred where a victim was injured or killed because of a failure to see or grab a throw line tossed to him/her, the courts may decide that because throw bags are a fairly established and relatively inexpensive safety device, the failure to carry and use one for rescues constituted negligence on the part of the leader (and/or agency).

Although the circumstances involved a different sort of safety device, an example of such a finding occurred in *Ware's Taxi Ltd. v. Gilliham*,[10] where the defendant taxi company was found negligent for not installing a commonly used, inexpensive safety device to keep children from opening car doors while the vehicle is in motion.

The standard of care when dealing with participants classified as minors is, of course, somewhat higher than that owed an adult participant or group. Recent case law indicates that adult participants will more often than not be held personally liable for assuming most, if not all inherent risks in the activity as it will be presupposed that they are of sufficient age, intelligence and experience to be aware of these risks and their potential consequences.[11] In dealing with child participants, however, the standard of the careful parent laid down by Lord Esher,[12] although slightly modified, is still the model recognized by commonwealth courts.

In the outdoor education case example of *Moddejonge v. Huron County Board of Education*,[13] a school outdoor education coordinator was found negligent for allowing a number of girls who could not swim to wade in an unmarked swimming area with a steep drop-off of irregular outline. Despite his cautions, two students drowned when one girl who could swim attempted to rescue the second of two nonswimmers who had gotten into the deep water over the drop-off area. The coordinator, himself a holder of a Master's Degree in outdoor education, was a nonswimmer and had failed to secure a lifeguard or any lifesaving equipment (such as poles, ropes or other reaching or throwing assists, a paddleboard or boat, etc.) before permitting the girls to wade in the area.

In applying the careful parent standard to this case, Justice Pennell stated that,

> ... a reasonably careful parent would have been unlikely to permit his daughter, who was unable to swim, to go into this particular body of water without exercising more care for her safety or ensuring that someone else did so on his behalf.[14]

It was held that the defendant had failed to meet his duty and his inability to foresee the likelihood of one or more of the nonswimmers, drifting into the deep water was attributable as the proximate cause of the accident which eventuated. He failed in his duty to take precautions to protect the girls from the real danger they were in.

The careful parent standard of care was also applied to a downhill ski instructor in the British Columbia decision in *Taylor v. R.*[15] In this case, the 14-year-old female plaintiff fell at a spot on the hill not visible from above and she was subsequently injured when another skier ran into her. The court concluded that in addition to the fact that very few skiers had been injured in that particular location on the hill (only 2 out of 229 accidents reported that year), the reasonably prudent parent would not hesitate to take his or her teenage daughter down that same hill. In essence, they decided that the inherent risks involved in descending downhill ski slopes are not above the evaluation and assessment capabilities of the ordinary parent, and that a ski instructor's expert technical knowledge was not necessary to predict and, if necessary, avoid hazardous areas.[16]

The standard of the careful parent has been modified in recent years to account for a number of factors in addition to the teacher-student relationship. Although the careful parent test "remains the appropriate standard for such cases... it is not... a standard which can be applied in the same manner and to the same extent in every case."[17] Justice McIntyre, in the proceedings of the Supreme Court of Canada deciding on the

Meyers case, supported qualifications to the original test, as presented in *McKay* v. *Board of Govan School Unit No. 29*[18] and reiterated in *Thornton* v. *Board of School Trustees of School Division No. 57 (Prince George)*.[19] In discussing these qualifications of the standard, McIntyre stated:

> It (the standard) has, no doubt, become somewhat qualified in modern times because of the greater variety of activities conducted in schools, with probably larger groups of students using more complicated and more dangerous equipment that formerly. . . . Its application will vary from case to case and will depend upon the number of students being supervised at any given time, the nature of the exercise or activity in progress, the age and degree of skill and training which the students may have received in connection with such activity, the nature and condition of the equipment in use at the time, the competency and capacity of the students involved, and a host of other matters. . .[20]

As a quick review of these qualifications will demonstrate, they are all directly applicable to the outdoor education/recreation situation. In looking at the "greater variety of activities" being pursued, outdoor education can boast additions to traditional outdoor programs emphasizing hiking, snowshoeing and canoeing, of activities such as rock climbing, kayaking, mountain biking and cross-country skiing among other rising adventure pursuits. Because of recent innovations in equipment and skill technologies, children are now exposed to more complicated and in some ways, more hazardous outdoor equipment than formerly. For example, high technology camping equipment such as naphtha or compressed gas stoves and lanterns pose new dangers.

Two other examples of qualifications to the test which may be more peculiar to the less clearly defined outdoor education circumstance than a regular school situation, but which would definitely be considered in evaluating the potential negligence of an outdoor leader include:

1. The actual training and certification of the leader. The standard of care expected of a certified mountain guide would be somewhat higher than that of a schoolteacher taking a class backpacking in the mountains.
2. Knowledge and employment of safety equipment and procedures designed to eliminate or significantly reduce the real risk of injury present in the situation. For example, first aid knowledge and a well

stocked first aid kit may be deemed vital in dealing with a back-country accident.

In physical training accidents, indoor or outdoor, the courts must consider much more than just how a prudent parent would have conducted the activity in question. Even though Canadian courts continue to adhere to this standard, they have recognized the need to temper it with consideration of the contemporary physical educators' circumstances. In time it is likely that increasing litigation will lead to a raising of the standard to that of the careful physical educator[21] or outdoor leader as the case may be.

In brief then, an outdoor leader facing tort charges would be evaluated largely on the basis of the foresight exercised in predicting the likelihood of a student/participant being injured, in the activity being pursued, and in the manner he or she was directing it.

In dealing with adult participants, the leader would be held to the standard of the reasonably prudent outdoor leader (the reasonable person with the defendant's outdoor knowledge and training). However, and although open to some interpretation, children are owed a standard concomitant with that expected of the reasonably careful parent.

DUTIES OF THE OUTDOOR LEADER

In order for a litigation to proceed against an outdoor leader, the injured plaintiff must show that the injury(ies) was proximately caused by the breach of one or more duties (standards of care) owed by that leader. These duties may be related to the instructor/guide's personal competence and qualifications or they may be directed at specific responsibilities this individual accepts in guiding, supervising and instructing participants, and in ensuring that adequate safety precautions have been taken prior to and during their participation and in the event of an accident or emergency situation.

Outdoor Leader Qualifications

The public or private agency hiring outdoor leaders/guides must be confident that they have the qualifications (the technical knowledge and skill, physical fitness, age, experience, judgment) and certification(s) required by law and common sense to do the job. In the case of *Walton* v. *Vancou-*

ver,[22] a school board was held liable for allowing an unqualified teacher to supervise a shooting competition during which a rifle backfired and injured a student.

In the *Moddejonge* case, the outdoor education coordinator supervising a group of girls swimming was neither qualified (he was a non-swimmer), nor certified (as an aquatics lifesaver) to be placing himself in the role of lifeguard.[23] Instructor qualifications have also been implicated as a cause of death in British[24] and American[25] outdoor education accidents. The latter of these was one of many actions against American Outward Bound schools, most of which run programs in a very similar manner to those seen in Canadian Outward Bound Schools. In this particular case, an instructor's qualifications were questioned when a 20-year-old woman was killed by a falling rock while she was rock climbing with the school.[26]

Instructors/leaders should not only teach/lead in their areas of competency, but also at a level well below their own level of ability. For example, little safety margin would be present where an intermediate paddler was found leading a kayaking trip on a difficult (class 3 to 4) whitewater river. Outdoor leaders who lead programs solely because of the challenge they find in the activity are a hazard to the program participants and themselves. And of course, the more dangerous the activity or the level of pursuit, the higher the expectations will be of a leader's qualifications and certifications. Therefore, both the agency hiring and placing outdoor instructors/guides and the leaders themselves have a duty to know the leader's capabilities and limits of performance and leadership.

Knowing one's limits and operating within them is one example of how outdoor leaders demonstrate their judgmental abilities. Other examples may be seen in the way they assess and relate risks to participant abilities in developing a strategy to safely supervise and instruct each program they run. Contrary to the somewhat unrealistic policies of most schoolboards and many agencies who strive to make everything completely "safe" for their charges, one of the ideals of outdoor education/recreation is an underlying philosophical challenge of preparing individuals to evaluate and accept risks in relation to their own abilities to deal with them.[27]

RISK ASSESSMENT The outdoor leader has a duty to assess the real risks inherent to participation in a given activity pursuit, with an identifiable group using certain equipment in the particular environmental circumstances found on the proposed site or travel route. Risk factors worthy of assessment in any outdoor program situation include weather (for example, exposure to sun, heat, cold, wind, precipitation) and the chance of someone becoming unexplainedly ill during the program. Most other factors are rather activity specific. For example, the leader taking a group out high country hiking may be concerned about water availability and quality, wild animals, poisonous plants and rockfalls or landslides while the canoe trip leader will be more concerned with water level, volume and obstacles and possible cold water immersion by participants.

In assessing each particular risk factor (as well as likely combinations of such) the leader must consider both the likelihood of anyone being injured and the potential severity of injury(ies) which may result from accepting that risk.[28] Also, risk assessments cannot occur in isolation from participant capability assessments. Each hazard must be evaluated to determine both the likelihood and potential magnitude of risk posed for *each* participant as well as for the group as a unit.

A tragic accident in the United States illustrates the need for careful attention to risk assessment of weather factors. In mid May of 1986, seven youths and two adults died of hypothermia while on a day hike up Mount Hood in Oregon. They were part of a group of 18 (15 students, 2 adult leaders and a guide) engaged on a Oregon Episcopal School required outdoor program called "Basecamp."[29]

The objective of this aspect of the program was to ascend 3,428 meter Mount Hood. While Mount Hood is recognized as the second most climbed peak in the world (next to Mount Fuji), with over 10,000 ascents per year, it is also respected as being far from safe and predictable. Sixty people have died on the mountain in the last century.[30]

The Oregon Episcopal group started out in the early hours of the morning. The day broke pleasantly enough, given that storm warnings had caused at least four other professional guides to cancel trips with their clients. Six members of the group (including one of the adults) turned back early for various reasons. At about 4:00 in the afternoon, and three hours after their planned return to the foot of the mountain, the group was hit by a ferocious late-spring blizzard (90 kmph winds resulted in a −50° windchill and total whiteout conditions).[31]

While within a few hundred feet of the peak, the group was forced to beat a hasty retreat. Unfortunately, at about 2,530 meters, one of the boys became hypothermic and the group stopped to warm him. After an hour of trying to warm the youth, the futility of the effort was realized and a decision was made to dig in.

The next day, as the storm continued to rage, the leader and one student walked down to get help. The incredible intensity of the wind prevented helicopters and snow-cats from initiating a search until the next day. Helicopter searchers found the bodies of three 15-year-old members of the group on the surface, but the blowing snow had obliterated their tracks and there was no trace of the remainder of the group.[32]

Finally, late on the third day of searching, a 23-man walking probe line located the eight people still in their cave. Of these, only two were to live, one suffering the loss of his lower legs.

While many of the surviving students and representatives of the school maintained no one was to blame for the tragedy, a number of parents of the deceased youths and external observers were not as forgiving. Knowledge of a suspected storm on a mountain known for its unpredictable weather was the most commonly cited factor. Others accused the trip guide of inadequate leadership and of failing to take enough equipment.[33] One opinionated postmortem stated that:

> . . . the Hood fiasco tells a tale replete with bad judgement and avoidable error: too large a party with too little expertise; a dangerously slow ascent pushed dangerously long into the face of a predicted major storm; a descent dogged by hypothermia; a cave digging so haphazard the party lost its packs (with lifesaving stove and sleeping bags) under snowdrifts while they scooped out their shelter; a guide taking off to launch a rescue without ensuring he could relocate the party he was leaving behind, and so on.[34]

The results of the ensuing inquiry and any lawsuits eventuating out of the incident (none decided at the time of this writing) are, of course, of no significant legal influence in Canada. However, the facts of this incident, as described, are of substantial instructional import to those responsible for assessing weather and other environmental risks in relation to the skill and experience of such groups.

PARTICIPANT CAPABILITY ASSESSMENT   Although most participants, especially more mature and experienced ones, often have a fairly good idea of their capabilities, it is the outdoor leader's duty to determine these independently.[35] The leader has a duty to know the general abilities and rates of progression of groups at various levels of proficiency and even more importantly the leader must know and appreciate the possible consequences of participation for each individual in his care.[36] Consequently, in an American case (therefore not binding in Canada), a college was found fully liable when a freshman nonswimmer taking a required course in swimming drowned.

Despite the fact that he held himself out as a swimmer when the class separated itself into swimmers and nonswimmers, the courts held that:

> Under these circumstances, the deceased who... was an unskilled swimmer who could barely stay afloat, did not, as a matter of law assume the risk of death by drowning... [T]he deceased, by separating himself into the group who could swim, did not represent that he was, or assume the position of the skilled in swimming, but was entitled to assume that his instructors knew he was not and would exercise ordinary care to protect him.[37]

Normally, one of the most important aspects of participant evaluation will be an assessment of their physical abilities and limitations. This may be ascertained through statement of health forms and fitness tests related to the activity. The importance of such evaluation was borne out in a survey carried out on accidents reported in Banff National Park from 1974-1980. This survey concluded that pre-existing medical problems and conditions was the second largest cause of backcountry hiking and backpacking accidents during that period of time, second only to off-trail accidents by inexperienced and unprepared travellers.[38] The *Dziwenka* case, where a deaf-mute student was injured while using a power saw in an industrial arts class, demonstrates conclusively the need to identify and program in accordance with individual participants' abilities and limitations.

In terms of technical knowledge and skill assessment, the courts have stated that an instructor "should quickly ascertain how far advanced the student has progressed and what ability the student possesses."[39] New participants require constant, ongoing evaluation[40] and feedback in order to develop their skills.

In *McWilliam v. Thunder Bay Flying Club*,[41] it was held that a formal evaluation of an advanced student's skills was not necessary and the instructor flying in a plane with such a student was held not liable for failing to prevent a crash caused by the latter stalling the plane in midair.

In addition to an evaluation of physical fitness and skill parameters, consideration of the participant's mental set and ability should not be overlooked. Where a participant expresses anxiety concerning a particular activity, the courts may hold that he or she was not psychologically prepared for it.[42] Conversely, if the participant displays enthusiasm for the activity, this may be construed as inferring a mental readiness for that exercise.[43] However, neither mental attitude displayed by the participant would conclusively indicate the activity's appropriateness or lack of such.[44] The outdoor educator must take the time to personally assess this.[45] The outdoor leader must also have some knowledge of the different mechanisms people employ when dealing with mental and emotional stress and he or she must be aware of how to employ these techniques within the group to decrease unfounded perceived stresses (or to increase them when an individual or group displays overconfidence).

In addition, where an outdoor leader encourages a participant to perform a given task (such as paddling down a potentially hazardous rapid) by intentionally understating the risk and lulling the individual into a false sense of competence, that leader may be liable for any injuries sustained by the participant while attempting that task.[46] The courts would be very likely to construe such comments as negligent misrepresentations of the real risk to the participant. It should be noted that it is an extremely unwise practice to require, force or otherwise coerce any individual into doing anything he or she expresses a strong fear or disapproval of.

The experienced instructor is aware that people learn differently. While some may be aggressive free learners with lots of personal initiative and a high risk threshold, others in the same group may be at the other end of the learning continuum. These dependant learners must often be "spoon fed" and slowly and cautiously nurtured so as to avoid exceeding their comfort level.

Once the outdoor leader has looked at all possible environmental risks and participant characteristics, consideration must be given to these two types of factors as they relate to each other, before determining the group's course of action. When the leader has assessed the theoretical knowledge and technical skills of a group as being sufficiently high, he or she may be permitted to democratically make his or her own risk assessments and choose subsequent courses of action. However, the leader almost always retains ultimate responsibility for the possible consequences of the group's decisions, especially if the participants are minors. The duty to terminate or modify a significantly risky pursuit will remain in the leader's hands. This remains true because the group will very rarely have the leader's experience and knowledge of the hazard and the particular travel area. Before arriving at a level involving shared decision-making, the leader must have done much assessing of the participants' physical, mental and social skills in similar risk situations and be confident of them.

Regardless of who appears to be making the decisions, the leader must be certain that the course of action selected is congruent with his or her assessment of the party's ability to handle the particular situation. A risk worthy of avoidance with a group of novices may be retainable as is or in some reduced form for a more experienced party. For example, while an icy river swollen with spring floodwaters may be perceived as too hazardous for a class of neophyte paddlers, an intermediate group wearing wetsuits and helmets and carrying extra floatation in their boats may actually seek this risk.

Early in 1972, six youths lost their lives while on an Edinburgh Education Authority sponsored training hike on the Cairngorm Plateau in Scotland.[47] The six, part of a group of seven being led by an assistant instructor, walked into a blizzard and the resultant heavy snowfall and whiteout conditions kept them stranded in bivouacs for two nights, less than a kilometer from their destination cabin of the first night. It took a full day for the program instructor, leading another group in the same area, to realize the other party's absence, and bad weather and pending darkness precluded the search until late the second day. A helicopter pilot finally spotted the assistant instructor and led a search party to the remainder of her group, buried in the snow.

A report outlining the judicial fatal accidents enquiry which followed the tragedy cited the instructor's underestimation of the Cairngorms as a dangerous mountain group and his naivety in taking children into the area in the winter as the most serious charge to emerge from the enquiry.[48] Numerous "expert" witnesses stated that they considered these mountains too hazardous for such expeditions, particularly due to the likelihood of severe weather, in featureless terrain from which retreat is difficult. In bad weather, this area was perceived as a tremendous challenge for seasoned mountaineers, let alone young climbers trying to gain experience.

Leader qualification was also brought under question, in reference to the assistant instructor placed in charge of the group. A number of authorities questioned thought she was "too young, insufficiently qualified and not experienced enough to take charge of parties of school children."[49] Other factors which were deemed to have contributed to the disaster included the lead instructor's failure to perceive the dangerous conditions pending and to reunite the group when the weather deteriorated and numerous minor errors in judgment made by the assistant instructor while following the instructor's directions without question.

Despite all of these allegations, the jury concluded in their findings that "there was no one area of serious negligence," and that the accident had resulted from the "cumulative effect of a number of miscalculations."[50]

It must be noted that no lawsuits succeeded this judicial enquiry, and enquiries themselves do not yield any binding law. However, many excellent points did evolve which are worthy of consideration by all outdoor leaders attempting to match environmental risk assessments to participant needs and capabilities.

Navigation and Guidance

Even leaders who are careful not to overextend their participants' resources by carefully matching their abilities with the planned activity and environment, may be negligent in the manner in which they guide their charges or in the way they conduct their program. The fact that outdoor leaders often run their programs in a transient manner, sometimes leading participants many kilometers in a day (regardless of travel mode), indicates that they have a number of specific decision-making duties to perform throughout each trek. Unlike most other physical activity programmers who function in relatively fixed, easily definable environments (such as gymnasia or playing fields), outdoor leaders must combine their educational duties with those of a navigator and guide. As navigators, they must be able to make necessary route choices, both before and during each day's travel. Good orienteering skills and route hazard evaluation are difficult to acquire and require much time and experience travelling in the type(s) of terrain that one will eventually lead in.

The recent British Columbia case of *Lowry et al.* v. *Canadian Mountain Holidays Ltd. et al.*[51] supported at appeal[52] clearly indicates the need for great care in areas with inherently hazardous terrain. This case involved a fatal heli-skiing avalanche accident which occurred on 23 February 1981, on the Sundance run in the Purcell Mountains. Heli-skiing has become a very popular activity in B.C. and Alberta as skiers are able to ski high altitude virgin powder without the time and effort associated with climbing up to it. The helicopter shuttles the skiers up the mountain after each run. As a result, experienced, competent skiers can ski many runs in a single day, easily adding up to as much as 15,000 vertical meters.

The defendant, Canadian Mountain Holidays (CMH) heli-ski operation, was well aware of the potential hazards of avalanches in mountainous terrain, and took definite steps to ensure that guests appreciated this risk. All clients were supplied with a copy of the CMH Heli-Skiing Handbook prior to applying for a heli-ski package. Included in this handbook was a detailed description of the hazard, steps that CMH staff take to avoid it, and a disclaimer noting that avalanches are an inherent risk participants must "share" with CMH. This section even noted that the operation has had 5 avalanche fatalities in 16 years of operation, and that the use of *Skadi* avalanche transceivers had facilitated the rapid rescue of a number of other potential victims.[53]

On the day in question, four groups went out under the direction of R. Kaser and three other guides. Kaser's group, which was involved in the accident, consisted of ten skiers including Kaser. While the weather had been cloudy and unsettled, it had broken enough that morning to allow all four groups to ski a reasonably safe line down the Sundance run earlier that morning. The limited flying conditions restricted the groups to lower runs for the rest of the morning and early afternoon.

When the weather broke, the groups returned to the Sundance area, with one other group preceding Kaser's on an uneventful traverse of the bench slightly higher than that taken in the morning. Kaser's group, following the line taken in the morning, likely triggered an avalanche which broke loose from the steep slope above. Kaser and one other skier managed to ski to the relative safety of a shallow ridge, where the avalanche split and flowed around them on both sides. Five skiers were caught up in the right branch of the avalanche path and came to rest on the lower bench. The three remaining skiers were carried by the left and main body of the slab avalanche over a section of cliffs and gullies to the valley floor some 500 meters below.

When the avalanche stopped moving, three skiers were partially buried but were able to dig themselves out. A fourth was partially buried and injured and required assistance. A fifth, also partially buried, was dug out by skiers from the first group who climbed back up to help. Three skiers, Lowry and Rossman, who had been caught in the right branch, and Rondeau, who had disappeared in the left one, could not be seen.

Kaser immediately radioed for assistance. Everyone present began a transceiver search, and located the three men within 10 minutes. But, due to the difficulty encountered in digging through the dense avalanche debris, it took an additional 10 to 30 minutes to dig out the victims and they were all pronounced dead by a doctor at the scene.[54]

The wife of Lowry and the wife and children of Rondeau subsequently brought a law suit against CMH and its guide Kaser under the *Family Compensation Act*.[55] The plaintiffs contended that the defendants negligently conducted their heli-ski operation "in an area, and at a time when ... the danger of serious avalanches was readily predictable."[56] The defendants countered that they were not negligent, that they had followed reasonable and accepted practices, that the avalanche in question was not reasonably predictable, and that the victims had voluntarily assumed any risks present.

At trial, both the plaintiffs and defendants counted heavily on expert technical testimony regarding avalanche forecasting in general, and the CMH's procedures at the time in question in particular. The court eventually found little difference in the final version of the evidence provided by each of these expert technical witnesses.[57]

After 10 days of evidence, the court was able to establish the following facts and opinions:

1. Heavy storm conditions had prevailed for some 10 days prior to February 23rd, and the high winds in the last 2 or 3 days had changed from a prevailing westerly direction to a southerly direction.
2. The slope where the avalanche occurred was, at the fracture line, approximately 48°—a comparatively steep slope, and one, when snow-loaded with unstable shearing, markedly susceptible to avalanche.

3. ...there had been numerous natural avalanches in the week of February 14 to 21, with the peak of such activity on February 17. There had in this period not been an avalanche from the slope above the Sundance run, a known avalanche area.

4. There was at the fracture line site an accumulation of fresh wind-drifted snow, as the site was, with a southerly wind blowing, in the lee of a ridge.

5. Underneath the layer of drifted snow referred to in 4, above, was a slab layer of wind-packed snow [sitting] on top of a raincrust. The existence of the raincrust should have been known. Also, it should have been known that there existed the danger of a slab layer sliding over the raincrust.

6. There was unstable layering, shown in the snow profile taken at the fracture line site ... on February 24, such that one should deduce from it that the area was avalanche prone.

7. No snow profiles, full or hasty pit type, had been taken in the windswept vicinity of the Sundance run, or anywhere in the area at the 2,590 to 2,740 meter level.

8. The closest profile taken was that at the Arborite weather station, altitude 2,040 meters, 2 days prior to the accident.[58]

The court surmised that a reasonably prudent guide would have considered all the aforementioned factors except number 6 without digging any snow profiles. And even a hasty profile pit dug in the vicinity of the Sundance run, or at a similar elevation anywhere nearby, would have indicated the unstable layering present. Justice Gould concluded that had the guide known these 8 factors, which he should have, "he would have never taken the group on a traverse of the Sundance run when he did."[59]

Canadian Mountain Holidays' defense was undoubtably injured by the fact that it had failed to meet the snow profile monitoring guidelines established in the heli-ski guide *Operators Manual*[60] written by Hans Gmoser, the founder and president of CMH.

This manual stated that weather and snow profile

observations must be carried out and recorded continuously from the beginning to the end of the operating season. The snow cover conditions shall be monitored by making full snow profile observations at selected study plots and hasty pits as close as possible to avalanche starting zones. The frequency of profiles and the location of hasty pits must take into consideration the local terrain and weather.[61]

In evaluating these policies and the actions taken by CMH staff in this case, the courts found negligence on the part of the employees of CMH on two grounds:
1. Failure to take any kind of snow profile in the vicinity of the Sundance run.
2. Failure to interpret reasonably and competently available evidence that indicated avalanche propensity at Sundance.[62]

The four defenses presented by CMH and Kaser were dealt with individually and collectively. The court had established negligence, which negated the defendants' claim that there had not been any. The claim that an avalanche was not reasonably foreseeable was dismissed as a totally invalid defense, as the "high danger of avalanches was at the forefront of contemplation by both parties from the very commencement of their relationship."[63]

The defense of *volenti non fit injuria* was dismissed because there was no express release or waiver signed by the victims. While Lowry and Rondeau were deemed to have accepted the physical risks involved in heli-skiing, they had taken no action to accept the legal risks involved if negligence was found.[64]

In attaching some liability to the guide Kaser, the court reverted to another publication put out by one of CMH's proponents in this case. *The ABC of Avalanche Safety*[65] was perceived to be a good written resource of the general safety rules any senior heli-skiing guide should know. Although the court did not suggest that Kaser had seen this particular publication prior to the accident, it did raise some of the general rules which appeared to have been ignored in this case. For example, Kaser was believed to have failed by exposing more than one man to avalanche danger at a time,[66] and by leading his skiers across and down the avalanche path and not more safely above or below this known track.[67] Finally, the judge mentioned Kaser following another group across the slope and noted another rule which contains the admonition that one cannot assume a slope is safe simply because it did not slide when the first skier traversed it.[68]

In short, the court believed that Kaser should have been familiar with the essence of these guidelines, and that he failed to operate according to them. Because Canadian Mountain Holidays' clients were required to follow their guide's orders explicitly, there was a finding of liability against Kaser, as well as against CMH.[69]

The issue of quantifying damages was dealt with at a later time, and was set at $200,000 to Lowry's wife, and $500,000 to Rondeau's wife and seven children.

This case has set a very onerous precedent for all outdoor leaders in Canada. While it will hopefully result in increased time and thought being devoted to sound route selection, it may also have the undesirable effect of scaring off many careful operators who fear the consequences of making an honest error in the art/science of assessing environmental hazards.

Supervision

Supervision refers to the general duty to oversee the participants from the time the outdoor leader assumes responsibility for them until the program is complete and the leader and group part company. In the interim, the degree of supervision administered by the leader varies, as it is neither essential nor desirable that the participants be watched every minute of the day. Factors affecting the tightness of supervision required include: the nature of the activity, the real risk present in the situation, the age, experience and technical expertise of the participants themselves.

For example, in *Sholtes* v. *Stranaghan*,[70] an experienced outdoorsman employed a professional guide to accompany him on hunting, fishing and animal photography expeditions. Although the guide always escorted the plaintiff on hunting trips, he did not always go along on the latter's fishing and photography excursions. When the plaintiff was mauled by a grizzly bear while on a photography outing, he tried to claim damages against the guide for breaching his duty of care by allowing him to be "out in the wilds alone."[71] The courts dismissed the action and held that the guide/outfitter's standard of care "depended upon the knowledge and experience of the person who hired him."[72] In this case, he was justified in allowing the experienced plaintiff to pursue a low risk activity (photography) without his direct supervision.

Although the duty to supervise will be higher with children, especially with young children, the courts have tempered the need to prevent unnecessary accidents[73] with the impossibility and undesirability of watching every child continuously. In a British school case, Justice McNair stated that "a balance must be struck between the meticulous supervision of children every moment at school and the desirable object of encouraging sturdy independence as they grow up."[74] The duty to supervise children in a given situation was shortly thereafter held to be that which an "ordinary and prudent schoolmaster or mistress"[75] would observe in that same situation.

While *general* supervision (where participants may summon the leader for assistance if they require it) may be adequate where risk is low and participant skill high, *specific* (close and concentrated) supervision is necessary when participants are attempting skills for the first time or practising inherently dangerous activities where foreseeable accidents may result in serious injury. In outdoor education situations where a group is geographically spread out but where risk is still fairly high, many leaders employ a "buddy" system where participants keep an eye on one another. For example, while on a canoe trip a leader may make partners in a boat responsible for one another and may also make each craft responsible for the boat directly behind it. This practice allows the boats to spread out so they will not run into one another, but keeps everyone within sight of at least one, if not two other craft. It should be noted, however, that although this type of system may help the leader keep a group together, that leader retains ultimate responsibility for all participants; this duty cannot be delegated.

The outdoor leader also has a duty to supervise most closely those participants engaged in the most dangerous activity. In the *Dziwenka* case, an industrial arts teacher was held liable for not remaining close to the only student using a potentially dangerous tool in the class.[76] In giving his reasons for the finding, Justice Laskin stated:

> ... he could have stayed with the plaintiff until the job was done with the unguarded saw... I do not find it improbable that the accident would not have happened if the instructor had directly supervised the operation. ... [77]

In the *Moddejonge* case, part of the outdoor coordinator's liability for the drownings of the 2 students was based on the fact that he had wandered some distance up the beach from the place he had left his group of girls wading.[78] His distance from the group significantly increased the time it took for him to react to the situation.

Charlesworth states that a "greater degree of supervision is required during hours of instruction than during hours of recreation."[79] In the outdoor education situation, this is certainly true and the statement may also be extended to reduce the standard of care required during free time, meal times and at night when leaders and participants are sleeping. A leader could hardly be faulted if a participant out sleepwalking in the middle of the night wandered over a cliff some distance from his or her tent. Again, only the standard of the reasonable outdoor leader (or parent if the participant is a minor) need be met.

One of the major objectives of outdoor education is to provide participants with sufficient knowledge and skill that they may pursue the activities they are trained in independently upon completion of the program or course (or series thereof). One of the methods a number of agencies (for example, Outward Bound Schools, some universities) use to facilitate the development of this self-sufficiency is by including a soloing component (group, individual or both) during the program. Supervision during such aspects of programs may be within whistle range or so distant as to be virtually nonexistent, again depending on the leader's perceptions of the participants' skills and judgment in relation to the real risk present in the environment (except where agency policy dictates the level required).

In 1978, three young adults drowned while ocean kayaking off the Baja peninsula in California.[80] They were part of a group of nine, engaged in the final training expedition of an Outward Bound program, and they were travelling without the accompaniment of their instructors. The instructors, according to Outward Bound School procedure, were to travel separately and make once-daily checks on the progress of the group at predetermined locations.

The Baja general weather pattern, while far from predictable, usually consists of calm predawn weather, with winds picking up to often violent levels by late morning. While fully knowledgeable of this pattern, the group succumbed to the natural tendency to break camp slowly when faced with the cool chill of morning and the calm sea ahead. As a result, they had been on the ocean less than an hour when a violent windstorm blew up. The accompanying five meter swells overturned all but one of the kayaks, leaving six of the group in the water clinging to their craft for over 15 hours before they finally managed to kick their way to the rocky shore.

Two of the three drowned students' parents brought lawsuits against the Southwest Outward Bound School on behalf of their children, citing negligence in a number of areas. Among their allegations, they claimed that the course was not reasonably safe for the students, that the area selected was very dangerous and known for its storms and that the students were inadequately supervised. In reviewing the supervision question, it was learned that a second Outward Bound group, travelling independently, returned to shore when the winds picked up and sought out the instructors. After directing this group to either portage or attempt the ocean again, the two instructors claimed that they took their motorized sailboat through the area where the first group was having trouble. The plaintiffs denied this and said that no attempt was made to summon help until almost noon the following day when a fishing vessel who rescued the survivors contacted the harbormaster.

It is almost certain that the absence of an instructor contributed to the late start of the group and the subsequent disaster. According to an interview with one of the female survivors:

> The instructors had us out by the crack of dawn every day that we went on the water. . . . We didn't have an instructor cracking the whip so we just took a little longer.[81]

This case should bring to bear for the outdoor educator the importance of instilling the value of self-determined exploration, while treading carefully the thin line between adventure and misadventure. The case was eventually settled out of court. Being of American origin, it would not have held any precedential power in Canadian courts even if it had been fully litigated. However, it nevertheless leaves outdoor leaders with an important message concerning the importance of providing at least general supervision during all programs. The instructors in this unfortunate tragedy could have averted the disaster by keeping an eye, however distant, on their charges and moving in to render assistance when the group found itself in trouble.

It should be remembered that in order for a plaintiff to convince a court of law that an accident resulted from a lack of adequate supervision, it must be demonstrated that the same or a similar accident would have been unlikely had supervision been more specific and direct in the situation.[82] A participant injured tripping over a root while hiking is unlikely to win an action raised by claiming the leader was in front of the group at the time, instead of watching him or her walk. Also, an instructor does not have a duty to stop everyone in a group from proceeding with the activity while giving individual attention to a particular participant experiencing problems with equipment or skill techniques.[83]

In brief, an outdoor leader has a duty to provide supervision equivalent to that which would be expected of a reasonably prudent leader, or parent where children are involved. The need for specific, close supervision will be highest with young, inexperienced participants engaged in potentially risky pursuits and will decrease as the participants' age and skill level increases, and/or the real risk present in the situation decreases.

Instruction

Virtually all outdoor leaders are involved as instructors, if only through the example they set for their participants. Those who are hired for their outdoor activity instructional skills assume a great duty to teach their students the activity pursuit comprehensively and safely. In addition to teaching physical activities, the outdoor instructor has a duty to teach some of the scientific theory relevant to the pursuit before and/or during the students' engagement in it. For example, when teaching river canoeing, films, slides and/or discussion of topics such as the reading of rivers, river grading systems and the biomechanical principles of efficient paddling are all integrally related to the learning of the activity.

A functional understanding of important elements related to an activity is crucial to providing students with an understanding and appreciation of risks inherent to involvement in the activity. This understanding and appreciation of risks is an important prerequisite to the delivery of essential cautions and warnings concerning the handling of these risks.[84]

It is prudent to make sure that *every* participant hears these warnings; the more frequently they are delivered the better. A factor the courts may consider in a case would be the length of time expired since the last warning was issued regarding a particular risk which eventuated in an accident. Warnings need not be presented to each individual separately; a group communication of them is sufficient as long as any members not present at the group session are individually cautioned when they arrive. Although these warnings will not absolve instructors of negligence should they fail to take adequate care in one or more of their other duties, they certainly provide favorable evidence and place much onus on plaintiff participants (especially adults) to show that they did not assume the risk voluntarily.[85]

For example, in the *Michalak*[86] case a university student suffered a back injury as a result of a fall from a high ropes course. The court believed that one of the four grounds for negligence on the part of the defendants was the instructor's failure to emphasize sufficiently the need to maintain a secure grip on the Tarzan-Swing rope during the swing down. While the co-ordinating professor claimed that such cautions were unnecessary as the normal tendency was to grip the rope as strongly as possible, the court disagreed and believed the absence of a warning here constituted inadequate instruction.

One of the major general duties of all instructors is to ensure that safe and proper techniques are taught. In *Olsen* v. *Corry*,[87] an aviation apprentice sued the defendant aviation company for injuries he sustained while swinging a plane's propeller to help start the plane. He won the suit, based on his claim that no safe procedural system for starting engines was taught or enforced at the aerodrome.[88]

In *Starr and McNulty* v. *Crone*,[89] a father was found negligent in failing to teach his son proper and safe use of a firearm, resulting in the 15-year-old shooting another youth. Justice Wilson stated that:

> ... it is negligent to entrust a dangerous weapon to a young boy unless it is proved: (a) That he was properly and thoroughly trained in the use of the weapon, with particular regard to using it safely and carefully; (b) That the boy was of an age, character and intelligence so that the father might safely assume the boy would apprehend and obey the instructions given him.[90]

This same standard of care was found wanting in *School Division of Assiniboine South No. 3* v. *Hoffer et al.*,[91] where a father taught his son a modified and unsafe technique for starting his snowmobile with the kickstand down, resulting in the son losing control of the machine and its contributing to the damage of a school building.

Again, a safe and proper technique will normally be that which has either been customarily used by a large percentage of outdoor leaders in the area without mishap, and/or one which the agency has adopted to safely fit the particular environmental variables they are operating with. Unlike a school gymnasium, outdoor program sites vary tremendously in their nature and in the elements of risk present. An important consideration in court is sure to be the forethought the outdoor educator can show he used in planning his program in the manner he chose.

Justice Wilson's comment in the *Starr* case also brings up the importance of gearing explanations and instructions to the individual participant's level of comprehension.[92] The *School Division of Assiniboine South No. 3* case also indicated that instructors must not only gear their instructions to the participants' level of understanding, but must also be convinced of the students' physical ability to safely follow the directions given.[93]

Lack of proper instruction and supervision were found to have contributed to the injuries sustained by a 9-year-old plaintiff injured when he fell off a snowmobile he was a passenger on, being subsequently struck by a second machine.[94] In addition to finding both young drivers negligent and the plaintiff contributorily negligent, the courts held both drivers' fathers equally negligent in failing to teach the boys the safe and careful use of these dangerous machines in a manner which they could understand, appreciate and physically carry out.[95]

Instructions and explanations may be related to any number of aspects concerning the environment, the skills involved in the activity, safety precautions particular to individual skills or general emergency procedures to be carried out in the event of an accident. Often a verbal description will suffice, but where concepts are difficult to visualize, instructors should employ more illustrative visual and where possible experiential teaching methods.

In addition to verbal instructions, one of the most common instructional methods employed in teaching skills is the performance of a demonstration. In the *McKay* case, where a teenage youth was seriously injured while attempting a stunt on the parallel bars, part of the teacher's liability was attributed to the fact that he "had described the exercise but had not demonstrated it."[96] Demonstrations need not be perfect, but must be technically correct, which points to the importance of instructors practising their own skills and maintaining them at a high level.

It is not essential that the instructor personally perform all demonstrations; an assistant and/or skilled participant is adequate and often better as this frees the instructor to point out various elements of the skill, to demonstrate proper spotting position and so on. For example, it is perfectly acceptable for a canoeing instructor to remain on shore with the students while an assistant and/or skilled other demonstrates how to ferry a canoe across a rapid. From a close position on shore the instructor can point out how the water acts on the hull of the craft when the paddlers lean downstream and can illustrate uses for this skill in crossing a stream. This procedure also saves time, as much of the instruction occurs concomitantly with the demonstration; the instructor is close enough to the students that the instructor need not yell to be heard over the sound of the river.

Probably the most essential concern with instruction is that it be progressive in degree of difficulty. In outdoor education situations, progression may and should be utilized: (a) between the skills taught before telemarking; (b) within each skill taught; and (c) within the environment in which the skill is practised. To illustrate, a cross-country ski instructor would typically teach the diagonal stride before introducing the more complex one-step double pole, a skill which presumes reasonable mastery of the diagonal stride. In teaching the diagonal stride, progressive exercises would be selected to emphasize side-to-side weightshift and forward glide, first without poles, and later with poles. In considering progression in the practice environment, a considerate instructor will allow the class to largely master the diagonal stride on flat or rolling terrain before adapting the easy skill to steeper uphill slopes. The same categories of instructional progressions may be considered regardless of the outdoor activity pursuit being taught, only the specific skills, skill components, and environmental variables will change. In the *Murray* case,[97] the physical education teacher was not held liable for injuries a 12-year-old student sustained while breaking up a human gymnastic pyramid, largely because:

> ...there is an element of danger in all sports and even in the less dangerous ones, but at the same time that element of danger can be reduced to a minimum when the participants observe the rules of the game, play with reasonable prudence and care after having, in the proper cases, been progressively trained and coached in such exercises.[98]

Yet another important consideration regarding the use of progressive training is the importance of allowing time for *each* student to master one progression before going on to the next.[99] All too often, instructors progress their groups at the rate of the *average* student, often placing the less physically adept in situations with more skill components and/or environmental variables than they are physically and/or psychologically prepared to cope. Countless examples of failures to meet this duty in outdoor education situations, on occasion with near disastrous results exist, probably within one's own experiences. For example, some years ago, the author recalls taking a general month-long spring outdoor adventure course which included a one-day introduction to kayaking. After spending less than two hours learning and practising the basics on a nearby lake, the entire group was dropped in a class 2 to 3 river (in spring flood) with a lead instructor (who admitted she always grew grey hairs on this day of the course) and an assistant instructor the group had never seen before. Within five minutes, one boat had tipped and broached against a partially submerged stump (it later took 10 people hauling on a rope to free it) and the paddler was left on shore to make his way back to the center alone. Upon returning to the center, the author looked for the abandoned paddler and found him, right where he had been left, staring at his semi-submerged kayak in a state of shock. Although an avid outdoorsman, at last contact he had not sat in a kayak since that day.

The lesson to be drawn from this incident and similar ones is that unless special alternatives are allowed within a program (such as extra sessions for the less experienced or slower learners, selection of an area with enough variety that everyone can work at his own level) then a group may only progress as fast as its slowest member.

Finally, while students are engaged in learning new skills, it is wise to avoid initiating any elements of competition or grading between them. This point was brought out in the *Meyers* case,[100] as students received higher marks for completing more complicated gymnastics maneuvers. This fact was believed to contribute to the plaintiff youth attempting a rather dangerous maneuver he had never tried previously:

> He had not been told not to try it. In fact he had been virtually invited to do so, since higher marks could be obtained by the performance of Level Two exercises.[101]

An illustration of the importance of a number of these elements of instruction can be found in the facts leading to the recent decision in *Smith v. Horizon Aero Sports Ltd. et al.*,[102] where the plaintiff was rendered a paraplegic in a sport parachuting instructional class. Near the end of a short four-hour introductory session, the plaintiff and her class were taken up in a plane to attempt their first jumps. The plaintiff, although visibly anxious, was permitted to make her jump. She mentally froze as soon as she left the plane, immediately forgetting all of her previous instruction. As a result, she failed to steer her canopy to the safe landing area and instead landed in a tree, fell to the ground and broke her back.

One of the factors Justice Spencer used in attributing negligence to the school included the instructor's failure to adequately describe and discuss a number of elements of the upcoming jump, resulting in the plaintiff being excessively unfamiliar with the procedure and concomitantly overstressed by the situation.

The plaintiff was not shown a diagram or photograph of the drop zone so that she knew what to look for from the air. . . . Although told there would be a rush of wind, its strength and effect were not brought home to her. Although told she might have to turn to find the arrow (held up by a co-instructor on the ground directing jumpers to the landing area), she was not told that because they would be dropped upwind it was probable she would have to do that. There was insufficient testing and questioning to ensure that she grasped the essentials of the jump thoroughly enough to perform it safely. I do not say it is necessary to provide written tests. Verbal testing should suffice but it was inadequately done in this instance. The subject of canopy control was passed over too quickly in favour of concentration upon other elements of the jump.[103]

Although not finding the school or instructor negligent for attempting to prepare jumpers in only four hours, the trial judge stated that the

. . . shortness of the course which is deliberately designed to whet the appetites of novices so that they may jump with the minimal involvement of time puts on those who teach it a heavy onus to ensure that each individual novice has learned well enough to jump safely.[104]

Finally, although no overt competition was present, the court stated that

Having gone through the training and come to the point of the jump there are probably strong peer group pressures on the student to complete the task. I find it to be part of a jump master's duties to tell an alarmed student that she does not have to jump unless she is quite ready and that no one will think the worse of her if she declines.[105]

In fact, this court believed that it was the jump master's duty to prohibit any jumper who he thought was not "physically and emotionally in a condition to exercise clear and quick judgment," even if the jumper felt personally ready to proceed.[106] Parallels can be drawn with other outoor activities demanding participant commital, the easiest perhaps being the paddler about to run a rapid for the first time.

In summary, an outdoor leader has numerous duties to meet while instructing others in outdoor living and travel skills. The instructor has a foremost general duty to progressively teach participants the activity, using a variety of recognized teaching methodologies. While doing so, care must be taken to ensure that each student has the intellectual, physical and emotional capability to perform the progressions taught at a safe level.

Provision of Safety Measures

A fourth and final category of duties, integrally related to the duties pertaining to guidance, supervisory and instructional responsibilities, are those varied but essential duties collectively considered safety precautions. The types of safety measures employed will vary slightly depending on the activity, group, equipment and environment, but most of the factors considered here have warranted some attention in a wide variety of outdoor programs.

The first duty involves the need for outdoor educators to know their participants, both the general characteristics and propensities of the age group being dealt with[107] and any specific outstanding propensities displayed by any one participant.[108] Usually pertaining to children or the mentally disabled, this duty would be reflected in responsibilities to create and enforce necessary rules and regulations which facilitate organization and control of the group. Such rules and regulations may concern camp boundaries, unsupervised equipment use, horseplay during programs and so on and will most likely be appreciated by participants as they lay important guidelines for the activity.

Another large area requiring frequent, careful safety analysis involves the equipment used by the participants. It should be maintained in good repair and replaced when it becomes unsafe or obsolete. Leaders employed by agencies using unsafe equipment or procrastinating in the purchase of needed replacement equipment, would be wise to protect themselves from liability by writing their supervisors requesting new equipment and retaining copies for their personal records.

Another important equipment consideration is the need to carry adequate amounts of quality personal technical equipment (for example, lifejackets, paddles, ski boots, ski poles) if advertising the provision of such. In the recent case of *Delaney et al.* v. *Cascade River Holidays Ltd. et al.*,[109] upheld at appeal, the defendant whitewater rafting outfit was found negligent in failing to provide three plaintiffs (who drowned while engaged in one of the defendant's guided rafting excursions) with lifejackets meeting required buoyancy specifications for this type of usage. The crew and passengers were wearing Department of Transport small craft approved lifejackets affording 9.5 kgs of buoyancy.

However, the president of the corporate defendant admitted that he had previously recognized the inadequacy of these personal floatation devices when used in the cold, turbulent waters of the Fraser River, and although he knew where he could obtain Ministry of Transport approved lifejackets with 13.6 kg of buoyancy, he "made no effort to purchase those jackets before the tragedy but continued to provide passengers with personal floatation devices which were inadequate for whitewater rivers."[110] While not claiming that jackets with a higher buoyancy ratio would have prevented the tragedy, Justice Callighan stated that:

> ... based on the evidence before me they [the jackets] may have averted or reduced the loss of life that occurred when the crew and passengers were swept from the motorized raft.[111]

In this particular case, despite the defendant's apparent negligence, the plaintiff's estate was barred recovery because the plaintiff had signed a disclaimer which expressly excluded the company from liability, including that caused by its own negligence. Regardless, outdoor leaders or agency directors should note their responsibility to provide high quality equipment, suitable for the type of use it is likely to receive. Also, such equipment must be stocked in a variety of sizes to meet various participants' needs. In addition to detrimentally affecting learning, improperly fitting equipment can be hazardous. A lifejacket that is so large it slips over the head of the wearer is dangerous, as is a pair of cross-country ski boots so small that they constrict circulation and promote premature frostbite of the feet.

That equipment should only be utilized in the manner for which it was intended was borne out in the *Thornton* case,[112] where a teenager was rendered a quadriplegic doing somersaults in a gymnastics class. He gained momentum by jumping from a vaulting horse down onto a springboard and on a bad rebound from the board overshot his landing mats and landed on his head. Outdoor educators will have the same duty this youth's physical education teacher was held to owe: the duty to use suitable equipment for each planned activity and not to use equipment for purposes other than those for which it was intended without careful analysis of the potential risks involved in doing so. Innovation and improvisation of equipment are admirable, but they must be rationally considered.

The *Meyers* case set out in law the duty for physical educators to provide adequate protective landing surfaces for students working at heights, in this case on rings. Part of young Meyers's temporary quadriplegia was attributed to a finding that:

> ... on a balance of probabilities... there had been inadequate matting beneath the rings at the time of the accident, and inadequate supervision of the exercise room where the accident took place.[113]

In the *Michalak*[114] case, the Nova Scotia Supreme Court noted that greater safety protection needed to be provided for students engaged in the high ropes course. While participants were secured in a short waist belt attached to the main swinging rope, a full body harness was deemed the proper standard for such an event.[115]

This case also provided an illustration of the importance of checking equipment frequently. Yet another basis of negligence in this case was the court's perception that the instructor had not checked the knots on the safety rope attached to the Tarzan-Swing after each use, to ensure that the safety rope would not slip.[116] Application of these standards to other climbing/rappelling related activities should appear quite obvious.

In the *Moddejonge* outdoor education case,[117] a failure to provide adequate aquatic lifesaving equipment was found to be a contributing cause in the deaths of two girls swimming in an unmarked beach area. With technology at its present level, vast innovations and improvements have been made in the types and designs of various pieces of lightweight, compact lifesaving equipment used in each activity pursuit. For example, the wilderness highcountry ski leader may soon not only be admired for providing complete lifesaving gear, but indeed expected to provide or require all participants to provide such apparatus as electronic transceivers, avalanche probes and shovels.

Yet another useful and widely utilized technique to promote safety in many outdoor education/recreation settings is the "buddy" system, where two or more individuals are made reciprocally responsible for one another. A canoeing example was already described, but similar systems are also appropriate on, for example, winter ski or snowshoe treks where partners watch each other for signs of frostnip, hypothermia, or exhaustion. However, leaders are again reminded that when employing such systems, they cannot delegate their personal responsibility to their participants;[118] in the event of an accident involving negligence the instructor not one or more of the participants will be held liable.

A final area of concern is the importance of planning and preparing for emergencies which may arise during the program. As many outdoor education/recreation programs are conducted in wildlands some distance from normal life support systems, a plan of action which can be quickly implemented by a well-trained leader, using the human and equipment resources at hand, may make the difference between life and death or the remaining quality of a life saved. The fact that accidents **will** happen is a given; where, when, how and how serious are the only questions which need to be asked. Given this knowledge, the outdoor leader has a duty to develop a set of emergency procedures, including contingencies, to initiate in the event of an accident. These procedures must include first aid knowledge and equipment, a communication system and/or designated evacuation routes. Rescue from the outside may be facilitated by leaving route cards and estimated times of arrival with the agency or another responsible source. Some parks have mandatory backcountry permit systems in place and a failure to register in these areas may mean paying the full cost of any searches or rescues necessitated (at 60 dollars plus per minute for helicopter time, this is an expense few agencies could afford to incur). Leaders should carry statement of health cards on each participant, indicating any predisposing conditions or susceptibilities which may be useful in rendering first aid. Participants engaging in strenuous wilderness travel, especially if they are middle-aged or older or in questionable health, should be required to undergo a complete physical examination prior to beginning the program.

Perhaps one final incident example will serve to tie many of these precautions to risk and participant evaluations and subsequent program design and operation. On 12 June 1978, 12 boys and a teacher were found drowned in Lake Témiscamingue.[119] They had been engaged in a wilderness canoe trip run by the Ontario St. John's Boys School when a storm suddenly blew up on the lake causing some of their boats to capsize. In the ensuing efforts to save these boys, the rest of the expedition's boats also tipped and the waves and cold water claimed the lives of those who could not make it to shore. Some of the contributing factors cited in the coroner's report included:

1. The absence of a chain of command and contingency plans should one of the four leader steersmen be unable to complete the trip.
2. There was no communication system (walkie talkies, whistles, etc.) between the canoes or between the group and civilization.
3. No route card or plans had been drawn up; "it was simply hoped to cover about 65 kilometers a day."[120]
4. No one in the group had travelled the route previously and they relied solely on two copies of a small-scale topographical map.
5. No emergency procedures had been established and the group carried no rescue equipment (such as inflatable rafts).
6. Neither the leaders nor any of the 27 boys (aged 12 to 14 years) had had a medical checkup prior to this planned 3-week expedition and none had been required to undergo any pretrip physical conditioning, swimming, canoe rescue or lifesaving training.
7. Many of the boys were nonswimmers, and the leaders could not identify which boys could swim and which could not.
8. Neither the leaders nor any of the boys had paddled a canoe since the previous summer, 8 months prior to the day they set out.
9. A social the night before, all-night driving, an early start and the lack of a hot breakfast or lunch did nothing to ensure the endurance of the participants or instructors that day.
10. One of the steersmen was unqualified to accept this role and the students acting as bowsmen in the 22-foot canoes had received no prior training in paddling in this important position.[121]

And in their summary statement:

We feel that for boys from 12 to 14 years of age, this entire expedition constituted an exaggerated and pointless challenge.[122]

In addition, later studies of the modified 22-foot Selkirk canoes used on the expedition (all of which overturned, either unexplainedly or in the attempt to effect rescues of swimmers) found this craft highly unstable and considered safe only for "experienced paddlers in calm water."[123]

Despite the almost incredible list of duties and subsequent standards which the St. John's School and its leaders failed to meet, the coroner's inquest arrived at the verdict that the 13 members of the party "died violently and accidentally" and because "no criminal responsibility was involved," the issue was dropped. None of the boys' parents sued the school, due largely to the excellent school/parent relationship which existed. It could be speculated that if one or more of the boys had been seriously injured, but not killed, the parents may have been more inclined (if not almost compelled) to sue in order to recover the damages necessary for extended medical care. However, this incident well illustrates the tremendous importance of outdoor leaders striving to establish and maintain strong, trusting relationships with their students or participants and their families.

The only recommendation the inquest evolved was a desire to see such activities regulated through provincial legislation.[124] Although most outdoor leaders in Canada would prefer not to be subject to statutory regulations and constraints placed on their activities, the need for higher and more consistent standards of care both within and between provinces has become quite evident.

The most glaring recent example of the institution of a regulatory system is that currently being implemented in the whitewater rafting industry in B.C. Following the deaths of 12 people in three separate accidents on B.C. rivers in the summer of 1987, the provincial government tightened the reins on licensed rafting operators. Potential guide candidates must now pass a vigorous battery of written and practical tests. Also, in addition to the newly stated regulation requiring guides to become certified, there are rules requiring guides to be familiar with the river they plan to run prior to taking clients on it, to decide when a given reach is runnable or not, when helmets and wetsuits will be worn by clients and the extent of prefloat safety briefings offered.[125]

In this particular case the rafting operators themselves recognized the problems of inconsistent guide qualification and operating standards and worked with government to evolve regulations which would improve safety while not regulating the operators out of business.[126] However, as professional outdoor outfitters in some provinces can attest, where a group of people offer goods and/or services without any internal regulation or policing, an external body (usually government) will step in and impose what it perceives are steps necessary for public protection. As these imposed standards may not always prove as desirable as self-determined regulations, outdoor leaders would do well to improve their professional credibility by establishing, disseminating and encouraging adoption of their own guidelines or standards.[127]

7 VICARIOUS LIABILITY

THE RELATIONSHIP BETWEEN OUTDOOR EDUCATION/RECREATION LEADERSHIP AND PROGRAMMING ORGANIZATIONS

IN OUTDOOR ACTIVITY PURSUITS, there are a number of sports-governing and leadership-certifying bodies and professional associations operating quite independently of outdoor education/recreation delivery agencies and boards, and therefore rather immune to the liability allegations these agencies may be open to. However, these higher level organizations are often granted authority to develop instructor/leader qualification standards (as per various certifications and certification levels), which are used as guidelines by agencies involved in outdoor education/recreation leadership development or those interested in hiring "certified" leaders for their programs. For the individual outdoor leader, this means that qualifications may be sanctioned from a variety of sources over and above the agency the leader is employed by. For example, a cross-country ski tour leader may be influenced by training and direction received from any or all of the following sources:

Canadian Ski Association—Sports Governing Body (and in this case, also Leadership Certifying Body).

University—Leadership Training Agency; agency through which the cross-country tour leader was trained.

YMCA (and its executive director)—Program Delivery Agency: employs outdoor leaders (for example, tour leaders).

Outdoor Program Director—Supervises outdoor leaders (for example, tour leaders).

Outdoor Leader—Cross-Country Ski Tour Leader One.

For the cross-country ski instructor, the top level of this hierarchy of sorts (in this case the Canadian Ski Association), would be replaced by the Canadian Association of Nordic Ski Instructors (CANSI), a professional association and certifying body nationally sanctioned to develop and organize cross-country ski instructors in Canada.

To date there are no examples of successful lawsuits against any leadership certifying body or agency for insufficient or improper training of outdoor leaders. This follows the well-established principle that a teacher is not liable for the subsequent use of the knowledge and skills passed on to students as long as recognized theories and methods are taught. The theories and skills taught need not of necessity be the most popular currently, or even the most correct, but they should not be contrary to long standing custom. For example, if a first-aid instructor taught a class to administer sugar to a victim displaying signs and symptoms of insulin shock, insulin to one appearing to be in a diabetic coma, and insulin if unsure, the instructor could be negligent. This procedure is the exact opposite of that customarily taught by virtually all emergency medical training agencies and institutions involving administration of insulin to a victim diagnosed in insulin shock, sugar to one in a diabetic coma, and sugar if unsure. If a student taught and examined in the incorrect first-aid method were to subsequently cause further injury to a diabetic patient, the instructing agency could be liable for that victim's damages. Such incidences of obviously negligent instruction are rare and the unlikelihood of a specific related accident coincidentally arising later in the leader's career makes such suits even less likely. However, organizations developing leadership certification course curricula and agencies presenting these courses to prospective outdoor leaders should be aware of their responsibility to teach reasonably safe and proper techniques.

THE LIABILITY OF OUTDOOR EDUCATION/RECREATION PROGRAM DELIVERY AGENCIES AND BOARDS

A program delivery agency or recreation or school board may be held liable for injuries sustained by a participant or student "on the basis of a personal fault or because of the agency's vicarious liability"[1] for the conduct of the outdoor leaders it employs. Personal liability may readily be distinguished from that arising through a vicarious relationship.

> A person is not, subject to well known exceptions, generally liable in tort except where he has intentionally or negligently caused some loss or damage to the plaintiff. But the result of vicarious liablity is to make one person compensate another for loss not due to his fault at all, although it may be due to the fault of his servant, agent or independent contractor.[2]

Boards may be personally liable for breaching statutes contained in their province's *School* or *Education Act*[3] (if they have one), or for failing to meet their statutory or common law duty to maintain their equipment, buildings and grounds in a safe condition.[4] They may also be held liable for failing to meet the standard of care required in ensuring adequate supervision[5] (keeping leader-participant ratios low enough for safety) and qualified instructors.[6] But that form of "personal" liability

> ... is really another way of saying that some servant or official of the defendant, at some time, and in some way... failed to do something which ought to have been done, and that this was the cause of the accident.[7]

For example, in the case of *Smith* v. *Horizon Aero Sports Ltd. et al.*,[8] where a parachuting student was rendered a paraplegic on her first jump, the plaintiff attempted to attribute some of the liability to the Canadian Sport Parachuting Association (CSPA). She claimed that the CSPA misled her through their brochure which indicated sport parachuting was safer than she later believed it to be, and that they failed in their duty to require adequate prejump training, to provide qualified instructors and to supervise Horizon Aero Sport's personnel and teaching methods more closely.[9]

Justice Spencer countered each of her arguments in finding the defendant CSPA not negligent, and stated that he held such voluntary nonprofit organizations to a lower standard of care than any other person. He believed that:

> ... it is in the interest of society that voluntary efforts directed towards promoting excellence and safety in any field of endeavor are to

be encouraged. If the standard expected from a nonprofit organization is put too high, such organizations may depart the field. In my judgment, the standard to be expected of them may be compared to the standard expected from a rescuer—another form of volunteer. A rescuer does not become liable towards a victim who he is trying to help unless what he does worsens the victim's plight: see *Horsley et al.* v. *MacLaren et al.* (1970), 22 D.L.R. (3d) 545, [1972] S.C.R. 441. The plaintiff suffered harm because of negligent training in canopy control and negligent supervision. CSPA was not responsible for either of those. . . . [10]

The facts in this case clearly illustrate a failure on the part of the instructor to assess the plaintiff's readiness to jump and to act accordingly, and as he was certified by the CSPA, this case can be used as an example of the problem of teaching and evaluating leadership. The outdoor pursuits certifying bodies presently involved in leadership development in Canada are little more than technical skill training institutions. None has found a method of accurately teaching and/or assessing a prospective outdoor leader's judgmental capabilities,[11] the very core of all leadership in the outdoors.

However, it should be noted that a number of outdoor leadership sports governing and certifying bodies and professional associations (for example, Coaching Association of Canada (CAC), Canadian Ski Association (CSA), Canadian Association of Nordic Ski Instructors (CANSI)) have taken a positive active role in providing their certified members with insurance coverage while these leaders are working in the activity pursuit for which they have been certified.

THE CONCEPT OF VICARIOUS LIABILITY

The doctrine of vicarious liablity is a form of strict liability, wherein an employer "is called upon to make good, loss(es)" resulting from the tortious conduct of his employees, "even though he is not personally at fault."[12] It has been interpreted that this concept evolved because "the employer, having put matters into motion, should be liable if the motion that he has originated leads to damage to another."[13] Other justifications providing the rationale for vicarious liability include:

1. As an employer "employs others to advance the company's or agency's own economic interests," the employer should "be placed under a corresponding liability for losses incurred in the course of the enterprise."[14]
2. The employer selects employees and should therefore be accountable if they are inadequately hired or supervised.[15]
3. The employer is much more likely to have a capacity to bear the economic loss of damages than is an employee.[16] Such losses are normally covered by insurance and the employer may pay the cost of higher insurance premiums by increasing the price of the product or service, thereby distributing the cost to that sector of the population purchasing that good or service.[17] If the employer happens to be an agent of a federal, provincial or municipal government or a school board, the cost may be distributed through taxation increases.
4. The doctrine is also supported for its admonitory value in accident prevention.[18] It not only effectively places deterrent pressures at higher organizational levels, emphasizing the need for safety conscious supervision, but provides the employer with legal incentive to discipline employees not meeting imposed standards.

In short, the application of vicarious liability follows the tenets of tort liability in that it is a form of legal accountability oriented toward the just compensation of accident victims. In this case, employers are held legally accountable for the tortious wrongs of their employees, in part because of the master-servant relationship and in part due to their greater capacity to bear the risks inherent to the operation and to distribute the potential losses incurred through these risks.

The Test for Vicarious Liability

In order to impose vicarious liability upon an employer, the plaintiff must show that the injury(ies) was due to the negligent act or omission of an employee (whether paid or volunteer), performing some recognized duty for the defendant employer.[19] The limits of an agency's or, recreation or school board's vicarious liability will therefore be defined through a two part test. First, a master-servant (employer-employee) relationship must be proven, often referred to as a contract of service. Once this relationship has been established, it must be determined if the tortious conduct occurred within the scope of the servant's employment.

ORGANIZATIONAL CONTROL   The question usually raised when attempting to define the employer-employee relationship is whether the employee was working under a contract *of* service or a contract *for* service.[20] This distinction basically involves the determination of whether the employee was a "servant" of the employer or an independent contractor. While doctors, lawyers and some entertainment professionals are often hired as independent contractors, school teachers and most (not all) outdoor instructors/guides will be employed under a contract of service.

Historically, and even in some quite recent cases, the determination of a contract *of* versus a contract *for* service was held to be a control test. The question to be answered was:

Does the employer control the activities of the employee by saying not only *what* is to be done but also *how* it is to be done?[21]

If such control could be shown, then a contract of service existed. If not, the employee was considered an independent contractor operating under a contract for service. For example, in *Rheaume v. Gowland*,[22] a rifle club allowed a man to live on its property in an attempt to control trespassing and vandalism. This volunteer "resident manager" was merely instructed to telephone the R.C.M.P. in the event of trouble, and when he negligently shot a trespasser, the courts held him personally liable for taking this unauthorized duty upon himself.

In modern times, the application of the control test has been largely modified due to the high degree of technical specialization of many servants, making employer understanding and subsequent control of how various jobs are to be performed an unreasonable expectation.[23] In the mid 1960s, Lord Parker admonished the control test.

... clearly, superintendence and control cannot be the decisive test when one is dealing with a professional man, or a man of some particular skill and experience.[24]

Today the question of control over the manner of task performance is only one factor considered indicative of the employer's organizational control over the employee. Other criteria include such incidental and collateral matters as:

...the employer's power of selection of the person concerned, the nature of the payment fixed (wages or salary), the employer's rights in respect of suspension or dismissal, the degree of skill required, whether the employee is integrated into the business,[25] whether the man performing the services provides his own equipment, whether he hires his own helpers and what degree of financial risk he takes...[26]

In outdoor education/recreation situations other factors indicative of an employer's organizational control may include the employer's right to make stipulations regarding program content, methodology and location and the provision and directions regarding use of specific safety equipment and devices. Most outdoor leaders are employed under contracts *of* service. This is true, if for no other reason than the majority of outdoor educators are schoolteachers employed under such contracts by various urban and rural municipal school boards and county councils.

However, a significant number of individuals across the country are operating outdoor adventure businesses as independent contractors. In these cases, the independent contractor provides the hiring agency or individual with the outdoor instructor/trip leader staff and often the outdoor equipment (such as canoes, paddles, lifejackets, shelters, cook stoves and utensils) and food. The independent contractor maintains organizational control over the staff selected and is the insured defendant in the event of a lawsuit. As long as the individual or group hiring this contractor has no controlling powers over the staff hired by the independent contractor, they cannot be held liable for any torts the staff may commit while running a program or leading a trip for them. The independent contractor will vicariously assume responsibility for any injuries sustained by program participants resulting from the negligent acts or omissions of the staff line outdoor leader(s) provided. Of course, this responsibility may be altered to some extent where the independent contractor gives the hiring agency the power to control what and especially how the program is run and what safety precautions are taken by the staff.[27]

A number of agencies the author is aware of have attempted to hire their staff under contracts for service, thereby relieving themselves of vicarious responsibility for these individuals' actions. They have argued that it is impossible for them to supervise outdoor leaders running programs in a variety of wildland locations simultaneously, and they therefore believe they have little control over how programs are run. This has been shown to be an invalid practice as

... the law is concerned with the nature of the contractual relationship. The terms of the contract, although relevant, cannot be used by the employer to convert a contract of service into a contract for service. Thus, merely using the words "independent contractor" to describe the employee's status will not eliminate liability if sufficient control is proven.[28]

Therefore, the only way an agency may legally avoid being vicariously liable for its outdoor instructor/guides, would be by completely relinquishing control over the method of participant supervision, instruction and most importantly, "the safety measures employed during the course of instruction."[29]

SCOPE OF EMPLOYMENT   In order for an employer to be held vicariously liable for the torts of an employee, the negligent act or omission must have transpired while the servant employee was working within the scope or course of his or her employment.[30] A reasonably clear distinction between an employee's allowable deviation from the job description and a blatant departure from it was drawn by Justice Lynsky when he stated:

> It is well settled law that a master is liable even for acts which he has not authorized provided they are so connected with the acts which he has authorized that they might rightly be regarded as modes, although improper modes, of doing them. On the other hand, if the unauthorized and wrongful act of the servant is not so connected with the authorized act as to be a mode of doing it but is an independent act the master is not responsible for, in such a case the servant is not acting in the course of his employment but has gone outside it.[31]

Hence, the employer's liability will extend through all acts the employees have been "expressly or implicitly authorized to perform,"[32] including the employees' freedom to deal with unforeseen circumstances not necessarily defined in the job contract. Implication of such authorization will be determined through an assessment of the decision-making discretion expressly granted the employee, the direction available from superiors, the duties typically performed by similar employees in other agencies and the duties and acts foreseeably incidental to performance of the duties expressly outlined by the employer.[33]

On occasion, an employer may successfully limit vicarious liability by expressly prohibiting certain acts or conduct. Such prohibitions must relate directly to the course of employment and not merely to the employee's conduct in performing duties within that course of employment (the manner, place or time of his acts).[34] For example, in the case of *C.P.R.* v. *Lockhart*,[35] a carpenter negligently injured a plaintiff while driving his own uninsured vehicle for business purposes. Although his company had expressly forbidden him to use his own car unless it was insured, they were still found vicariously liable because they had granted him permission to use his own car and he was doing so while performing duties within the scope of his employment.[36]

In a school case, a board was found not liable when a number of teachers took it upon themselves to grant their students a half-day holiday to attend a concert.[37] When a student was injured after being thrown from an overloaded truck the teachers were using to transport the students to the concert the board was absolved of liability as its employee teachers were acting outside their scope of employment and well beyond their authority. In discussing the law here, the court stated:

> There is no doubt that a School Board is liable in law for an accident due to a teacher's negligence if in a matter which may reasonably be regarded as falling within the scope of his employment. . . . [38]

In the *Moddejonge* case,[39] the courts found the outdoor education coordinator/teacher negligent in failing to supervise or provide adequate safety measures for a group of girls he took swimming. The court pointed to the vicarious liability of the defendant board.

> It is to be observed that McCauley (the teacher) was acting within the scope of his employment. It follows that the defendant board is also liable.[40]

Had the school board expressly prohibited him from taking students swimming, the outdoor education coordinator would have been solely liable. But as they merely placed parameters on his taking them swimming (e.g., not taking them unless a lifeguard and/or lifesaving equipment were present) they remained vicariously liable.

In conclusion, only rarely in outdoor education/recreation situations (such as where the outdoor leader is an independent contractor and/or where he or she is proven to be expressly operating outside the scope of employment) can an agency or board successfully avoid vicarious liability for the tortious acts of its employees. Although they may limit their liability to some extent by expressly delimiting the scope of their employees' duties, the limited benefits derivable from such a course of action hardly warrant these restrictions and the loss of trust and perceived autonomy they create. It would also be undesirable for agencies to advocate an open system, completely lacking direction and boundaries for employees. Rather, agencies and boards should take to heart their legal and ethical responsiblities to their participants and their employees, ensuring that their staff are well-qualified and their programs are run as safely as is practicable.

THE CASE OF NONINCORPORATED CLUBS AND ASSOCIATIONS

Quite often, outdoor instructors/guides find themselves belonging to or otherwise involved with one or more nonincorporated organizations in the guise of various outdoor clubs. These associations are little more than conglomerations of people with a common area of interest; they have no legal status and usually no insurance. These organizations operate on the premise that most members are adults who are personally responsible for the risks they take in pursuing the activity. While this may be true to some extent for experienced adults co-adventuring in wilderness areas, those clubs advertising education and/or competition as within their mandate must accept greater legal responsibility for the participants they attract. An absence of legal standing may have tremendous implications for the executives of these associations as well as for individual members.

Unless a club is legally incorporated under the *Societies Act*,[41] the members of the Board of Directors can be sued personally. In addition, such an organization does not have the capacity to buffer its members from legal accountability. Therefore, members must carry sufficient "liability insurance to personally protect themselves in case of a suit."[42] Unfortunately, other than homeowner's liability insurance which will afford some minimal coverage, few of these people are adequately protected from such suits. Tort law exists to compensate accident victims, and although the courts may tend toward holding volunteer, nonprofit organizations to a somewhat lower standard of care than the average person, this cannot be counted on where no other vehicle for compensation exists. Responsibility for checking whether an organization is incorporated and/or insured falls squarely on the shoulders of the individual outdoor leader volunteering to instruct and/or lead club members in outdoor ventures.

It would be prudent for such clubs or associations to acquire corporation status and join provincial and/or national associations which provide liability insurance to protect sanctioned members. Once an association has become incorporated and acquired insurance, "claims can not be made against the individual members or officers, only against the legal entity, the corporation."[43]

Associations and clubs in other activity pursuits are advised to look into the benefits and feasibility of providing the sorts of liability insurance protection discussed herein to their executive, instructors, trip leaders and/or other event organizers, officials and volunteers. Unfortunately, the recent liability insurance crisis has reduced the possibility of securing such insurance at reasonable premium rates.

COMMON ADVENTURE SITUATIONS

It has long been assumed that adults who consented to travel and recreate together in the out-of-doors each assumed the risks involved. While the individuals involved may belong to a common activity club, it is more likely that they are business associates, friends, or neighbors and that one has invited the other(s) along on an outing. Most readers should be able to relate to the frequency with which they themselves have invited or joined others in just such ventures. Most readers will therefore be duly surprised by the finding of the British Columbia Supreme Court, which ignored this basic assumption of personal responsibility and instead found negligence in a common adventure situation.

In this, the case of *Pawlak and Pawlak* v. *Doucette and Reinks*,[44] the defendant Doucette invited the other defendant Reinks and the plaintiff Pawlak to water-ski with him, using his motorboat. While both Doucette and Reinks were experienced water-skiers and ski-boat operators, Pawlak had never tried water-skiing prior to that date. Doucette asked Reinks to drive the boat while he assisted Pawlak, helping him to don a lifejacket and water-skis and explaining how to position himself in the water for take-off, how to hold the tow rope, and other points.

As Pawlak assumed the proper position the ski rope was tossed to him from the boat by the spotter Vaillencourt. The handle landed behind and to his left but as the boat eased away, the rope was drawn between Pawlak's skis. Unfortunately, while the handle was still behind Pawlak, someone on shore shouted "Go," and Reinks applied full power to the boat. On the evidence, as the boat surged forward, Pawlak grabbed for the rope. His left hand became entangled in the rope with the result that a number of his fingers were severed.[45]

The court apportioned the damages in the following manner: Reinks—55 percent, Doucette—30 percent, Pawlak—15 percent. The rationale for this apportionment is most interesting and instructive. Reinks, as the driver of the boat, had a duty to care for the plaintiff. He was "required to act with skill and judgment expected of a reasonable boatman."[46] Reinks was found negligent in failing to ensure that the skier was ready to proceed. Pawlak's injury was a reasonably foreseeable result. The learned judge believed that Reinks had no reason to believe that the "Go" shout had come from either Pawlak, whom he was watching at the time, or from Doucette, who had sat down a short distance away. In fact, the origin of this shout remained undetermined. He also failed in his duty to ascertain the plaintiff's skiing experience and to arrange a "system of signals to allow the skier to communicate with the operator of the boat."[47]

It was interesting to note that while the plaintiff introduced expert evidence and pamphlets produced by the Canadian Waterski Association directing proper water-ski conduct, the judge dismissed this evidence. He noted these guidelines were "not requirements of law," but "counsels of perfection" and instead held Reinks only to the conduct expected of a reasonable man in the circumstances.[48]

Likewise, although Doucette was liable for failing to execute his supervisory role to the standard of the reasonable person in that situation, he was not held to the standard expected of the professional water-ski instructor. However, he was deemed to be a "person of superior knowledge in comparison to the knowledge of the plaintiff vis-à-vis water-skiing."[49]

In identifying specific omissions made by Doucette, the judge noted his failure to ensure that the boat operator knew the skier was unaware of basic communication signals, and to ensure that the skier learned safety practices common to the activity.[50] Some of Doucette's liability was also vicariously assumed for the negligence of Reinks, because it was Doucette's boat and it was being operated for his purposes.[51]

The defendants failed in their claim that Pawlak had voluntarily assumed the inherent risks in the activity and therefore could not collect. The negligent operation of the boat did not, in the court's opinion, constitute an inherent risk to the sport. However, Pawlak was found contributorily negligent for failing to take reasonable care for his own protection. The judge believed that Pawlak's entanglement in the rope was a product at least in part of his positive action in grabbing the rope, and wrapping it around his hand.[52] It was perceived that the plaintiff's past experience around mechanical objects and moving cables and ropes should have made him more aware than the average person of the risks involved in grabbing a moving rope. It was believed that his actions in this case fell below the acceptable standard.

This case, while only tried at the Provincial Supreme Court level, has tremendous implications for all outdoor leaders whose recreational pursuits often transcend those of their professional preparation and involvement. By its finding against Doucette and Reinks, this court has made a general statement that those with greater experience will be responsible for those with less, regardless of the presence or absence of a formal teacher/student or guide/follower relationship. As trained instructors/leaders will usually have more experience than those who accompany them on recreational outdoor excursions, they will concomitantly have an implied duty to care for those less experienced comrades.

The insurance the professional outdoor leader carries will not apply to such nonbusiness related activities, but there is some potential for insurance coverage in such situations through personal property and liability insurance where the leader is a homeowner.

8 RISK MANAGEMENT

DEFINITION AND CONCEPTS OF RISK

IT WOULD SUPERFICIALLY appear that attaching a definition to the word *risk* is an easy enough task. This definition would consist of the notion of uncertainty of outcome and the possibility that the outcome may be unfavorable. However, economists, statisticians, educationalists, decision theorists, and insurance theorists have grappled with attempts to arrive at a commonly acceptable definition and have been unable to do so. As one pertinent result, many of the problems related to dealing with the insurance industry stem from the different perspective with which they define and approach risk compared to the view that outdoor practitioners have.

In reviewing half a dozen insurance textbooks, the most precise and acceptable definition found was that risk is "the possibility of an adverse deviation from a desired outcome that is expected or hoped for."[1] This definition readily incorporates the notions of uncertainty and possible loss. An even simpler definition is that risk is an expression of possible loss. The possible loss to which we refer in outdoor activity situations may involve loss of equipment, life, or quality thereof through injury, and financial loss, which may accrue through lawsuits or settlements. Or perhaps the loss may simply involve a decrease in satisfaction and in enjoyment of the activity at that time and potentially in the future. We appreciate the adage "nothing ventured—nothing gained," but also realize the fine line we tread in challenging participants in our program appropriately.

Objective Versus Subjective Risk

The definitions presented describe objective risks only. Risk is a state of the external environment and the possibility of loss exists whether the individual exposed to it realizes it or not.

In outdoor educational/recreational situations, leaders often make use of mental tricks played to increase or decrease the level of subjective or apparent risk. The river leader may play up the mighty rapid around the next bend (actually only a grade II riffle) to excite novice whitewater paddlers and to enhance their feelings of satisfaction upon successfully negotiating the rapid. Experienced climbers often joke with each other as they approach a particularly difficult pitch, to play down the risk and thereby reduce the tension developing in each. In these and many other situations, the individuals involved are employing tactics to help keep others optimally aroused; neither so bored that they become careless or unappreciative of the risks present, nor so overaroused that they become too nervous or scared to perform essential tasks.

WHAT ARE THE RISKS?

In returning to our definition of risk, the higher the *probability* of loss, obviously the greater the degree of risk present. A measure of the possible *size* of the loss must also be considered as one may be willing to accept the possibility of a number of small losses while fearing a catastrophic loss from a single event. The insurance industry employs a concept of expected value to relate the probability of a given loss and its potential size. Here the expected value of loss in a given situation is the probability of that particular loss multiplied by the amount of the likely loss.[2] When calculating the expected value of a single risk factor, this equation is relatively useless. It only becomes meaningful when a number of risks are considered in relation to each other.

Another inherent difficulty in applying this concept involves determination of the probability of loss. There do not appear to be any Canadian studies indicating the actual incidence of serious injuries and fatalities occurring as a result of outdoor education/recreation program involvement.

In a study by Meyer it was determined that a number of well-established full-time American adventure programs experienced a fatality rate of approximately o.5 per million student hours of exposure.[3] This he compared to the United States national accidental death rate (all causes, at work, home and play) of 0.1 per million hours of exposure, and that evident in automobile related fatalities (0.7 per million hours exposure). Meyer added that the outdoor programmer could also expect about 40 injuries per million hours of student involvement, again significantly less than motor vehicle travel or sports such as college football where one may expect more than 60 injuries per million hours of exposure. These rates were established using the American National Safety Council criteria for reporting industrial injury; that is, any injury that prevents the individual from performing regular job duties for one or more full calendar days.[4]

In 1984 an outdoor education/recreation database program was initiated in the U.S. The objective is to collect accident, injury and near miss data from programs across North America and annually summarize this data in such ways that it can be useful for staff training and ongoing program operation.[5] In addition to improving the overall safety of outdoor programs, the annual *National Safety Network* (NSN) *Review* may also be useful in communicating with and providing actuarial data for governing bodies and insuring agencies.[6] The NSN's cumulative injury rate for the 1984–86 period was 0.00038 or 38 serious injuries per 100,000 activity days. In the 1986 *Review*, the year for which the greatest amount of data was available, there were 210 serious injuries to participants, which translated to a rate of 48 per 100,000 participant days.[7] A serious injury was defined as one which caused the individual to be removed from activities for one half day or more, one which required medical attention, or one with long term medical complications.[8]

Interestingly, according to the 70 programs submitting data for the 1986 database, there were a total of 270 injuries (participants and staff). Of these, the agencies (and insurers) involved only paid medical expenses in 58 (21 percent), suggesting that a medical payment was made at a rate of one per 10,000 activity days. Fortunately, only four lawsuits were threatened or filed as a result of any of these injuries.[9]

It should be noted that Meyer and the National Safety Network only considered sanctioned program related accidents. Many, if not most, outdoor pursuit accidents occur in casual recreational situations where individuals are less prepared and equipped to deal with the real risks present in the environment. In fact, they are often completely or largely ignorant of the presence of risks inherent to the activity and environment. Many involve recreational vehicles (power boats, snowmobiles, all-terrain vehicles) and according to Canadian statistics, most involve alcohol.[10] For example, there are at least 600 accidental drownings in Canada each year and approximately 25 percent of these are boating related. National statistics are difficult to obtain, but statistics released in the province of Alberta indicated 48 drownings in 1984, 11 of which were small craft related. In these, alcohol was a major factor in all 11, and lifejackets were not worn by 9 of the 11 victims at the time of their capsize. More recent statistical summaries suggest this trend is not, unfortunately, in decline.[11]

There are tremendous differences in the approach taken by trained, qualified leaders leading groups of well equipped participants and that adopted by many uninformed and irresponsible recreationalists. However, these differences are rarely appreciated by the public or by insurance actuarial adjustors who commonly perceive all outdoor adventure activities as extremely risky ventures.

Another question which needs to be addressed in Canada concerns the specific activities and populations we need to be concerned with. Asked to list those activities perceived as involving high risk or "high care," outdoor practitioners will often mention pursuits such as rock climbing, whitewater canoeing/kayaking, downhill skiing, ski touring, hang gliding, spelunking, and scuba diving.

In Meyer's study, the greatest hazard seemed to be present in those activities associated with moving water (ocean and whitewater canoeing and kayaking, rapids swimming and river crossings).[12] Conversely, the National Safety Network data suggest backpacking accounted for more injuries than any other activity, while canoeing only accounted for 1.5 percent and kayaking only 1 percent in the 1986 database.[13] This interesting difference is likely accounted for by the data collection methods and sources used (for example, the volunteer nature of participation in the NSN database).

In considering boating accidents in Canada, while ocean and river paddling certainly do present a high frequency of accidents, the most frequent and catastrophic accidents occur on open lakes (for example, Lake Témiscamingue).[14] Dangerous wind and wave conditions often develop in large shallow lakes, swamping small craft, and these conditions combined with the ever-present Canadian cold water hazard, have claimed many lives.

According to Meyer, in the United States, the second most hazardous activities seem to be related to alpine mountaineering and expeditioning, where the primary hazards are rock falls, avalanches, hypothermia and lightning.[15] Increases in the number of people backpacking and skiing off established trails and being caught by falling rock or avalanches are certainly comparable in Canada. National Research Council statistics indicate an average of 7 avalanche fatalities per year in Canada, with 33 percent involving back country skiers and 26 percent involving climbers. Of the remaining fatalities, 11 percent involved downhill skiers in or near resorts and 12 percent involved other recreationalists (such as snowmobilers), 10 percent represented those caught on roads, and the final 6 percent were in buildings. At least another 18 people per year are caught in avalanches but survive according to statistics. There are probably at least twice as many who are caught in avalanches, but whose accidents are not reported to the Research Council. As participation rates continue to increase, these figures can only grow.[16]

Meyer reports rock climbing, ropes courses and expeditioning below timberline as the third most hazardous group of activities. Here, wet and slippery surfaces precipitating falls are the most common cause of injury.[17] These figures are borne out by a Canadian study which showed that falls were the most frequent cause of backcountry accidents in Banff National Park.[18] The NSN database is consistent with this finding, suggesting that tripping, slipping or being stepped on accounts for 27 percent of all injuries reported.[19]

In addition to identifying the activities concerned, Canadian research needs to be done to assess which participants have the greatest propensity for program related accidents and when. Meyer's American research did not indicate an appreciable difference in the injury/fatality rate of males versus females, or in younger versus older student participants. There did not appear to be a significant difference in rates in longer as opposed to shorter programs, although injuries seem to occur more frequently in the first half of any program. Winter programs were perceived as somewhat more risky, but the smaller data base may have affected the rates. Finally, far from being immune to fatal accidents, leaders appear to experience a higher mortality rate than program participants.[20]

The National Safety Network reports some similar and some contradictory findings based on its three years of data collection. According to the database, while no sex related data were presented, definite age trends were evident. While 80 percent of injuries to all participants occur in the 11-20 year age group, virtually all staff injuries occur in the over 21 categories. Very few adult participants are seriously injured while engaged in programs.[21] In looking at date and time related data, July was by far the most accident prone month (double the number in June or August) and if possible, Tuesdays and Wednesdays should be declared days off instead of Saturdays and Sundays as more accidents occur on these days. The two worst hours of the day are between 10:00-11:00 a.m. and 2:00-3:00 p.m., with 40 percent of all injuries occuring between 10:00-12:00 and 2:00-4:00 p.m.[22]

Again, consistent with Meyer's findings, instructors injury rates exceeded those of participants. The three year cumulative injury rate for participants was 0.00037 while that for staff was 0.00039. Given staff's higher age, fitness, knowledge, skill and experience levels, this finding is somewhat shocking and at this time, beyond explanation by either research source.[23]

All outdoor programming agencies should consider participation in the National Safety Network and should attempt to file accident reports following any injury accident. Close call data is also collected and shared, as this will often suggest likely subsequent accident situations. Agencies/associations are advised to keep the following safety statistics to determine the degree of risk present in their endeavors:

$$1. \text{ Frequency of Injury} = \frac{\text{Number of Injuries}}{\text{Total Number of Exposure Days}}$$

$$2. \text{ Severity} = \frac{\text{Number of Lost Days}}{\text{Total Number of Exposure Days}^{24}}$$

The keeping of accurate records of participants and staff (separately) will enable each agency/board to compare its rates with other general groups and industries and especially other outdoor programming agencies. This type of data, once collected and synthesized, may prove invaluable in encouraging agencies to reduce unacceptably high risk levels where they exist. Perhaps even more importantly today, these statistics may help persuade insurance underwriters that outdoor education/recreation organized programs are reasonable and insurable risks.

PURE VERSUS SPECULATIVE RISKS

Insurance theorists classify risks according to a number of distinctions, some measurable and some not. These dichotomies may be based on whether the risk is *financial* (liability) or *nonfinancial*. Risks may be *static* (predictable) or they may be subject to radical variations as through *dynamic* changes in the environment. Risks may be defined as *fundamental* when they affect large segments of the population (for example, unemployment, occupational disabilities) or *particular* when relatively few individuals suffer exposure annually (for example, individuals involved in outdoor activity accidents).[25]

In addition to the distinctions between financial and nonfinancial risks, probably the most useful differentiation is that made between *pure risk* and *speculative risk*. Pure risk describes situations which involve either a chance of loss or no loss, but not an opportunity to gain. Speculative risk, on the other hand, involves a calculated gamble where one also might lose, but one might gain.[26]

The distinction between pure and speculative risk is interesting because normally only pure risks are insurable.[27] Of course, all insurers view outdoor adventure programming as involving only pure risks—either you get sued or you do not. However, most outdoor programmers view the risks taken as being much more speculative in nature. They accept and even seek a certain level of risk in order to achieve individual and/or program challenge objectives. They attempt to calculate the risk present, then speculate on the potential for program success (and subsequent potential growth for the individual or program) as compared to the potential and probable severity of incurring a loss (such as having an accident). Again, there is lots of room at lower levels of participation for toying with subjective risks while largely avoiding real ones, but this is not the case at higher levels of participation. The men and women who climb Everest are speculators in the deepest sense of the word. They gamble that they can climb the mountain in spite of the tremendous objective hazards and achieve personal inner growth and satisfaction as well as public recognition and appreciation. Given the significant number of people who die on this mountain every year, these adventurers know they are risking their very lives for the potential speculated gains.

Pure risks may be personal (injury or death) or related to property (a paddler may lose a prized kayak in attempting to run a dangerous set of rapids or the boat may be stolen off a vehicle as the kayaker sleeps in a campground). They may involve liability risks (such as when an outdoor leader fails to avoid or otherwise deal with commonly known avalanche runs with the result that a number of participants are buried and seriously injured or killed). Finally, pure risks may arise vicariously (such as when the victims in the aforementioned avalanche accident sue the agency by which the leader was employed).[28]

All these types of pure risks may have financial implications for the agency and/or staff and should therefore be considered in evaluating the consequence of accepting program related risks. Agencies, associations, and individual leaders must consider the potential for a number of these types of pure risks to overlap in a given situation and to evaluate and manage the risk present accordingly.

METHODS OF MANAGING REAL RISK IN OUTDOOR ACTIVITY SITUATIONS

With the accepted knowledge that participation in outdoor programs involves greater risk of injury or death than day to day activities (with the exception of road travel) we must look for acceptable means of dealing with these inherent risks. As outdoor leaders we are largely spectators, seeking adequate risk to stimulate participants while avoiding likely accident precipitating situations, and we must learn a variety of flexible yet appropriate techniques for handling objective risks.

In dealing with program related risks, the outdoor organization director and/or staff should follow this process:

1. Determine objectives—program and individual.
2. Identify risks—physical, social, legal.
3. Evaluate risks—frequency, severity.
4. Consider alternative methods of handling the risk.
5. Select the most appropriate method.
6. Implement the decided method.
7. Review and evaluate.

In considering the alternatives available, there are basically five ways to deal with real risk in outdoor program situations: retain, reduce, avoid, transfer through insurance or transfer through participant assumption. By looking at these methods in a bit more detail, they can be placed in two decision making models which show when we may employ each technique.

Retention—Risk assumption or retention is probably the most common method of approaching risk. That is as it should be. What is important is that this retention is planned and intentional and not the involuntary result of a lack of consideration of the risks. An example of risk retention would be intentionally choosing to backpack in an area known for its variable weather.

Reduction—A loss reduction approach involves the employment of safety equipment and/or procedures which may reduce either the frequency and/or potential severity of accidents. For example, requiring cross-country ski tourers to wear glacier glasses above tree line may reduce both the incidence and potential severity of snowblindness.

Avoidance—Avoiding a risk involves making a conscious decision not to accept the specific risk present at that particular time. Portaging around an oft-paddled rapid when the river is in flood and the group is inexperienced is an example of a wise employment of this method under the circumstances.

Transferance through Insurance—In most, if not all, outdoor programs, there are a variety of risks which are perceived as undesirable but largely unpreventable in the drive to achieve program objectives. These are the risks which, while occurring infrequently, may be quite catastrophic in their consequences. An example inherent in most camping situations is the risk of a serious burn, either from a campfire or gas powered appliance (such as a stove or lamp). These risks are best covered through insurance.

Transfer through Participant Assumption—Where participants are informed, consenting adults, there are a number of high risk activity situations where they must be prepared to personally assume the risk of participation. This may be legally achieved through the use of responsibility release contracts (waivers). The people who choose to climb Mount Everest or do other high risk activities at environmental extremes must be willing to accept great objective risks inherent to participation at that level.

A useful exercise for leaders would be to itemize all of the risks frequently encountered in a particular program and identify how they have typically approached each of these risks in the past. Evaluation of these risks must always involve a consideration of the group. In assessing the readiness of the participants, the leader must consider their age, fitness, skill, knowledge, mental readiness, enthusiasm, and the support equipment available. Equipment adequacy may refer to the presence of appropriate clothing, ropes, hardware, first aid kit, or other safety and rescue apparatus.

Table 1 shows that the advisability of retaining a given static risk may change depending on the results of the preliminary participant readiness

TABLE 1   Risk Management Strategies Considering Participant
Readiness

	High		
		AVOID	TRANSFER
Real Risk Present			
		REDUCE	RETAIN
	Low		
		Low	High
		Participant Readiness	

TABLE 2   Risk Management Strategies Considering Accident Likelihood
and Potential Severity

	High		
		TRANSFER — INSURANCE — WAIVERS	AVOID
Anticipated Accident Severity			
		RETAIN	REDUCE
	Low		
		Low	High
		Anticipated Accident Frequency	

or capability assessment. In evaluating a specific risk, the risk assessor
must estimate the seriousness of the risk present, including the potential
for an accident to occur and its likely severity. This must again be done in
light of the magnitude of risk for each participant present.

According to Table 2 it is advisable to retain risks which are unlikely
to result in many accidents and where the injuries which may be sustained will not likely have serious consequences. But, where there is an
expected high incidence of serious injury, the risk should be avoided.

Only those risks which, while occurring infrequently, may have catastrophic consequences should be insured against. All too often, outdoor program delivering agencies/associations have carried excess insurance coverage for risks which should have been retained and/or reduced, and have often been inadequately covered for potentially serious, although infrequent, occurrences.

TRANSFERENCE OF RISK THROUGH THE USE OF WAIVERS

Waivers are agreements which allow a program participant the opportunity to take part in a program in exchange for a promise not to sue for negligence if the participant is injured as a result of that involvement. Lawyers, insurers and even educators have repeatedly made recommendations for the development and implementation of contracts designed to transfer most or all program risks to participants. Lawyers see a liability waiver as a valid contract which will help them win court cases or settlement negotiations, regardless of the issue of negligence.[29] Similarly, the insurance industry welcomes responsibility releases because through their use, expensive pay-outs can be avoided[30] without concern for claims of negligence. Outdoor education/recreation programmers are being increasingly directed by their lawyers and/or insurance agents to employ waiver forms. In fact, some agencies have been refused liability insurance without proof of application of such release forms.

Contrary to common belief, properly worded, signed waivers may very well hold up in court.[31] Many people sign these releases believing they are not worth the paper they are written on, but this is incorrect, and participants who are asked to sign waivers must be made aware of both the physical and legal implications. All waivers should be very strongly worded and should include a clause warning participants that they "may *DIE* participating in this activity."

While not ethically decrying the use of waivers, it does behoove us to seriously consider their appropriate applications, their legal limitations and their moral implications. From this educated position, we must each decide whether responsibility releases will form an essential short term risk management tool, necessitated by the insurance dilemma, or whether we can and should establish a long range systematic transference of our accountability to those who participate in our programs and services.

Limitations To The Application Of Waivers

CHILDREN

Waivers have only been held valid when signed by an adult participant and may only allow the participant to waive his or her own legal rights, not those of other family members. Also, waivers signed by or for anyone under 18 years of age have been found prejudicial against child plaintiffs and have been held null and void in court.[32]

As a substantial proportion of outdoor education/recreation programs involve child or adolescent participants, and as this group frequently lacks sufficient age, intelligence or experience to otherwise assume program related risks, this population poses a significant problem to risk management in outdoor adventure programming. Despite their legal impotence, agencies frequently include responsibility release clauses in registration or parental consent forms, hoping the parent will construe them as legally valid, and not bring suit.[33]

Some legal professionals are of the opinion that there may be exceptional situations where a waiver could be shown to be on the whole beneficial to a child and therefore binding. A youth's right to be protected from an agency's negligence may, in certain circumstances, need to be weighed against the benefits the child derives from, say, the opportunity to pursue development of his or her skiing or climbing skills. This debate has not been addressed in Canadian courts to date. However, some lawyers believe that a properly worded release form signed by the parent/guardian may force consideration of this issue in the courts. The perceived key is inclusion of a clause which has the parent recognize that "The said Release, Waiver and Assumption of Risk agreement is on the whole beneficial to my/our child."[34]

Requiring the parent to sign an agreement containing such a clause may benefit the agency/association in that it "would place the judge in the unenviable position of usurping parental discretion in the matter."[35]

In general, parental waivers may be beneficial to programming agencies/associations in that they may prevent the parents/guardians themselves from suing for any damages they may personally accrue as a result of an injury(ies) to their children. In addition, in some situations, parent signed release statements may become relevant if misrepresentation of the child is raised as an issue in court. This may occur where, for example, a parent registers a teenager in an advanced whitewater canoeing program. Perhaps in completing the application form, the parent misrepresents the previous canoeing training and/or skill of the child in order to have the youth accepted into the program. If the child were injured and the injury was found to be proximally caused by the undisclosed lack of training and/or skill, then the parent may, in fact, become a second defendant in an action by the youth against the agency.[36]

Similarly, a parental permission form and a waiver may be used in court in providing evidence to settle a factual disagreement. For example, frequently a statement of health form is administered in conjunction with the responsibility release. If the parents, for example, neglect to inform the agency of a child's known allergies, and the child subsequently suffers a severe anaphalactic reaction to a bee sting, then the agency will have a strong defense against the parents should the latter claim negligence.[37]

In sum, while waiver forms signed by an infant plaintiff are unlikely to hold up in court, parents may affect their own rights by signing responsibility release statements. This does still leave outdoor programming agencies and associations open to suit by the child plaintiff.

Some have suggested that the remedy may lie in simply not offering programs for those under 18 years of age. This is not a very realistic solution. Others have suggested that we have the child participant sign a waiver and assumption of risk, have the parent sign a waiver, assumption of risk and agreement to indemnify, have the program registrant's solicitor sign a statement declaring that the nature and legal effect of the agreement have been explained to the registrant prior to the signing of the release forms.[38] Except in a very few situations (such as elite competitive sport), this extremely cumbersome process would very likely mean a low registration rate.

Obviously, outdoor programmers cannot feel immune from claims of liability where child participants are involved. Methods of risk management other than waivers must form the basis of the organization's programming.

INSUFFICIENT NOTICE

The exclusionary provisions of a waiver form must be brought to the attention of the participant. Responsibility releases on the backs of ski lift tickets[39] or on a vague "Participate at Your Own Risk" sign[40] have not held up in Canadian courts. The waiver must be a *signed* document to have any hope of consideration in the courts. Even then, there is no assurance that the courts will hold a participant responsible for having read and appreciated a waiver clause prior to signing.[41] It is advisable to have a separate form constituting a waiver and assumption of risk as opposed to simply inserting a waiver clause on an entry or registration form.

Another concern is the time lapse between the signing of a disclaimer and the occurrence of an accident where the agency attempts to revive the waiver in its defense. The plaintiff could argue that even if the exclusion had been brought to the specific attention of the participant at one time, that this occurred so long ago that the individual was no longer cognizant of it at the time he or she participated in the activity and was injured.

While some legal authorities suggest once a year may be sufficient,[42] others believe a more frequent administration is necessary. It has been suggested, for example, that a waiver form can be reapplied several times during a program to serve as a lead-in tool for instructors. It can be used to summarize the program to date and to re-emphasize the challenges still faced by the group.[43] While frequent waiver reapplications may indeed be used in this fashion to further the participants' understanding and appreciation of risks to be faced, the negative tone set by excessive focus on the contract form may detract more from the program than it would add.

LACK OF DUE CONSIDERATION

The dictates of contract law state that a contract must illustrate consideration or benefit flowing between both parties entering into the agreement. In this regard, an agency or association could argue that it benefits by being relieved of liability while the participant benefits from being allowed to participate in the program or event.[44]

ADHESION CONTRACT

Waivers as a type of contract differ from those evolving out of negotiations between two parties of equal bargaining power. Therefore, while Canadian courts will honor release agreements, they do so only after careful scrutinization of the contents and consideration of the waiver's bias for the contractor.[45] At issue will be the presence of viable options for the participant. This particular issue is likely to receive ever-increasing attention as more and more agencies employ waivers and the opportunity to participate in an outdoor education/recreation activity without signing one becomes extremely limited or impossible. There must appear to be reasonable outdoor program alternatives available for the individual where participation is not contingent on signing a waiver.[46]

FUNDAMENTAL BREACH

A properly constructed waiver will state clearly and unequivocally that the agency and its representatives are not responsible for the safety of the participant.[47] Suppose a participant registers in a ski marathon event having explicitly been told that adequate safety precautions would be taken to ensure participants did not become lost on the course. If the participant subsequently made a wrong turn at an unclear trail junction, got lost, and in remaining out overnight suffered severe frostbite and hypothermia, the participant could claim that the contract made was fundamentally different from that which eventuated, and subsequently the disclaimer should be void.

In addition, the activity waivers which have been respected in Canadian courts have all extended the exclusionary provisions to cover incidents of agency/association negligence.[48] Cases involving reponsibility releases not including such a specific negligence clause have failed. Here, the plaintiffs have frequently been able to show that while they accepted the risks involved in participation in the activity, that agency/staff negligence is not a foreseeable inherent risk to such participation. The waivers in these cases have been dismissed and the plaintiffs have been awarded damages.[49]

Agency and association directors considering the inclusion of such an exclusionary clause should do so with full understanding of its potential ramifications for the participant. The issue facing outdoor program practitioners is their moral and professional, if not legal, obligation to the participant. While participants should be expected to assume risks inherent to an activity, is it right that they be barred recovery when they are injured due to staff or agency error? Such waivers may amount to the participant, often unknowingly, legally sanctioning agency or staff irresponsibility and negligence. No professional or paraprofessional discipline should be placed so far above accountability for their actions. The current insurance situation is leaving some agencies with few if any alternatives, but responsibility releases of this type should be avoided whenever other viable options exist. We must wonder when an insurance company refuses to provide coverage unless a valid waiver is utilized, if the programming agency might as well save the cost of the liability premiums because the insurer is attempting to eliminate any potential payouts on the policy. When a driver gets behind the wheel, everyone else on the road does not automatically sign a waiver to say that they will not sue if the individual happens to negligently cause an accident. The driver carries insurance to compensate anyone accidently injured by their negligence and this is the same reason outdoor programming agencies/associations want and need insurance.

Perhaps offering and/or requiring proof of adequate accident insurance coverage prior to participation in risky outdoor pursuits would alleviate much of the agency's real or perceived responsibility in the event of an injury accident. However, where no option exists except access to the agency's liability insurance, such clauses may be avoided to ensure some avenue of recompense in the event of the agency/staff negligence causing injury.

UNUSUAL RISK

The best waivers are those that list the most common foreseeable types of accidents and injuries which one may sustain while engaging in the activity(ies) of interest. By presenting such lists and then excluding the agency/association and its staff for any of those mentioned, the participant has an informed basis on which to sign the form. In reality, granted, this is very difficult to do, especially in survey courses where a wide variety of activities is attempted. The number of situations involving risk and the incredible list of injuries possible simply becomes too long and tedious.

Many waivers rather vaguely cover the eventuality of a participant claiming injury by a risk that could not be contemplated at the time the agreement was made. They refer to "all foreseeable and unforeseeable risks" in their exclusion clause,[50] and leave it to a court's discretion to decide whether they will accept such general notice.

Waivers are suspect contracts in the eyes of the courts and they will be strictly interpreted against the party employing them. Careful consideration will be given to the relative *knowledge* of the parties to the contract of the rights released or indemnified against, and the *foreseeability of the danger* from the viewpoint of both parties in conjunction with the burden of protecting against it.[51]

As such, general reference to "all risks, both foreseeable and unforeseeable" may not be viewed as adequate warning. The more specific the waiver, the better its chances of surviving judicial scrutiny.

DEGREE OF NEGLIGENCE

Where the defendant agency's standard of care is perceived to fall substantially below that accepted as reasonable, the courts may avoid recognition of a waiver. While a number of plaintiffs in outdoor education/recreation cases have claimed that a defendant programming agency and/or its staff were grossly negligent, no court in Canada has found any such defendant guilty of negligence so reckless, willful, or wanton as to negate the application of a waiver.[52] Outdoor adventure education programmers, however, should be aware of the fact that a waiver form which may protect the agency in circumstances involving common negligence may not hold up where the courts perceive that the agency's actions or omissions are so improper or inappropriate as to constitute gross negligence.

THE ANATOMY OF THE LEGAL LIABILITY WAIVER AND ASSUMPTION OF RISK FORM

While waivers are certainly not the be-all and end-all of risk management, if and when an agency feels compelled to apply one, that agency should do so with the confidence that it is delivering a clear and comprehensive document. The issues and principles discussed to this point should be thoughtfully considered before application of a waiver. We should not be using them simply because everyone else is. Rather, there should be a conscious decision made in light of the agency/association's overall risk management plan and the appropriateness of including a waiver in this program.

The actual contents of a waiver will vary depending upon the type of program or event involved. A waiver written for a student in a cycling class may not protect the agency in the event that that individual is injured in a special end-of-course cycle race event sponsored by the agency.

If it is to have a solid chance of being valid and binding, a waiver must include a number of components designed to inform the participants of the physical and legal risks they are taking and to have them acknowl-

in the activity. There are a number of important elements in a good waiver form:

1. Identification of the form by title (for example, Safety Affirmation and Release; Release, Waiver and Assumption of Risk).
2. Identification of parties participating by name and liability extensions (heirs and executors), and agency owner, director and staff.
3. Inclusion of a warning to read the waiver carefully in the preface and a statement acknowledging having done so prior to signing, near the end of the form.
4. Listing of all technical prerequisites to participation (certifications, skill level).
5. Participant acknowledgement of awareness of inherent risks of the activity and safety rules.
6. Identification of limits of course content and instructor responsibility for participant safety.
7. Participant agreement to adhere to safety and other rules stipulated by the agency or its staff.
8. Identification of participant's responsibility with regard to equipment adequacy and condition.
9. Identification of specific inherent risks involved in participation in the activity (such as unforeseeable environmental hazards, human error, equipment failure).
10. Inclusion of a comprehensive waiver clause holding the agency, all of its owners, operators and staff harmless from negligence suit by the participant, the participant's family, heirs or assigns.
11. Participant statement that she or he is of sufficient age and intelligence to sign the contract.
12. Participant agreement to avoid engagement under the influence of drugs or alcohol.
13. Permission for the agency or its staff to seek out appropriate medical aid in the event of an accident involving the participant.
14. Lines for the participant's and witness' signature and date following the illustrated waiver as evidence of acceptance of its terms by the participant.

See Appendix 1 for Sample Release, Waiver and Assumption of Risk Form.

In sum, in establishing a legally valid and morally correct system of transferring appropriate risks to participants, program delivery agencies and organizations should develop clear, concise, yet comprehensive

and organizations should develop clear, concise, yet comprehensive waiver and assumption of risk forms and parameters for their use and distribution.

Because of the current difficulties in securing adequate liability insurance, and subsequent increasing reliance on waivers, the legal limitations and ethical considerations of this risk management avenue must be clearly understood and appreciated. Organizations operating programs and premises with total reliance on waiver forms and no insurance backup are not completely immune from potential lawsuits.

Many agencies and boards have jumped on the waiver bandwagon as a result of the increasing price or unavailability of liability insurance. Some agencies falsely assume that an explicitly worded responsibility release protects them from all potential negligence suits, and so have relaxed their efforts to secure appropriate insurance. Such is not the case. Those earning a living administrating and/or leading outdoor programs should continue to work with the legal profession and insurance industry to include waivers and insurance as integral aspects of an optimum risk management program.

In closing, both the physical and legal risks the outdoor education/recreation practitioner faces are real. Through thoughtful risk and participant readiness assessments, the program director and/or leader should be able to determine the best way to handle the tremendous variety of risks confronting them and their participants.

The liability insurance crisis continues to seriously affect the ways we should be dealing with many program related risks. It is hoped that the factors creating this problem may be rectified in the near future and that we may eventually purchase liability insurance with premiums which reflect the actual risks they are intended to cover. In the meantime, agency directors and staff will have to carefully consider which of the remaining techniques: retention, reduction, avoidance, or transfer through participant assumption is most appropriate for handling each foreseeable program risk.

9 INSURANCE

THE MID 1980s LIABILITY INSURANCE CRISIS

IN 1983 THE CANADIAN Ski Association (CSA) paid $7,700 in premiums for 11 million dollars in liability coverage. In 1984, the CSA was forced to find a new insurer who agreed to provide the same coverage for $47,000 in premiums. When that policy expired in December 1985, the Association could not find liability insurance at any price. Across Canada, news reports carried stories of our national alpine ski team having to return home if coverage could not be secured soon. In January of 1986, the CSA managed to solve the problem by establishing an agreement with eight firms to provide a total of 5 million dollars in coverage for the astronomical premium of $245,000.[1] This expense was borne by all organized skiers in the nation, largely through increases in local club and provincial association memberships and competitive event fees.

December 1985 marked the last date the Canadian Sport Parachuting Association (CSPA) was able to obtain third party liability insurance. The 1986 offer to renew would cover only instructional parachuting, perceived as much safer than recreational and competitive jumping. Premiums for this reduced coverage went up over 300 percent from $9,600 to $30,000. Implications of the reduced coverage included Canada's forced withdrawal as sponsor of the August 1987 world championships, slated for Princeton, B.C., and the potential embarrassment of having to hold the 1986 Canadian championships in Oklahoma in conjunction with the American finals. At the time, it was believed that the insurance situation could conceivably eliminate all parachuting clubs and competitions in Canada.[2] The Canadian Recreational Canoeing Association, Association of Canadian Mountain Guides and most national and provincial outdoor activity associations were operating without liability insurance as of 1986, and many continue to do so. In Alberta, for example, only about half of the province's 80 sport and recreation associations were insured in 1988.[3]

School boards and municipal administrators have been faced with similar drastic increases, often in the order of three to four times the annual premiums paid only two years ago. The city of Red Deer, Alberta, faced more than a 400 percent increase, as its premiums jumped from $44,000 in 1984 to $179,000 in 1985, and its deductible was increased from $500 to $5,000. Kamloops, B.C., faced a 300 percent increase in its premium when its $46,145 policy expired in July of 1985. The new policy was offered by a different insurer as the original one simply refused to renew the policy.[4] These examples are indicative of a problem which was, and to some extent, still is being experienced coast to coast. Some municipalities have been forced to give up their insurance policies as the premiums have become too expensive. Similarly, the premiums for other small businesses and organizations remain very high.

The implications for municipal sponsored outdoor education/recreation related facilities and programs are significant. Everything from low supervised playgrounds and beaches to summer day camps and winter learn-to-ski programs remain in jeopardy of being closed or drastically cut back.

Taxpayers are being forced to carry the burden of the large premiums asked, or even of municipal self-insurance when the premiums are deemed unaffordably high. In this arrangement, no liability insurance is purchased on the chance that taxes need not be raised unless the municipality is sued, in which case they will be raised the following year to cover the damages. While often offering a viable alternative for large urban centers, this option will certainly leave the politicians and administrators of smaller communities extremely uncomfortable.

Property owners would be left not knowing whether they would have to face significant tax jumps from year to year. As it is, homeowners faced about a 20 percent increase in liability insurance in 1986 in Canada. Professionals such as doctors and lawyers were forced to pay up front increases up to 3,000 percent higher for error and omission protection. While somewhat softened in the late 1980s, neither the insurance industry nor the legal profession sees an early end to this far reaching and most serious dilemma.

Causes of the Crisis

Representatives of numerous provincial Bar Societies claim that the insurance industry is the author of its own misfortune. They believe that the current situation arose as a result of poor investment of premium income and excessive competition between insurance underwriters during the economic boom of the 1970s. In that decade, high interest rates helped investment income soar which attracted more companies into the insurance market. This created fierce competition which resulted in an overall reduction in premium income. As claims on policies increased and interest rates declined in the 1980s, the insurance industry was forced to reassess its risk acceptance policies and rate schedules.[5]

Legal professionals in Canada also contend that the rates have been distorted by a relatively small number of large verdicts and by fear—stemming from the explosion of liability suits in the United States. They say our rates are based on traditionally high first-judgment awards, not the usually smaller appeal settlements or those completed out of court. Also lacking is a consideration of the number of defendant victories in relation to claims made. Members of the insurance industry believe just as strongly that while underwriters may have been temporarily in err in judging risks, that unprecedented excesses in litigation and the size of awards granted were and are the real cause of the problem.

While everyone else was writing about an insurance crisis, John Lyndon, President of the Insurance Bureau of Canada, was writing about "The Courts and the Liability Crisis." Lyndon expressed shock and dismay at the rapid rate with which Canadians have moved from their stable predictable individualistic tendency towards the established American "doctrine of entitlement."[6] Americans are well known for their litigious nature.[7]

While nowhere near as trial happy in Canada, the insurance industry has been unsettled by a few unprecedented large awards granted at trial. While overturned at appeal with substantial reduction of damages, the most oft-cited of these was the $7 million award given a 14-year-old Brampton, Ontario, youth following a trail bike collision accident which rendered him a quadriplegic. The accident, which happened in 1977, occurred on some vacant city-owned land. The Ontario Supreme Court ordered the city of Brampton to pay $5.2 million of the damages for failing to post no trespassing signs and not fixing the dangerous curve on which the accident occurred. Although reversed upon appeal, with a reduction in damages to about half of the $7 million originally granted at trial, this case seriously escalated the fears of insurers at a time when they were already paranoid that damage awards were rising uncontrollably.

Implications of the Crisis

As of this writing, the insurance industry appears to be making a comeback, but gone forever are the low premiums of the 1970s. Edward Belton, President and Chief Executive Officer of the Insurers' Advisory Organization (IAO) stated that the third quarter in 1985 marked the first growth in the industry in a long time. However, he did not extend his optimism to liability markets. Due to the present perceived unpredictability of court decisions and the related uncertainty of claims costs, underwriters and their international reinsurance allies are shying away, afraid they cannot set realistic rates.[9] For example, large insurance corporations like Lloyd's of London, renowned for their insurance of high risk endeavors, are extremely leery of the situation and have cut back their reinsurance coverage substantially.

The types of policies likely to suffer the most and the longest will be those written for the smallest pools of perceived high risk liability insurance consumers. Therefore, while auto insurance represents a market with a tremendous number of users and hence, reasonably stable predictable risk sharing, recreation and sport and, more specifically, outdoor education/recreation agencies and associations, are much less secure. If an outdoor recreational activity association with 2,000 provincial members purchases a liability insurance policy for $2.00/member (a number of similar policies were available in 1984), the premium would be only $4,000. There are probably less than 100,000 people involved in such organizations across Canada which translates into only $200,000 in payment into all such policies. In a nation where many liability awards and settlements are approaching and exceeding the million dollar mark, it is not surprising to see an increasing scarcity of coverage.

In short, the relatively insignificant number of heterogeneous outdoor program delivery agencies and associations operating in Canada do not present an easily acceptable risk to most insurers. Understandably, the insurance industry's decision has been that liability insurance will be made increasingly less available to outdoor programmers. The premiums asked in any remaining policies will reflect the perceived potential claims cost and not necessarily the number of members contributing to the policy.

Potential Solutions to the Crisis

In 1985, then Federal Minister for Fitness and Amateur Sport, Otto Jelinek, responded to the problem and set up a commission to study the insurance crisis facing sport and recreation associations. The Commission began by surveying national sport governing bodies. Of 73 national associations contacted, 62 replied to the survey. Some interesting trends emerged from the data.

The total premiums paid by responding associations amounted to 1.5 million dollars for the 1985-86 period. However, this is likely a conservative estimate as not all groups noted their premiums. Startling to the researchers was the fact that only 47 of the 62 respondent associations had any form of comprehensive general liability insurance for that period. In addition, a number of the remaining groups had inadequate coverage for the risks they faced as employers or as tenants.[10]

Based on the findings of this survey and day to day discussions with associations resident at the National Sport and Recreation Centre, the Commission made the following conclusions:

1. Most national associations do not have adequate insurance;
2. With some exceptions, associations are generally inexperienced in insurance matters. Their volunteers often do not see insurance as a high priority. Yet associations have a regular, often urgent need for insurance;
3. Many associations are having great difficulty finding and maintaining liability coverage. With work they can secure general liability and even third-party (spectators) insurance, but liability insurance for participants is next to impossible to find;
4. Because associations previously found coverage easy to buy, few have done the careful risk management and the claims record-keeping now demanded by a far choosier insurance industry;
5. Associations have not used the purchasing power they could exercise by banding together and buying insurance collectively through a central agency or broker;
6. Some associations, such as the CAHA (Canadian Amateur Hockey Association), are proceeding with a form of self-insurance—

whereby a large some [sic] of money is deposited in a bank account to pay claims. The money comes from association dues or increased membership fees. With this "initial insurance" in place, the wealthier associations, at least, may be able to raise the rest of the coverage they need, but even this secondary insurance comes at a high price;

7. Where records exist, the claims against association policies are few. Sport, in other words, appears to be a good insurance risk.[11]

ACTUARIAL DATA In further studying the relationship of sport and recreation to the insurance industry, the Commission was astonished to discover that the industry did not have readily available information and statistics on sports' claims. Nor is there any sort of central information source within the insurance industry detailing the types and amounts of coverage available to sport and recreation, potential suppliers, and cost factors. The Commission was left totally perplexed in trying to determine how, without such information, the insurance industry could possibly analyze the risks of insuring sport and recreation activities and set competitive premiums.

The Task Force concluded that the insurance industry urgently needed to involve itself in more information collection and statistical analysis. It was decided that it was high time that insurance decisions were based on hard data, not the questionable "educated guesses" of brokers or the unfounded paranoia resulting from the unpredictable nature of liability claims.[12]

Since the publication of the Task Force findings, while the federal government has done little in the way of follow-through to solve the insurance availability and actual problems it identified, provincial sport/recreation councils and private insurers have to some extent picked up the ball. As of 1988, there were at least two private insurance corporations providing insurance to sport and recreation associations and agencies as needed across Canada, including participant liability.[13] The reliance on brokers with an expressed specialization in recreation and sport program and activity insurance should prove a positive step to centralizing the information and statistical analysis of accident and injury data. This improved data collection and synthesis should result in more accurate actuarial determination, free of the effects of guesswork and unfounded fears about our activities.

Within this objective, however, we cannot remain complacent with our belief that the insurers will do their job. At the very least, we need to require insurers to share their facts and figures up front. It is also important that time and energy be devoted to more and better outdoor activity accident data collection, synthesis and analysis. We need to ascertain exactly what and how severe the risks are in outdoor education/recreation activities as carried out in organized programs. Only by better program/club accident reporting can we hope that insurers will base their rates on relevant actuarials, and not on the combined total fatalities and injuries experienced in organized programs and unsupervised recreational situations. Widespread participation in the National Safety Network database may help achieve this objective. Even better would be the development of a solely Canadian database or an additional, separate analysis of the data received by the NSN from Canadian programs.

LEGISLATIVE REFORMS The courts have already established that voluntary not-for-profit organizations are held to a lower standard of care than the average individual.[14] The Department of Justice is currently reviewing the potential of eliminating suits against agency/board directors, unless they are found directly responsible for an accident.

The Federal Task Force Commission spent a good deal of time exploring legislative alternatives which involve statutory extension of Good Samaritan legislation. In the provinces with this legislation, any individual who attempts to rescue another who he sees injured or in peril is not liable for any injuries suffered by the victim, unless these are caused by the rescuer's gross negligence. In short, legislative immunity is offered voluntary rescuers who act without the legal duty to do so. While we have no Canadian provinces with a sport/recreation extension to this legislation, we do have a number of American examples to study.

In 1986, two states (Pennsylvania and New Jersey) developed a special form of good Samaritan legislation, dubbed "Little League" legislation. A number of other states have followed suit. In those states, coaches, managers and officials of amateur sport are immune from negligence suits "provided they have participated in a safety orientation and training program and have not been grossly or unduly negligent."[15]

Upon reviewing the American examples, the Canadian Task Force concluded that some version of provincial Little League legislation could potentially protect sport and recreation volunteers and/or all volunteer groups (for example, hospital candy stripers) from suit in normal circumstances. Such legislation would have the desired effect of substantially reducing their need for insurance.

In qualifying its recommendation for this legislation the Federal Task

Force recognized that institutions of such statutes would be a long term measure, requiring provincial legislative jurisdiction commitment and an exception to the Canadian tendency to accept with reluctance any statutory immunity beyond the bounds of the common law on negligence."[16] It may be many years before we see any movement in this direction, if we ever do. This writer is not optimistic that such bills would ever survive in Canadian legislatures. However, such legislation would be welcomed by most not-for-profit outdoor activity clubs and associations, and combined with the application of safety standards and accident insurance, they could provide a reasonable system of protection for volunteers and participants. Similarly, insurers and most volunteer sport and recreation delivery agencies and associations would welcome the legislative institution of participant waivers.[17] This alternative would have the effect of reducing an association's participant liability insurance. As noted, we are very unlikely to see this type of legislation enacted in Canada in the foreseeable future.

Other types of tort reform which have been suggested include placing limits on awards allowed for pain and suffering and/or for punitive damages. Apportionment legislation and practice could also be reviewed, so settlements would more accurately reflect blame and be less based upon a perceived capacity to bear the cost.

The insurance industry would dearly love to see a repeal of recent legislative changes to the *Court of Justice Act* and citation which requires the defendant in a case to disclose the limits of insurance coverage at examination for discovery. Insurers feel that this information disclosure predisposes judges to calculate larger awards than are often warranted simply because they know the insurance is accessible.[18] Of course, there may be occasions where such disclosure favors the defendant by reducing a potentially high award to keep it within the limits of the individual's insurance coverage.

Some insurance professionals would like to see lawyers contingency fees limited so they would have less incentive to seek a percentage of larger awards. Still others feel that if the loser in a suit was always forced to pay all the winner's court costs, as with the system employed in Europe and generally employed in Canada, the number of frivolous cases brought to court would be significantly decreased.[19]

INSURANCE POOLS Perhaps the easiest solution to the situation of too many small perceived high risk policies is to pool resources and find one company to provide a blanket policy. Sport B.C. and Sport Alberta, for example, have established such policies to provide third party liability coverage for all contributing amateur sports associations. There may still exist the potential for a single national policy to cover all provincial/territorial amateur recreational and competitive sports and outdoor pursuits collectively, for an even lower premium than each would pay for provincial coverage.

The Federal Task Force cited in its major recommendations that the federal government "create a central insurance service for national sport governing bodies." This could involve acting as an insurance broker for associations by creating a reciprocal self-insurance exchange and/or purchasing insurance collectively through a regular market mechanism.[20]

When a reciprocal self-insurance exchange is put in place, member associations form an unincorporated collective and contract with each other to spread their potential risks and losses. Each activity association contributes premiums on a per-member basis, on an activity-specific premium scale (for example, 50 cents per lawn bowler and $50.00 per sport parachutist). The subscribing associations pre-arrange the actual scale based on their collective expected payouts for that year, with each group receiving a rebate in premiums if the total claims remain below the total expected payout. Invested premium monies are used to hire risk managers and safety supervisors who ensure subscribers are adhering to their safety guidelines.[21]

In spite of the onerous preliminary task of performing actuarial studies of each sport or activity association's risks and assignment of risk ratings for each activity on a scale found agreeable by all members of the reciprocal exchange,[22] the existence of current examples suggests these are not unmanageable obstacles. The Task Force concluded that reciprocal exchanges would work well in a collective of small to intermediate sized associations, whose risks tend to represent relatively small losses and where credit worthy subscribers can promptly report their claims.[23] Advantages of sport/recreation reciprocal exchanges include: their relative ease of institution (no legislation required, short 30-60 day start-up period, absence of initial capitalization required, saving of agents' or brokers' fees, subscriber cash flow planning facilitated by early advance warning of premiums required, and economical professional management of the exchange possible).

Disadvantages of such a system include: additional costs to associations when claims exceed premiums, and up to a three-year commitment to participate in the exchange required, which may leave large members torn if available commercial insurance costs drop substantially during that period.[24] Paul Conrad of the Alberta Sport Council noted that while Alberta recreation associations have made some good use of their exchange (administered by the Council), that now that private insurers are making affordable and complete coverage available, his provincial Council is considering a move away from the provision of this service.[25]

The second alternative suggested, collective purchasing through regular market mechanisms, involves spreading the risks of organized sport and recreation nationally by taking a coordinated collective stance in approaching insurers. The tremendous number of participants involved (6.5 million) in relatively low risk activities would bring the participant premiums down to an extremely low rate. Insurers would fight for the opportunity to insure such a collective, especially if the numbers were ensured by a federal dictate requiring compulsory participation in the collective by all sport and recreation governing bodies.[26] In the 2 years following publication of the Task Force recommendations, nothing was done to further the national implementation of either a reciprocal exchange or a collective insurance purchase by recreation and sport groups. A few private insurance companies in B.C., Alberta, and Ontario have picked up the slack and are currently providing insurance to most of the sport and recreation associations in the country seeking it, thus forming informal collectives.

A permanent solution of the problem will not likely be achieved through adoption of any one of the suggestions presented. A combination of concessions will likely have to be made by insurance consumers, the insurance industry and the legal system. In doing our part to facilitate more reasonable insurance coverage of outdoor activity programs, practitioners and administrators need to keep and share accurate accident statistics. Outdoor risk managers can also improve their position with regard to insurance by only insuring against relevant risks and utilizing other more appropriate methods of dealing with risks where possible.

PURCHASING EFFECTIVE LIABILITY INSURANCE

Who Pays the Premiums?

The individual outdoor leader may purchase his or her own insurance (such as professional liability), and this is recommended if operating as an independent contractor, if involved in one or more nonincorporated associations or if otherwise not protected through another policy. However, the leader is most often covered by one or more other sources. It is the personal responsibility of each leader to review agency or board and/or certifying body policy, where applicable, to ensure that it affords sufficient coverage, and to request increases in protection where they are found wanting, or to purchase personal liability insurance to cover these areas of potential exposure.

Almost all outdoor leaders in the employ of an outdoor education and/or recreation program delivery agency or board will be vicariously protected by that organization's insurance policy. In addition to property insurance, most agencies will carry substantial liability insurance to protect themselves from damages claimed due to personal liability (such as breach of statutory or common law occupiers' duties, inadequate provision of a sufficient number of qualified staff) and vicarious liability (due to tortious acts or omissions committed by their staff).

In addition, a number of sports governing and certifying bodies and professional agencies have taken upon themselves the responsibility of providing their members with liability insurance. The Canadian Ski Association (CSA) indemnifies downhill and cross-country ski instructors and coaches and tour leaders, the Canadian Association of Nordic Ski Instructors (CANSI) insures cross-country ski instructors and the Coaching Association of Canada (CAC) has purchased a policy to offer to certified individuals functioning as coaches in any sanctioned sport. As the insurance crisis continues to plague these organizations, the certified leader should check on the insurance status of these and any other certifying bodies providing coverage in the past.

There is the possibility that such coverages may prove redundant for leaders already covered by their agency's or board's policies. However, overcoverage is certainly preferable to inadequate protection. Normally, the agency vicariously liable would be called upon to make damage restitution through its policy first, but this will depend upon examination of the terms of the contracts and the history of the accident and may involve some compromise between the two insurers. Insurance provided by the other certifying organizations mentioned would be used when the leader was teaching a certification program, working without sponsorship or if the agency vicariously liable decided to in turn sue the leader, for example, for lack of qualifications. It is established law that any employer held vicariously liable has the option of claiming the loss from the employee, but this is rarely pursued as few employees have access to sufficient financial resources to indemnify the agency.[27] Although such follow-up claims may become more likely for individuals with this back-up insurance, to date, there have been no cases to demonstrate this recourse.

Where the leader is voluntarily guiding members of a nonincorporated, uninsured club or association, or is involved in a recreational co-adventure, the leader's personal property and liability insurance may provide some protection for nonautomobile liability exposures. Where the leader owns property he or she will usually have purchased comprehensive personal liability insurance as part of a standard policy. The personal liability section of the comprehensive policy provides liability coverage for matters related to the premises as well as for the personal activities of the insured and his or her family, both on and away from the insured premises.[28] Outdoor leaders are encouraged to learn the range and limitations of their policy and to discuss any possible desirable endorsements to their policy with their insurers.

A final option is that participants may purchase their own no-fault accident insurance which pays when they are injured, whether or not the agency was liable. Many school boards historically made such coverage available for students and "Camper's Insurance" can be purchased to provide coverage for campers injured while involved in camp activities.[29] Provision of better accident insurance for participants is a major recommendation by the Insurance Council of Canada.[30]

Suffice to say that most individuals working in the outdoor education/recreation field will probably be insured from one or more sources. More crucial questions to ask are what type(s) of insurance is protecting the individual and his or her agency or board and does it adequately cover the actual risks leaders and participants may be exposed to in foreseeable courses of events?

Definitions and Principles of Liability Insurance

According to the *Canadian and British Insurance Companies Act* liability insurance is defined as:

(1) insurance against liability arising out of:
— bodily injury to, or the death of a person, or
— the loss, or damage to property, and includes:
(a) insurance agent's expense arising of the bodily injury to a

person other than the insured or a member of his/her family but does not include:

(b) insurance coming within the class of aircraft insurance, automobile insurance, or employer's liability insurance.[31]

While there exists the potential for claims based on loss or damage of personal property or equipment, most liability claims faced by outdoor educational/recreational agencies and staff will result from personal injury actions. When considering the purchase of insurance, the agency should review the particular risks it is dealing with and determine the appropriateness and viability of purchasing protection. It is very important for the program risk manager to be prepared, and it is almost essential that a competent, experienced agent or broker interested in the agency's insurance requirements be consulted for advice and recommendations. While the insurance industry is taking steps to help make insurance particulars easier for lay people to understand, at this time it is likely that only an insurance professional will be able to interpret policy terms, conditions, and exclusions for the purchaser.

Given the tremendous expense involved in insuring against all of the risks an outdoor programming agency will face, time and energy spent discussing and applying techniques to avoid insurance where appropriate and to minimize premiums where possible will undoubtedly be well spent.

Risks which tend to eventuate in frequent injuries involving relatively minor damage should be retained, but not be insured against. If the losses may be easily absorbed in the operations budget of a single year, then they are not worth the price of the insurance to cover them. Unless the agency is very big or very rich, it is important that this be a conscious, planned retention program, and not unconscious because the risk had not been identified and assessed.

The number of insurance claims made, and hence the cost of premiums, may also be significantly reduced through the employment of a funded reserve (self-insurance) and/or the use of deductibles. Self-insurance differs from noninsurance in that foreseeable losses have been estimated and a special fund set aside to cover them.[32]

Often, very large agencies, such as federal and provincial governments, are self-insured, while most other municipalities and nongovernment organizations purchase policies from commercial insurance companies. The cost of insuring all federal and provincial government activities, agents and vehicles annually would be astronomic; covering losses as necessary from general funds is much less expensive in the long run. When claims are paid out, the loss is simply distributed through the public by increases in taxation in the following fiscal year.

Deductibles involve the retention of risks to a certain point and subsequent transfer to an insurer of all others above that level. These two methods help keep an agency or board's interactions with its insurance carrier to a minimum and therefore keep administrative maintenance costs down. Higher deductibles are most suitable when the frequency and size of losses are largely predictable.[33]

As previously mentioned, always insure where the risk of potential loss is *severe* even if the *probability* of loss is small.[34] Insurance should be used for those risks which have been identified and evaluated as essential to the achievement of program objectives, but which the outdoor agency or board does not have the financial capacity to retain. All too often, agencies and boards have insured themselves against the relatively more frequent but less significant losses (for example, broken limbs) and left themselves unprotected from the large, catastrophic losses (for example, quadriplegia, paraplegia, major burns).

Other common errors related to insurance selection and management may relate to a failure on behalf of the insured agency/organization to periodically review its liability insurance policy and bring it up to date. One private outdoor organization program director admitted that after four years of simply renewing his agency's policy, he finally took the time to carefully read the package. He discovered that the policy did not protect the agency against suits arising through participation or instruction in any physical training, sport, or athletic activity or contest (about 90 percent of the agency's program). The policy was a third party policy only, and did not cover suits arising from injuries sustained by any program registrants, most of whom were youths. The director claimed that the policy was in place when he was hired, so he just assumed it was adequate. Perhaps it was only luck which prevented a serious injury to a participant which could have led to a lawsuit.

Perhaps this agency, while most certainly under-insured for the period described, had been careful in adopting loss-prevention techniques and had reduced the potential of lawsuits through its program risk management. Another organization, well-known nationally for its youth outdoor programs, has always been considered much more lax in its management of risks. Because it uses volunteer leaders with very little required program and/or leadership related training, the organization must carry a large liability insurance policy to pay out on the numerous settlements it agrees to annually. The organization director claims that if he increased the training requirements of program leaders, many potential leaders would not get involved, and the program and the participants would be the ones to suffer. While this may be true to some extent, economically as well as ethically it makes more sense to require certain qualifications or to train leaders to a reasonable level of competency.

Hiring capable leadership staff is just one example of ways an agency can reduce risks. Others may relate to the location/route participants are taken to or along, the safety equipment carried, clothing used and other factors. Reducing the number and size of claims made against a policy or on similar policies should have the desired effect of decreasing the premiums required for any such coverages.

Types of Liability Insurance Coverage

It should be remembered that not all risks can be transferred to an insurer through any single policy. It is up to the purchaser to find the policy, or combination of policies, which best covers potential catastrophic losses. It is not the intent of this book to deal with the various insurance contracts available in any depth; there are certainly almost as many policies as there are insurance companies to write them. However, there are a number of relatively standard policies available. A brief review of their common provisions may be of use and interest.

Every liability insurance policy written provides coverage based on the following four factors:

1. Interrelationship among three parties.
   A *claimant* sues the *insured*, and following a court decision, the *insurer* pays the damages awarded which are within the limits of the policy.
2. Distinctive insurance categorization of liability and labelling of damages.
   The claim must arise from the type of liability insured against (i.e., negligence) and the type of damages (e.g., special, general, punitive, etc.).
3. Division of liability hazards.
   Occupiers' liability or vicarious liability are examples.
4. Claims response at one of two levels, primary or excess.

Excess policies respond to cover the differences when a liability claim covered by another policy exceeds the limits of the primary policy.[35]

Virtually every policy written has one or more exclusions, even so-called "all-risk" contracts. While "named-peril" contracts identify the risks the insured is protected against, all-risk policies merely spell out the exclusions rather than the perils covered, and any peril not excluded is covered. In either case, be sure to confirm that all foreseeable risks are covered.

In the case of outdoor instructors and guides, where program premises often cannot be specified precisely, coverage must be general enough to cover the leaders wherever they may be working.

In addition to insuring the agency, provision must be made for employees and volunteers working for the agency. A cross liability clause is required when there is more than one name (entity) insured by a policy.

Comprehensive General Liability Policies

Typically, an outdoor programming agency or board will seek to purchase a comprehensive general liability policy (CGL) which covers a variety of risks in one contract. CGL policies are issued on an all-risk basis. In addition to providing indemnity from personal injuries and/or property damage, among other risks, it is usually possible to combine the policy with a comprehensive automobile liability policy.

The limits of the policy must be based on foreseeable claims, but outdoor programming agencies and boards should carry at least one million dollars' worth of comprehensive general liability insurance. Additional coverage should, where appropriate, be secured through an umbrella policy.

It is crucial to consider who the likely claimants will be and to provide coverage accordingly. Policies which cover registered program participants are called second party policies. There are also policies which exclude participants and restrict coverage to claims from unassociated others affected by the operation. For example, it was earlier noted that the Canadian Sport Parachuting Association has traditionally carried third party liability insurance to indemnify it when jumpers landed on and/or otherwise damaged other people's property. When they tried to renew their policy in 1986, the insurer only wanted to cover the association for claims from jumpers injured during instructional parachuting classes, thus offering only second party liability insurance for a particular segment of the membership.[36] Sport parachuting is perhaps unique in its propensity to raise claims from third parties not associated with the activity. For most other outdoor agencies or groups, second party liability insurance protection is very highly desirable, if not essential.

Another example may help to clarify this distinction. Members of the Canadian Ski Association, Alberta Division (CSA-AD), are covered under two separate policies. The first is the national second party policy mentioned, which provides $5,000,000 in insurance coverage for participating athletes. The board is currently reviewing the possibility of replacing or supplementing this policy with an accident insurance policy to cover competitive skiers. The second source of coverage for skiers in Alberta is a third party policy (including nonowned automobile insurance), which protects directors, participants, coaches, managers, trainers, chaperones, and team officials from liability claims made by others outside the association. This $2,000,000 policy was arranged by Sport Alberta, and cost the CSA-AD 25 cents per member.

Unfortunately, neither the national CSA second party policy, nor the Sport Alberta third party policy appears to clearly state coverage for participants involved in educational or recreational programs (except Jackrabbit ski youth participants). Both policies restrict their descriptions to competitive skiing events, primarily downhill. Participants in club sanctioned cross-country and downhill programs seem to be lacking coverage.

It is obvious that third party liability coverage is desirable where competition spectators may be injured, as for example, at an alpine ski race. However, this coverage may be just as valuable in recreational situations, as for example, where a bystander is injured while trying to rescue a capsized canoe belonging to the outdoor agency, or where a group of cross-country skiers on a club tour negligently triggers an avalanche which buries an unsuspecting skier below.

In reviewing the terms of the contract, the purchase should also ensure that the CGL is written on an *occurrence* and not a narrower *accident* basis. An occurrence is defined as "an accident including continuous or repeated exposure to conditions, which results in bodily injury or property damage neither expected nor intended from the standpoint of the insured."[37]

Hence, the occurrence based policy would cover damages resulting from the effects of prolonged environmental conditions (heat, cold, altitude) where an accident policy may not. It is not necessary for the loss to result from any sudden act caused by the insured.

The difference between an accident and an occurrence based policy is just one example of the types of confusing terminology insurance policies are fraught with. Fortunately, the insurance industry has recognized the problems associated with its jargon, and is attempting to take steps to rectify these concerns. It started with the rewriting of the comprehensive general liability policy form. Implemented by the Insurance Bureau of Canada in 1987, the new policy is referred to as a *Commercial General Liability Policy* (to remove any misconceptions of its having an all-encompassing nature).[38]

The new CGL is being designed to remove some of the policy form ambiguity which has been raised in insurance litigation in the United States and Canada. The most significant change is likely to be the change from an "occurrence" based claim to a "claims made" basis. The primary difference here is that under an occurrence-based form, the policy was triggered when the injury or property loss was sustained, and it could therefore be compounded over a number of subsequent years. In contrast, under a claims-made policy (previously restricted to professional liability policies), the policy responds only from the time that the claim is made against the insured, regardless of when the loss occurred, and so is more limiting.[39] While the reasons for this change are not particularly relevant, readers should be familiar with this new modification.

The move towards more simple wording throughout the policy may result in additional confusion and litigation until it is sorted out through judicial interpretation. While this process will undoubtedly take a period of years, the new plain language commercial policy wording, scope and limitations will eventually become familiar to those in the insurance industry, and hopefully to those of us seeking to purchase liability insurance.

Additional Types of Liability Insurance

A Comprehensive General Liability policy will not necessarily provide complete protection to the insured. Sometimes specific types of risks inherent to the operations cannot be included in a typical CGL policy and must be covered through separate policies or through the inclusion of endorsements or riders to the CGL policy. Examples of such endorsements and riders include: personal injury endorsements, for injuries not occurring from physical injury or property damage (such as libel); contractual liability endorsements for contract related concerns (lease of premises); occurrence based property damage liability endorsements, which border on the applicability of the common "accident" coverage; and tenants' legal liability endorsement for property damage claims made against tenants renting property which is the subject of the claim. Other common endorsements may be related to employers' liability (to idemnify an employer for work related injuries sustained by employees) and employer-employee related matters.[40]

Liability coverage may also be extended by the addition of specialized liability insurance policies. Potentially relevant examples may include: director and office liability policies to cover against any errors and omissions committed in directing or administrating the operation (usually related specifically to financial loss); municipal errors and omissions policies, which indemnify councillors, board, commission members and statutory positions as well as employees of the municipality; and errors and omissions policies, which deal with any specialized hazards and the higher standard of care expected of those with specialized skills and knowledge.[41] It may be possible for professional outdoor leaders to purchase professional liability insurance, and this would be recommended where the individual is not adequately covered through other sources.

In addition, the standard comprehensive general liability policy may prove inadequate in terms of the limits or dollar amounts of insurance provided. The most common method of expanding insurance protection to cover potential catastrophic losses is through an excess liability policy or an umbrella policy. While the excess policy will usually contain terms, conditions, and exclusions identical to those written in its primary policy, an umbrella policy may actually provide a much broader coverage than that of the CGL it supplements. In either case, an excess or umbrella policy will respond, subject to its own limits, when a claim exceeds the limits of the primary policy. These policies will pay the difference when the comprehensive general policy has been exhausted.[42]

Third party nonowned automobile insurance is also often included in a rider with a CGL. This type of insurance applies when a vehicle, not owned or licensed by the insured agency, is being used on agency business. If someone in another vehicle claims personal injury and/or property damage against the agency's/board's agent driver following an accident, the third party insurance will cover the driver. In effect, this coverage protects all employees or volunteers using their own vehicles on agency/association related business. Typically, the driver's own auto insurance would be drawn on first, if relevant, with the agency's CGL insurance picking up any difference which may remain after the driver's policy is exhausted.[43]

In summary, while the existing price of liability insurance may render this entire discussion somewhat academic to some administrators, small business entrepreneurs and associations, it is hoped that this situation will continue to improve in the future. We have seen that while there are other methods of dealing with program related risks, transference through the purchase of suitable liability insurance is the most appropriate solution in dealing with some types of risks.

Purchasing liability insurance to cover unretainable risks can be a difficult venture, complicated by the tremendous variety of policies and clauses available. When selecting insurance, it is best to be familiar with some of the principles and policy particulars which they will have to know when selecting insurance. Probably the best advice one can give the outdoor agency or board is to:

1. Identify and evaluate risks to determine which require transfer;
2. Employ legal assistance to determine what types of coverage are recommended;
3. Shop around to see what protection is available on the insurance market, and at what price;
4. Carefully review all contracts to be sure of all exclusions; and
5. Ask lots of questions to clarify areas which appear unclear.

Insurance is a necessary measure designed to protect the assets and, in the case of business enterprises, the earning capacity of the entity. The peace of mind it offers the agency or board and the individual employee is usually well worth the premiums. Again, and especially as insurance companies lean toward preferred risks, the emphasis must be placed on sound staff selection and the development of practical, positively affirmative outdoor programs, employing insurance coverage as a support system and not as a panacea. Agencies and boards must be prepared to settle claims resulting not only from personal errors made in the administration of their outdoor programs and residential sites, but also for those arising from the negligent conduct of any employees of the agency or board.

The purchase of accident and liability insurance, although obviously a

"Band-Aid" approach to treating activities with inherent risk, does facilitate the compensation of accident victims and the enduring solvency of agencies and boards providing potentially dangerous activities such as outdoor pursuits. Without this support system, the financial destruction of many innocent accident victims and/or the individuals and agencies liable for their care would be inevitable.

10　MOTOR VEHICLE LIABILITY

LIABILITY FOR ACCIDENTS OCCURRING DURING TRAVEL

ACTUAL LIABILITY FOR INJURIES sustained by participants during travel to and from or between program sites will depend on the relationship between the driver and the passengers at the time of the accident and who the vehicle used was owned and insured by.

The only way an agency or board may completely avoid incurring liability for accidents occurring during travel is by employing an independent contractor to drive a personal or company vehicle while transporting students or participants. Chartering buses or taxis, or using public transit buses where convenient, are all examples of transferring to others the risks involved in transportation. The degree of organizational control the agency or board holds over the driver of the vehicle will be the the criterion used to establish whether the driver indeed was employed as an independent contractor. In *Baldwin* v. *Lyons et al.*,[1] a school board was held not to be vicariously liable for a bus accident. The board had little control over the driver, as it merely recommended the route and the exercise of caution and discipline by the driver. However, in *Tyler* v. *Board of Ardath*,[2] the school board was vicariously liable as it "controlled the route and was empowered to discontinue use of the van at any time without notice to the contractor" and to prohibit the driver's assigning the contract without consent.[3]

As the employment of independent contractors is not always convenient, and often totally unfeasible for remote programs, outdoor leaders should use agency/board owned and insured vehicles as their next preferred option. The agency will almost always be vicariously liable for accidents eventuating out of the negligent operation of its own vehicles used by its employees in the course of their employment.[4] In many cases this protection will extend to participants and others who may not be directly affiliated with the agency but who may be involved in one or more of its sponsored events.[5]

When program logistics necessitate that students/participants drive each other, it would be especially prudent to screen the drivers' records, check the condition of the vehicles ("especially the lights and brakes"), designate the "route, speed limits and driving conditions" and "make certain that there is appropriate and sufficient insurance coverage on the drivers and the automobiles."[6] One writer has even recommended that where private vehicles are used, the agency require drivers to "sign a statement verifying that their insurance covers liability for injury to passengers."[7]

AUTOMOBILE INSURANCE

All standard owner's automobile insurance policies provide coverage for:
1. Third Party Liability arising out of:
    (a) Bodily injury or death of a person (except in Quebec); or
    (b) Damage or loss of property caused by an automobile.
2. Accident Benefits to the insured including:
    (a) Bodily injury or death benefits for the insured regardless of accident blame;
    (b) Uninsured motorist coverage where the accident is caused by an unidentified or uninsured motorist.
3. Loss of or Damage to Insured Automobile where:
    (a) The policy holder selects coverage for his or her own insured automobile (e.g. collision, comprehensive); and
    (b) Where the policy indemnifies against vehicle loss or damages regardless of blame.

The terms and provisions of the standard owner's automobile policy are quite consistent across all the provinces and territories, with the notable exception of the province of Quebec. Unlike the rest of the country, in Quebec an injured third party cannot take legal action for negligence against the driver responsible. Instead, the injured victim is automatically paid accident benefits, without having to establish fault. The only time an accident involving bodily injury may end up in the courts is when one or more of the drivers or vehicles is from outside Quebec.[8]

When a vehicle is insured in Canada, the owner (individual, association, or organization) is covered along with anyone else who drives the automobile with the owner's permission. On long trips or during vehicle shuttles, this extension becomes important to outdoor leaders using their own or agency vehicles. For example, the length of trip or necessary shuttles may dictate the need for participants and/or other volunteers to operate program vehicles. When an agency/organization owned vehicle is involved, unless the employer/director has explicitly denied permission for others to drive, the owner's policy would protect these various drivers.[9]

The vehicle to which the owner's policy relates would indicate the described automobile, a temporary substitute vehicle or one which has been newly acquired. In the latter case, a fleet endorsement will provide automatic coverage. This policy will also cover sitations where the employee will be temporarily driving his or her own or another vehicle (not owned by the agency/association) instead of the program vehicle furnished by the organization. However, here the policy will only respond if the driver has no or inadequate insurance, and will pick up those damages exceeding the limits of the driver's own policy[10]

Even if the agency does not possess its own fleet of vehicles, it is encouraged to purchase nonowned automobile liability insurance to protect itself and its employees when its servants use an automobile not owned by the agency (employee-owned, leased, rented, borrowed), but at the time of an accident being used in the business of the agency. This type of policy may also be utilized when a staff member or participant is using a private vehicle to transport others involved in one of the agency's sponsored programs. However, it should be remembered that the driver's personal automobile insurance will be applied to all accidents first,[11] with the agency's or board's policy covering damages exceeding the limits of the driver's insurance protection.

The instructor/leader who even only occasionally drives participants should make sure sufficient liability insurance is carried (one million dollars is an absolute minimum), and the individual may reasonably increase this up to two million in protection before it would become more economical to purchase a separate excess automobile insurance policy.

GRATUITOUS PASSENGER STATUS

Where staff or participants voluntarily utilize their own vehicles to transport others involved in a particular program, the question they most often want answered concerns the limits of their liability for their passengers, if the latter are completely gratuitous, and/or if they share in the vehicle expenses incurred over the trip.

According to statutory re-enactments remaining in a few provinces:

> No person transported by the owner or driver of a motor vehicle as his guest without payment for the transportation has any cause of action for damages against the owner or driver for injury, death or loss, in case of accident, unless (a) the accident was caused by the gross negligence or wilful and wanton misconduct of the owner or operator of the motor vehicle, and (b) the gross negligence or wilful and wanton misconduct contributed to the injury, death or loss for which the action is brought.[12]

The statute excluding the right of gratuitous passengers to legal action against the driver for negligence was intended to protect generous drivers from litigation and to keep insurance premiums down by restricting recovery. It was also designed to eliminate "collusion between driver and passenger in seeking satisfaction from insurance companies in a situation where it is not in the former's interest to resist allegations of negligence for the sake of protecting his own purse."[13] Professor Linden criticizes these explanations, saying that insurance premiums should reflect the cost of compensating unfortunate victims.[14]

In Canada, most provinces (for example, Ontario, British Columbia, Alberta) have abolished their gratuitous passenger legislation and others are in the process of abolishing it. Quebec has never barred guest passengers from recovery. Drivers are encouraged to check their provincial statutes for the relevant legislation and their insurance contracts, as regardless of the existence or absence of statutory support, these contracts will identify whether the insured driver will be covered in such situations.

Occasionally, it must be established whether the passenger was in fact riding in a gratuitous capacity. In the leading Canadian case in the area, *Oulette* v. *Johnson*,[15] the Supreme Court of Canada found a driver liable when he charged the plaintiff for regularly driving him to and from work. The two dollars the passenger had paid for each round trip was based on the amount previously charged by the driver for this service and not on the actual cost of gas and oil. Judgment for the plaintiff was upheld on the grounds that at the time of the accident, the vehicle was being "operated in the business of carrying passengers for compensation."[16]

However, if a passenger merely shares the calculated gas and oil expense of a trip, the courts may hold the driver not liable. In *Teasdale* v. *MacIntyre*,[17] the Supreme Court of Canada found the driver not liable for injuries sustained by his gratuitous passenger, based on the fact that the two students had agreed to equally share the expenses they would incur in taking an automobile holiday together. Justice Spence commented in regards to the social rather than commercial intent of the venture.

> ... I am unable to regard the evidence in this case... as showing that there had occurred "an arrangement of a commercial nature" .... There was in my opinion, no element of a contract of carriage. The arrangement, rather, in my view, was that of a joint adventure, not, in this particular case, an adventure in trade but an adventure in recreation.[18]

Grey areas still seem to exist where individuals car pool ("I'll drive us to the river this weekend, and you can do it next time") or share driving under similar arrangements. Legal confusion may also arise when there are a number of vehicles being driven to the same destination and the group decides to have all their passengers pay their driver a set fee, regardless of whose vehicle they ride in and whether it uses slightly more or less gas than the other vehicles. While this arbitrary sum would certainly be based solely on an equitable sharing of the driver's gas, oil and expenses, it is not certain whether the courts would apply the statute.

It would be ethically desirable for drivers to accept a predetermined sum based on expenses, thereby throwing the legislation into question, and, hopefully leaving an avenue of compensation to the injured passenger. However, if an accident should occur and a passenger be injured, this practice may have some hazards for the driver. The risk he or she will take is that the courts may find that if the passenger was not riding in a gratuitous capacity, the driver must have been driving for "compensation" (implying a commercial venture). In this case, it is unclear whether the individual's personal automobile insurance will pay the damages awarded. The insurer may balk and claim that the driver did not have a commercial policy (that used for buses, taxis) or rider. Therefore the driver may be ineligible for insurance coverage and may be personally responsible for any damages awarded.

It will be up to each driver to choose whether he or she wishes to take advantage of the statutes and insurance contract provision, where these exist, to avoid liability, or, conversely, to be held personally accountable for negligence. In sum, in those few provinces retaining gratuitous passenger legislation, drivers may remain protected from legal liability should their negligence result in injury to a passenger(s), as long as money contributed by the passenger(s) is based on actual gas and oil expenditures for the trip and not on an arbitrary figure. However, when one considers statutory and common law judicial hesitance to prevent worthy compensation of innocent accident victims, drivers are again strongly encouraged to carry sufficient automobile liability insurance to cover such events.

11 RESCUE AND EMERGENCY SITUATIONS

—
—
—

THE OUTDOOR LEADER AS RESCUER

DUE TO THE INEVITABILITY of backcountry accidents and the relative unavailability of immediate support systems (search and rescue, ambulances), outdoor leaders must be prepared to deal with any of a variety of potential emergency situations which may occur while they are running programs in various wildland settings. Because of the actual and/or perceived superior knowledge and experience participants and other backcountry users attribute to outdoor leaders, they will usually be expected to assume the primary leadership role in any emergency which occurs in their general proximity. The duty to initiate rescue attempts or to provide first aid measures will depend upon the relationship (and subsequent duty of care) of the outdoor leader and imperiled person or persons.

Duty to Rescue Participants

It stands to reason that when outdoor instructors or guides place their students or participants in dangerous situations, or allow such situations to develop without intervening, they cannot evade their responsibility to assist those they have placed in peril.[1] However, in reality, the leader would have this duty regardless of the cause of the accident and the presence or absence of negligence on the leader's behalf. The outdoor leader-client relationship would be viewed in the same light as that of shipmasters and their passengers and other such associations where the former has an imposed duty to take affirmative action for the benefit of those they have accepted responsibility for.

This duty was first identified in the *Canada Shipping Act*,[2] where it was stated that:

> The master or person in charge of a vessel shall, so far as he can do so without serious danger to his own vessel, her crew and passengers, if any, render assistance to every person... who is found at sea and in danger of being lost, and if he fails to do so he is liable.[3]

Although this statute imposes a general duty to aid anyone in trouble, over the years, strong support grew for a more specific

> duty of affirmative care, including aid and rescue, incidental to certain special relations, like that of employer and employee, carrier and passenger, and occupier and his lawful visitors, and others who the law has come to attach exceptional obligations of protective care, because of the peculiar vantage by one party to such a relation in preventing accidents and a corresponding dependence by the other on such help.[4]

This obligation can be attributed to the fact that the individual assuming the duty "normally derives some economic advantage from the relationship."[5] It is important to understand the concepts of misfeasance and nonfeasance and the present trend in Canadian courts toward categorizing rescuer conduct where an affirmative duty exists as misfeasant rather than nonfeasant. Misfeasance may be differentiated from nonfeasance in that the former implies a situation involving a positive duty to care.

> Unless the court finds that there was a "duty" in the defendant to take positive action, there will be no liability imposed, even if harm to someone else is foreseeable and preventable.[6]

In principle, liability may attach to misfeasance, but at present there is no liability for nonfeasance. In the outdoor education/recreation context, this could mean that a leader would be misfeasant (and therefore potentially liable) for failing to aid a program participant in danger. However, where a stranger faced the same jeopardy, a failure to act in the affirmative by rendering aid would only constitute nonfeasance and hence, no liability could be affixed.

In practice, though, it is not always easy to distinguish in such situations because a "failure to act can sometimes take on attributes of positive conduct."[7] In addition, some provinces have enacted legislation requiring individuals to render aid and the common law courts have supported this trend by imposing civil liability for breach of these statutes.

Because of the obvious duty to care for participants in the outdoor leader's charge, liability for misfeasance, which indicates the existence of a greater standard of care than nonfeasance, will usually be imposed upon him if he is negligent. The reason for defining such failures to take positive action as misfeasance lies in the underlying premise that there has generally been no liability for nonfeasance.[8]

The Standard of Care Expected in Emergency Situations Involving Participants

Having established a legal duty to initiate rescue operations or first aid measures in the event of an accident involving an outdoor leader's participants, the next issue to be addressed concerns the standard of care which the leader's emergency responses are required to meet. The query raised in a recent Canadian boating rescue case was:

> What would the reasonable boat operator do in the circumstances, attributing to such person the reasonable skill and experience required of the master of a cabin cruiser who is responsible for the safety and rescue of his passengers?[9]

In this, the case of *Matthews et al.* v. *MacLaren et al.*,[10] also called "The Ogopogo," the defendant took some friends for a ride on his cabin cruiser named *The Ogopogo*. When one passenger, Matthews, unexplainably fell overboard into the 7° Celsius water of Lake Ontario, another summoned MacLaren who immediately put the boat in reverse and backed up toward Matthews, cutting the engines so the boat could drift to him. MacLaren repeated this procedure again when the boat drifted away and the life rings and other personal floatation devices thrown to Matthews by other passengers went unnoticed by the apparently unconscious man in the water.

As the craft again drew close to Matthews's still unresponsive body, another passenger, Horsley, removed his clothing and without notice or explanation dove in to attempt to rescue the first victim. Unfortunately, it appears that the shock of the cold water caused him to have a heart attack and although MacLaren recovered his body reasonably quickly, Horsley could not be resuscitated. Although Matthews's body disappeared from view and was never recovered, it was assumed that his heart also succumbed to the icy water upon immersion.

At trial, Matthews's family was denied recovery on the grounds that "the defendant's negligence... was not the cause of Matthews's death and there can therefore be no liability."[11] After it was somewhat extraneously proven that MacLaren had a legal duty to initiate the rescue he voluntarily undertook, the court settled down to establish whether or not he had been negligent in performing this rescue. Although it was agreed that MacLaren could in no way be faulted for Matthews' falling overboard, serious questions were raised concerning his sobriety at the time of the accident and the errors in judgment he showed in repeatedly backing the cruiser to the victim rather than approaching him "bow-on" in the approved procedural fashion. Expert police testimony also stated that MacLaren was intoxicated at the time of the accident and he himself admitted to committing an error in judgment in his selection of an incorrect rescue procedure.[12] However, the pathologist's report forced the court to conclude that "on the balance of probabilities, it had not been shown that Matthews's life could have been saved"[13] through the employment of the recommended procedure and the defendant was therefore relieved of liability.

As the duty of the outdoor leader or guide directly parallels that of the ship's captain, it may safely be said that the leader will be held negligent if he or she does that which a reasonable outdoor leader with similar training and experience would not do, or fails to do that which the reasonably prudent leader would, given the same training and circumstances. Because outdoor instructors and guides as a group have such a tremendous range of qualifications and certifications, each case will of necessity have to be tried according to its particular fact situation and the qualifications of the individual(s) involved. However, it is reasonably safe to assume that the standard of care expected to be provided by someone with extensive knowledge, training, or certification (such as Wilderness Emergency Care, equivalent to extensive ambulance paramedic training but with an outdoor accident orientation) will be somewhat higher than that expected of a leader holding only a general emergency first aid certificate (such as St. John's Ambulance or Canadian Red Cross emergency care). The lack of judicial precedent makes it impossible to identify the variations in the standard of care actually required by individuals with different levels of training and experience in this area. However, it should be remembered that all outdoor leaders will be expected to have acquired some training in this area, and to act as the "reasonable person" with like training would. Certified or not, the question raised in court would be "what was done and how did it affect the victim?"

In an emergency situation, the outdoor leader would be wise to have an assistant leader or participant record the leader's dictations of what was done and how the victim responded. In addition to the possibility of this treatment record proving valuable once the victim has been handed over to other medical care, it may be vital in the ascertainment of whether the leader acted negligently or not, should a legal action be brought.

It is hoped that rather than shying away from additional training in order to avoid the imposition of a higher standard of care, readers will see their moral obligation to achieve and maintain a high standard of excellence in the area of emergency rescue and first aid. The need for a high level of skill and knowledge in this area is as important as technical proficiency in the activity pursuit involved. The fact that the leader has a legal as well as a moral obligation to initiate emergency procedures in the event of an accident carries with it the onus to be prepared to face this responsibility with the confidence attendant to competence.

The need for frequent, realistic in-service training has been brought to bear in at least one swimming pool accident. On 17 January 1975, a young girl drowned in a supervised YMCA swimming pool in west Edmonton.[14] At the subsequent public inquiry it was learned that the supervising lifeguard was adequately certified as a lifesaver, holding his Royal Life Saving Society Bronze Medallion, Bronze Cross and Senior Resuscitation Awards, but that he should not have been allowed to work in the position of lifeguard because he did not meet the minimum age requirement of 18. However, even his extensive lifesaving qualifications were brought into question when a material witness stated that after pulling the victim from the pool, the young guard froze when she began vomiting and ceased to treat her. He was allegedly in such a state of shock that he could not even verbally respond to an onlooker, completely untrained in artificial respiration, when the latter took over resuscitation attempts.

An expert technical witness gave numerous recommendations, the majority of which related to the updating of standards for lifeguards and the legislation of these standards, increasing the frequency of mandatory recertification examinations for all certified guards and the institution of in-service training at all pools to keep guards finely tuned.[15] All of these recommendations were adopted by the jury in delivering their verdict at the inquest.[16]

The duty of affirmative action owed by an outdoor leader to the program participants is not unlike that owed by a lifeguard to the pool's patrons. The results of this particular inquest, although not yielding binding law, apply directly to outdoor education/recreation and demonstrate that although the acquisition of emergency and first aid certification may prove one way of attaining the required knowledge and skill, only through continuous practice and retraining can the outdoor leader be reasonably confident of correct application of that knowledge and skill in an emergency situation.

The Duty to Rescue Others

Although the outdoor leader has a relatively clear obligation to protect participants from harm and to care for them should they be injured or in some other danger, the same duty is not as clearly owed a stranger whom the outdoor leader finds imperiled. Historically, not only was the law not encouraging toward good Samaritans, it actually deterred them by exposing them to civil liability when their rescue attempts failed and by affording them no avenue of recompense should they be injured while attempting to aid another.[17]

Today, although both of these negative sanctions have been largely removed in both statute and common law, the individual is still rarely under a legal obligation to come to the rescue of a stranger to whom no initial identifiable duty was owed[18] and who was not through his or her conduct placed in harm's way. The most common examples of pure legally acceptable nonfeasance may be found in motor vehicle accidents where many people, including doctors and registered nurses have been known to pass an accident scene without offering aid.[19] Also, more than once a skilled swimmer has ignored a plea for help from a drowning person,[20] again without legal repercussion. It appears clear that although statutory and common law are "prepared to support altruistic action, they have stopped short of compelling it."[21]

Therefore, the outdoor leader leading a backpacking expedition who came upon a solitary backcountry traveller who has fallen and broken a leg could technically walk on by with no fear of legal reprisal. However, as noted, the law regarding nonfeasance is in a state of transition and should not be relied on as a source of legal protection. It is suspected that this poses an academic question only, as it would be a rare leader who could, without conscience, ignore the call to aid another in trouble.

The Standard of Care Expected When Rescuing Others

The provinces of Alberta,[22] Saskatchewan[23] and Nova Scotia[24] have enacted legislation to protect any person rendering emergency first aid assistance from civil liability actions, unless they are found grossly negligent. The *Alberta Act*, the first of its kind in Canada, states that:

> If, in respect of a person who is ill, injured or unconscious as the result of an accident or other emergency,
>
> (a) a physician, professional medical assistant, or registered nurse voluntarily and without expectation of compensation or reward renders emergency medical services or first aid assistance and the services or assistance are not rendered at a hospital or other place having adequate medical facilities and equipment, or
>
> (b) a person other than a person mentioned in clause (a) voluntarily renders emergency first aid assistance and that assistance is rendered at the immediate scene of the accident or emergency,
>
> the physician, professional medical assistant, registered nurse or other person is not liable for damages for injuries to or the death of that person alleged to have been caused by an act or omission on his part in rendering the medical services or first aid assistance, unless it is established that the injuries or death were caused by gross negligence on his part.[25]

Although most provinces (for example, British Columbia, Ontario) do not possess such statutes, the common law may be relied upon to give guidance in these provinces. Case law has demonstrated that although a duty will be imposed upon a would-be rescuer to complete a rescue initiated,[26] the standard of care required in such situations appears quite low. As long as the defendant's conduct does not worsen the plaintiff's position noticeably, thereby constituting misfeasance, the rescuer is under no legal obligation to significantly improve the status of the imperiled victim.[27] To hold otherwise would have the undesirable effect of discouraging assistance for fear of incurring liability if the most expeditious methods were not employed.[28]

The recent Canadian case of *Horsley et al.* v. *MacLaren et al.*[29] also clearly demonstrates the favor the courts are currently showing would-be rescuers, even when their attempts fail. Although the plaintiff, Horsley et al., was denied tort recovery after Horsley died of a heart attack while attempting to save a friend who had fallen off a yacht into Lake Ontario, the Supreme Court of Canada did not base its decision on Horsley's negligence as a rescuer. Rather, the case was decided on the grounds that no blame for the initial accident could be attached to the defendant whose own rescue attempts, although showing poor judgment, were not legally misfeasant. The driver, MacLaren, could therefore not be held liable for injuries or death sustained by others who risked their lives attempting to rescue the imperiled man.

In the Court of Appeal, Justice Jessup adopted the test set out in the *East Suffolk Rivers Catchment Board* case, contending that:

> ... where a person gratuitously and without any duty to do so undertakes to confer a benefit upon or go to the aid of another, he incurs no liability unless what he does worsens the condition of that other.[30]

Justice Schroeder supported this position and stated that:

> ... if a person embarks upon a rescue, and does not carry it through, he is not under any liability to the person to whose aid he has come as long as discontinuance of his efforts did not leave the other in a worse condition than when he took charge.[31]

The purpose of the law cited in these cases, supporting statute in a few provinces, is to encourage rescue efforts by reducing the risk of liability for failing at such. The statutory exclusion of protection for grossly negligent rescuers helps deter the inept from engaging in careless or foolhardy rescue operations. As this appears to be a fairly sound way of encouraging would-be rescuers, while retaining some control over their conduct, it is hoped that other provinces will see fit to enact such legislation.

Therefore, in summary, if an outdoor leader is negligent in creating, or failing to reasonably foresee, a dangerous situation which results in the imperilment of a participant or someone else, the leader will be legally obligated to assist them. As the law has created what amounts to a duty of affirmative action, a leader will have a duty to attempt to assist any of his or her participants who land in harm's way. Finally, the outdoor leader is under no legal obligation to assist an imperiled stranger whom he or she encountered. However, others will turn to the leader in such situations and this fact combined with the individual's conscience will often call the leader to action. As long as nothing grossly negligent is done, resulting in a significant worsening of the victim's condition, statutory and/or common law will protect the leader from liability and the latter will provide recompense should the leader be injured in the rescue effort.

THE OUTDOOR LEADER'S LIABILITY FOR OTHER RESCUERS

As the *Horsley* case so vividly illustrated, if the defendant's negligence cannot be shown to have been a contributing factor in an endangered person's plight, then that defendant cannot be held liable for the injury or death of a third party who attempts to rescue that person.[32] In that case, expert witnesses called upon to establish the defendant MacLaren's breach of duty in failing to adhere to established rescue procedures were not able to convince the Supreme Court of Canada that this failure constituted more that an error in judgment; he was not found negligent. If he had been found negligent, it is very likely that Horsley's estate would have succeeded in attaining at least partial compensation. In some aspects this case demonstrated what Professor Linden described as rather "exceptional facts"[33] which may have led to a very different decision today, especially with regard to Canada's current trend in apportioning liability.

Canada has been an international leader in rescuer compensation law. In the 1910 Manitoba Court of Appeal decision in *Seymour v. Winnipeg Electric Railway*,[34] Justice Richards, after recognizing that "the promptings of humanity towards the saving of a life are amongst the noblest instincts of mankind," stated that:

> ... the trend of modern legal thought is toward holding that those who risk their safety in attempting to rescue others who are put in peril by the negligence of third persons are entitled to claim such compensation from such third persons for injuries they may receive in such attempts.[35]

This was the first case known where a plaintiff rescuer was not barred tort recovery due to voluntary assumption of the risk involved in the rescue or "on the grounds that the defendant was not the cause of their loss."[36] However, notwithstanding Canadian leadership in this area, it was not until the early 1920s that Justice Cardozo established the precedent for all common law nations when he made the following oft-quoted statement:

> Danger invites rescue. The cry of distress is the summons to relief. The law does not ignore these reactions of the mind in tracing conduct to its consequences. It recognizes them as normal. It places their effects within the range of the natural and probable. The wrong that imperils life is a wrong to the imperilled victim; it is a wrong also to his rescuer. . . . The risk of rescue, if only it be not wanton, is born of the occasion. The emergency begets the man. The wrongdoer may not have foreseen the coming of a deliverer. He is accountable as if he had.[37]

Although *Wagner* was an American case and Cardozo's judgment therefore had no binding power on any commonwealth courts, the later cases in these countries which adopted it regardless, set their own precedents for future decisions in this area. It is now generally accepted that if an individual breaches a duty owed another and the latter is subsequently placed in a position of danger, it is completely foreseeable that a third party happening upon the situation may attempt to render aid and may be injured as a result. The negligent defendant will be liable to both.

Therefore, in the outdoor education case of *Moddejonge* v. *Huron County Board of Education*,[38] the outdoor education program coordinator was held not only liable for the death of a nonswimming student who drowned due to his negligence, but also for a second girl who could swim, but who drowned when she attempted to rescue the panicking nonswimmer who had drifted out over her head. Even as recently as in this case the courts reiterated Cardozo's statement in giving their decision and justifying it. In relating this precedent to the case at hand, Justice Pennell claimed that:

> The initial act that set the events in motion was the negligence of the defendant. One of the links of causation was that someone might thereby be exposed to danger and that someone else might react to the impulse to rescue.[39]

As a natural extension of the law stated here, it should be noted that "a person is not only liable to those injured while rescuing persons that he places in danger, but, if he gets *himself* into trouble, he owes a duty to someone who comes to his aid."[40] This fact has several implications for the outdoor leader. Not only does it explain how the leader may secure restitution should he or she be injured while rescuing another, injured or in danger through no fault of the outdoor leader's, but it is certainly of great relevance to the outdoor leader whose carelessness places his or her own person in a hazardous position. To hypothetically alter the facts of the *Moddejonge* case, for example, if it had been the outdoor educator himself (a nonswimmer in the real case) who had been wading and drifted into deep water, he would have been liable for any injury to or death of his would-be rescuer.

The same could be said of the leader who is careless in scouting a river and negligently ends up pinned under a sweeper or log jam while paddling, or one who negligently skis across a known avalanche slope and is caught. Rescuers often place themselves at great risk attempting to recover people (or their remains) from such hazardous locations as the three illustrated. People who knowingly flirt with nature's powers must be prepared to accept responsibility for themselves and others injured in the process. Although people do not have a duty to preserve their own safety, "if by his own carelessness a man puts himself into a position of peril of a kind that invites rescue, he would in law be liable for any injury caused to someone who he ought to have foreseen would attempt to come to his aid."[41]

The effect of the liability one owes to potential rescuers should instill an even greater moral responsibility to exercise prudence in outdoor leadership and activity situations than one would normally perceive. When leaders place themselves and/or their participants (who may even voluntarily wish to assume the inherent risks) in a high risk situation, innocent others who may foreseeably offer their assistance when the leader and/or group overextends itself, must be considered in weighing the utility of that action versus its possible and probable costs. As the courts have repeatedly demonstrated, rarely will the defendant leader and/or participant be able to claim that the rescuer(s) voluntarily assumed the risks involved in performing rescue operations.

THE CONTRIBUTORILY NEGLIGENT RESCUER

While few recent cases exist where an injured would-be rescuer has been denied recovery based on voluntary assumption of risk, the defendant's lack of duty and/or the rescuer's own negligence in carrying out the rescue operation does not make this result an impossibility. The courts have been largely reticent in finding altruistic rescuers who have been injured during their acts of heroism guilty of contributory negligence, especially when those they came to aid were imperiled through another's negligence. However, not all rescuers will necessarily find such legal shelter. The common law will only protect those rescuers who respond to a reasonable perceived danger to a person(s) or goods and whose conduct is reasonable given the circumstances.[42]

In terms of the first criterion, it is not necessary for the plaintiff rescuer to prove that there was actual danger, only that there was a "reasonable belief that someone was in peril."[43] It would not matter if the rescue attempt had no hope of success because the party to be saved was already dead[44] or perhaps was never really in any danger. For example, in *Ould* v. *Butler's Wharf*,[45] a workman pushed a fellow worker out of the path of a crane hook he believed was about to strike him. Upon being pushed, the workman dropped a case of rubber he was carrying on the would-be rescuer's foot. Although in hindsight there was no danger to the workman, the courts allowed the rescuer recovery for his injury because although futile, his rescue attempt was not altogether unreasonable.[46] Again, it was believed that the common law should foster rescue efforts and not discourage them.

Also, it appears to matter little whether the rescuer responded instinctively or through a rationalized decision to act. "Courage deserves no lesser reward because danger is deliberately faced... [b]ut to be a 'rescuer,' he must have acted in an emergency."[47] For example, in *Brandon* v. *Osborne, Garrett and Co.*,[48] a man's wife was injured when she attempted to pull her husband away after he was struck by glass, which, due to the defendant's negligence, fell from a skylight in his shop. In passing judgment for the wife, Justice Swift referred to the reasonable person test in these terms:

> If she [the wife] did something which a reasonable person in the circumstances ought not to have done she would not be entitled to damages, but if what she did was done instinctively and was in the circumstances a natural and proper thing to do, I think she is entitled to recover.[49]

In the *Horsley* case,[50] compensation was refused by the Supreme Court of Canada, not because his rescue attempt was perceived as "futile, reckless, rash, wanton or foolhardy,"[51] but because the imperilment of the first man overboard could not be attributed to any negligence of the defendant. However, among a number of reasons the earlier Court of Appeal judges used to reverse the trial decision and deny Horsley's right to action was the fact that he was an unforeseeable rescuer who placed himself in the same situation as the victim he sought to aid, without taking any "precautions for his own safety by donning a lifejacket or attaching a rope to himself."[52]

Professor Linden referred to the Court of Appeal's findings as a sad misuse of the foresight theory.[53] Rather than dismissing Horsley's action, Linden advocated an apportionment of damages, thereby rewarding his admirable efforts while penalizing him for the contributory negligence he displayed.[54] As Canadian courts have demonstrated an ever-increasing tendency to divide assessments according to liability between the parties involved, this would be a more likely outcome in similar cases in the future.

In the *Moddejonge* swimming case,[55] Justice Pennell stated that:

> It was delicately argued that the efforts of Geraldine Moddejonge constituted a rash and futile gesture: that reasonableness did not attach to her response. Upon this, the rescue of Sandra Thompson is sufficient answer. One must not approach the problem with the wisdom that comes after the event. Justice is not to be measured in such scales. To Geraldine Moddejonge duty did not hug the shore of safety. Duty did not give her a choice. She accepted it. She discharged it. More need not be said. The law will give her actions a sanctuary.[56]

Undoubtedly, the Moddejonge girl was ignorant of recognized lifesaving procedures, or in the stress of the emergency presenting itself, did not take the time to wait for the drowning victim's panic to subside in exhaustion before extending assistance. But the courts have been and will remain reluctant to construe such errors in judgment as reflective of negligence.

In conclusion, as with all contributory negligence claims specific to rescue situations, the onus placed upon the defendant to prove that the rescuer was foolhardy or reckless will be a difficult one. The courts will continue to support rescuers by compensating them when they are injured risking their safety to assist others. It is hoped that the law in this area will likewise encourage people working or recreating in potentially dangerous areas to take extra care to avoid accidents resulting in liability to other participants and/or to those innocent others who may come on the scene to render emergency aid.

12 DEFENDING AGAINST CLAIMS OF NEGLIGENCE IN OUTDOOR EDUCATION/RECREATION SITUATIONS

DESPITE THE HIGH STANDARD of care expected of those holding themselves out as outdoor leaders, certainly not all claims of negligence brought against outdoor instructors/guides and programming agencies in Canadian civil courts will succeed. The defendant outdoor leader, and vicariously the program delivery agency, will have ample opportunity to review the situation with their counsel to determine whether they think they have any legally acceptable defense(s) to present in the case.

DEFENDING AGAINST THE CRITERIA FOR NEGLIGENCE

Five criteria have been outlined for a cause of action to proceed in negligence law:

1. The defendant must have had a duty to care for the plaintiff.
2. The defendant must have breached that duty through a failure to meet an established standard of care.
3. The plaintiff must have incurred one or more physical or mental injuries.
4. There must be a proximate connection between the defendant's conduct and the plaintiff's injury(ies).
5. The plaintiff must not have acted in a manner prejudicial to his or her action (i.e., volenti).[1]

The plaintiff will try to establish that all five of the elements above were present. The plaintiff will attempt to provide sufficient evidence to establish at least a *prima facie* case (a case established by sufficient evidence by the plaintiff which can be overthrown by equal or greater rebutting evidence produced by the defense). If succeeding, then the defendant(s) must present evidence which proves he or she should not be liable, that some other defendant is liable, and/or that even if the defendant(s) is liable, the plaintiff has overestimated the damages.

A wide variety of arguments may be available to the defendant in rebutting the plaintiff's claim that all five negligence criteria have been sufficiently met.

No Duty of Care

Claims that no duty was owed the plaintiff may be made by either the leader, the agency or both. The leader and agency may, for example, collectively and severally claim that the accident occurred at a time and/or in a place where they were not responsible for the plaintiff.

That an agency cannot be liable for injuries to a plaintiff outside the time period for which it has accepted this duty was shown in *Scoffield et al.* v. *Public School Board of No. 20 North York*.[2] Here a young girl was injured in a tobogganing accident which occurred on school property 15 minutes before school was scheduled to start for the day. The case was dismissed on the grounds that teachers did not have a duty to supervise the schoolyard at that time and because there was no evidence to show that supervision could have prevented the accident.[3]

Therefore, outdoor leaders may expect to be liable for their participants 24 hours a day when running extended programs, especially with children, but they will not be responsible prior to or following the time identified for participants to be under the direction and supervision of the leaders and/or the agency. Usually, unless transporting children to and from school on school buses or conducting an off-area field trip, schools are not liable for injuries sustained by students occurring outside the school grounds.[4] Use of this defense by an outdoor leader would depend greatly on where the program was being run. With the exception of some special circumstances (such as running a program in a park campsite area or other location where a different occupier may be liable for visitors' injuries caused by site related factors which that occupier had or should have had knowledge of), the outdoor leader is normally responsible for taking the environment as it is found and protecting participants from or warning them of obvious hazards.

Agencies such as governments often reduce or eliminate their duty to care by contracting themselves out of liability, especially in such "high risk" program areas as outdoor education/recreation. A good example is the exclusion of government responsibility for injuries sustained at ski resorts in the mountain parks. The Canadian Parks Service typically hands ski concessionaires responsibility for liability as part and parcel of the ski operator's lease package. Frequently, municipalities will remain "liable for defects in the premises" (for example, municipal parks) but other more specialized activity groups indemnify municipalities by securing their own liability insurance for activity related accidents.[5] This same approach has also been adopted by countless school boards over the last decade, probably in outdoor education more than in any other area of the curriculum.

In sum, although there are a few identifiable circumstances which may place the duty issue in question, in the majority of situations the relationship between the defendant outdoor leader and his or her agency of employ and the plaintiff are relatively easy to ascertain.

No Breach of Duty: Meeting the Required Standard of Care

Once a relationship between the plaintiff and the defendant has been established, the courts must ascertain whether the defendant met the standard of care required in the situation. Most often this will be accomplished by listening to the testimonials of "expert" outdoor program technical witnesses, called by either the plaintiff or defense to determine whether the outdoor leader and/or agency were performing their duties in a manner which the witnesses would consider reasonable given the defendant's particular situation.

In the Canadian case of *Sholtes* v. *Stranaghan et al.,*[6] for example, a guide/outfitter was taken to court by the experienced woodsman who had hired him, "for breaching his duty of care to the plaintiff"[7] by allowing him to go out in the bush alone where he was subsequently mauled by a grizzly bear. In deciding the case, the British Columbia Court of Appeal held that the "guide was justified in permitting the woodswise plaintiff to photograph and to fish alone." This judgment was based on the grounds that the "standard of care imposed on a guide/outfitter depended upon the knowledge and experience of the person who hired him."[8] In this particular case the guide did not breach his duty to care for the plaintiff and so the latter was barred from recovery.

An interesting and unique area of care centres on the judgment a leader must show in deciding when environmental factors are favorable or unfavorable for a particular program. Outdoor leaders are expected to possess some knowledge and experience in reading environmental conditions and the signs of natural hazards. Therefore, if the leader is ignorant of, or fails to properly assess, environmental conditions and subsequently takes participants "into a hazardous situation occasioned by the natural elements, then there is liability."[9] For example, the outdoor leader must be able to read the weather and know where to camp and where not to pitch when a thunderstorm is imminent; he or she must understand snow deposition, structure and metamorphism well enough to know when a given slope may be prone to avalanche,[10] and so on. For although lightning and avalanches may be considered completely natural phenomena, hazards such as these usually identify themselves in advance, and the leader who is aware of the predisposing signs can consistently prepare for or avoid them.

Often, in order to show that the required standard of care was met in the circumstances, the defendant must call in one or more reputable outdoor education practitioners to testify that the methods employed by the defendant at the time of the accident have been used by themselves and/or other agencies which they are aware of, over a significant period of time and without serious mishap; in other words, to illustrate a *custom*.

The more established the custom (that is, the greater the number of outdoor leaders using it and the greater the length of time it has been in use), the greater the likelihood of its providing the defendant with a valid defense. However, the courts will not accept an inherently dangerous practice, regardless of how widespread its application. Here the defendant will likely be made an example to all practitioners using the disapproved method.

For example, in the case of *Michalak* v. *Dalhousie College and University, Governers of,*[11] the defendant professor who had designed the high ropes course on which the student was injured claimed that the course had been fashioned after ones successfully used at various Outward Bound schools. In finding against Dalhousie, the courts ignored the custom defense presented and made the university accountable for what it perceived was a dangerous practice.[12]

Also, because of the tremendous variability in environmental situations, outdoor leadership and participant skill levels, teaching methodologies used and so on across the country, adherence to custom is often a difficult thing to prove (or disprove). Occasionally a very good practice will be adopted because it suits a particular leader's or agency's situation, but because it lacks widespread application, it may be more difficult to justify in a court of law.

Therefore, in brief, although the outdoor leader and/or agency may on occasion be called upon to justify a particular act or practice and show that it met the standard of care required in a particular situation, most cases will involve the defendant in proving that there was adherence to an established custom previously regarded as being safe and sound.

The Absence of Legitimate Damage

Rarely is the existence of physical injury a disputed aspect of an education/recreation related case. There do not appear to be any cases considering the issue of questionable damage in this area.

In terms of mental and emotional damages, the potential defendant should be aware that where the plaintiff demonstrates one or more physical symptoms resulting from nervous shock (such as cardiac arrest, a miscarriage or an identifiable psychiatric illness), traceable to the incident, the defendant may be liable for damages.[13] However, the courts do not permit claims for fright, sorrow, sadness or other such temporary emotional upsets resulting from a traumatic experience.[14] Therefore, if the required medical and/or psychological examinations do not yield evidence of a legitimate injury or illness deemed worthy of compensation, the defendant need not fear continuance of the case to trial.

No Proximate Causation: Meeting the Foreseeability Test

Application of the foreseeability test involves an evaluation of the likelihood of the reasonable outdoor leader pursuing the activity in the manner of the defendant after assessing the magnitude of risk (likelihood and potential gravity of injury) present for each participant. If the accident was caused by one or more factors which were not reasonably foreseeable by the outdoor leader, then that leader will not be liable. If, for example, a healthy looking tree unexplainably cracks in the cold and falls across a cross-country ski trail, injuring a skier, it is likely that this freak accident would be viewed as an *Act of God*, beyond the foreseeability and hence the control of the ski tour leader.

Not all unforeseeable accidents need be related to Acts of God. So-called "freak" accidents may occur due to human error alone (leader and/or participant), for example where a canoeist tips on a relatively easy stretch of river, but is seriously injured when his head strikes a large rock on the bottom. Or they may be due to human error acting in combination with human-influenced environmental factors. For example, in an unlitigated incident in 1979 in Alberta, a number of preteen schoolchildren were scalded in a wilderness steambath when one student, either accidentally or while acting on a dare, threw a bucketful of water on the red hot rocks. No one had previously foreseen the potential hazards of allowing youths to control the temperature of their own steambaths. But now, many outdoor leaders, hearing of this incident, have prevented its recurrence by tying the water bucket near the entranceway to the steambath and only allowing participants to use a cup or ladle to carry water from the container to the rocks.[15]

In sum, if the outdoor leader can demonstrate that the accident occurred as a result of the rapid onset of some unpredictable natural phenomenon or was otherwise the freakish catastrophic result of some unforeseeable (at least previously unforeseen) chain of events, then the leader may be able to show that his or her presence was incidental to an inevitable accident. If the accident was not foreseeable, then the defense will be successful. However, if the accident was foreseeable either through simple prediction by reading the natural signs, or through another imposed duty such as that requiring the leader to know the abilities and propensities of participants, then the defendant's conduct may be held as the proximate cause of the accident and he or she will be liable.

Prejudicial Conduct on the Part of the Plaintiff: Voluntary Assumption of Risk

When a plaintiff voluntarily assumes a risk and/or "the consequences of being exposed to the risk,"[16] the plaintiff is said to be volenti and will not have a right of action. Two bases for claims of volenti have been outlined: either (a) the plaintiff was not owed a duty by the defendant or (b) the plaintiff waived legal right to action while participating in an activity where he or she knew and appreciated the risks. Volenti in the first instance would simply illustrate an example of the application of the first criterion: the need to prove the existence of a duty of care at the time and in the place where the accident occurred. Although defendants in common adventure situations may state that injured co-recreationists were volenti on this basis (not necessarily successfully[17]), most outdoor education/recreation program cases will be argued on the grounds that the plaintiff voluntarily assumed the consequences of known and appreciated risks.[18] In so doing, it would be claimed that the plaintiff either had no right to legal action, or secondly that this right was knowingly waived even where the defendant may have negligently breached a duty owed.

In order to use this in his or her defense, a defendant will usually first try to show that the plaintiff was injured by something inherent to the activity (for example, falling while learning to ski), and not by something not normally encountered by individuals engaged in that particular activity (for example, skiing into a barbed wire fence the leader knew of but neglected to warn participants of). If this defense fails, the defendant can next argue that the "plaintiff knew of the physical risks involved in the particular situation, even if these were unusual, that he or she appreciated their nature, voluntarily incurred them, and expressly or implicitly agreed to assume the legal risk and waive any right of action."[12] There are Canadian outdoor education/recreation related cases which have been won by defendants on the grounds that the plaintiff was injured due to an assumed risk inherent to the activity, and by those who could prove that the plaintiffs waived their legal rights to action through contract.

To illustrate the first type of volenti defense, in *Dodd et al. v. Cook et al.*,[20] falling was held to be an inherent risk to skaters. In making its decision, the Ontario High Court stated that:

> Skating is not a dangerous sport in itself but the risk of being tripped or thrown off balance by other skaters and caused to fall is an ever present hazard. In skating as in any other game or sport the voluntary participant is assumed to take risks which are the necessary incidents thereof.[21]

But in a more recent skating case with a very similar fact situation to that in *Dodd*, the British Columbia Supreme Court[22] held that the 26-year-old plaintiff was aware of the risk of being bumped by someone while skating. However, she did not "expressly or implicitly agree to accept the risk of a blow inflicted by the negligent defendant who was skating erratically and at excessive speed."[23]

This same position has been applied in a number of downhill ski accidents. In *Fink* v. *Greeniaus*,[24] a skier was held negligent when he failed to take greater care skiing through a blind spot and subsequently collided with another skier. In dismissing the defendant's claim of volenti on the part of the plaintiff, Justice Van Camp stated:

> There was no evidence before me to support a finding that the plaintiff had voluntarily assumed the risk of the negligence that has been found. There was no express agreement nor can I imply it from the mere presence of the plaintiff on the slopes.[25]

Although the defendant proved that the plaintiff was fully aware and appreciative of the "nature of the risk she ran in crossing the slope, there was no evidence that she had released him from his responsibility" to ski with care.[26]

In the *Lowry et al.* v. *Canadian Mountain Holidays Ltd. et al.* case, the two skiers who were killed in an avalanche were held to have accepted the inherent physical risks associated with the activity, but not to have taken any action to relieve the defendant heli-ski operator from his legally defined reponsibilities.[27]

The *Siddal, Fink,* and *Lowry* cases all illustrate that a plaintiff may voluntarily assume risks inherent to the sport, while not necessarily assuming the legal consequences of those risks; in all three examples, the plaintiffs retained their legal right to action.

In *Turanec* v. *Ross*,[28] the courts further reduced the scope of volenti to the acceptance of risks which are obvious and essential to the activity. While the facts again revolved around a collision on a ski hill, the courts held that volenti did not apply.

> The key words qualifying the application of the principle of "volenti" are the words "obvious and necessary." That is, before the principle applies the risk being assumed must be "obvious," i.e., "foreseeable," and "necessary" for the accomplishment of the purpose of the sport. The risk of falling with the resultant injury is both foreseeable and necessary if one is to learn how to ski, skate, ride, tumble, etc. . . . . Turning to the present case, skiing is not a "bodily contact" sport. . . .
> There is nothing about the sport of skiing that renders skiing in close

contact with another skier either "obvious" or "necessary"; rather the converse applies...[29]

In this particular case the courts found the plaintiff 25 percent contributorily liable for failing to "ski under such control and keeping such lookout" that the defendant would have been unlikely to collide with him.[30]

It appears that inherent risks, those deemed obvious and necessary to the activity, will only be held as adequate defenses to negligence when the accident "is of the type that happens frequently, regularly and normally in the particular activity."[31] For example, many people fall down and injure legs or ankles while skiing; these are common injuries resulting from an inherent risk of skiing.

Even where the risks involved are inherent to participation in an activity at a certain level (for example, the risk of being trapped in a hydraulic keeper increases with the grade of whitewater paddled), participants can only be held responsible for assuming those hazards for which they were of sufficient age and experience to perceive, understand and appreciate. This places a tremendous onus on the outdoor leader to communicate with participants in a continuous fashion, explaining hazards, procedures for avoiding or reducing them and the dire consequences of failing to so recognize and deal with them. Explanations and warnings of this nature "should encompass the way in which a skill is performed, the necessity of warm-ups and progressions, reasons why certain safety rules have been set forth, and so on."[32] Leaders can help ensure that participants comprehend these explanations and warnings by quizzing their understanding of and responses to new or hypothetical situations based upon the real ones seen and experienced.

It is established in law that the older, more experienced and more skilled the participants are in the particular activity, the greater the responsibility for themselves and the more risk they may be held to have assumed.[33]

Therefore, rather than the more difficult and demanding risk sports being of greater risk liability-wise to the sponsor and leader, just the reverse is true. If only those who have the appropriate skill and experience level are allowed to participate, they assume most of the risks inherent in the activity for they are knowledgeable of the conditions un-

der which they participate, the nature of the activity and its requirements of them. The greater peril in sponsoring activities is with the beginners, where very competent leaders are required.[34]

For example, in *Tomlinson v. Manchester Corporation*,[35] a 12-year-
old girl inexperienced in gymnastics was injured attempting a vaulting
progression exercise. The teacher was held liable for failing to directly supervise such novice students who obviously lacked the skill and confidence to practice alone on the apparatus.[36] However, in *Butterworth* v.
Collegiate Institute Board of Etobicoke,[37] where a 14-year-old grade 10
boy with some gymnastics experience was injured when he fell while attempting a vault, the courts held him volens. In this case, the absence of
the teacher could not be cited as the cause of the accident and the court
said this of the youth's assumption of the risks of the activity:

> ... the infant plaintiff was conscious of the fact that previously he
> had been clumsy, and also conscious of the fact that on previous occa-
> sions boys had been helping, yet on the occasion of the accident know-
> ing he had been clumsy, knowing the horse, and knowing that there
> were no boys posted, he attempted the exercise.
> I am of the opinion that this goes far beyond mere knowledge of the
> danger. I think there is a clear perception of the existence of the dan-
> ger, and also a clear comprehension of the risk involved,[38]

and later,

> Boys of fourteen years of age are capable of and indeed should be held
> to exercise reasonable intelligence and care for their own safety.[39]

It should be noted that this position was not supported in the Supreme
Court decision in *Meyers et al. v. Peel County Board of Education*,[40]
where a 15-year-old gymnastics student was seriously injured in a fall
from the rings. The teacher and school board were found liable for failing
to properly supervise and to provide adequate protective matting and in
dismissing claims of volenti on the part of the student, the court said:

> Although [the plaintiff] may have assumed the risk of falling off the
> rings, he was entitled to expect that the defendants would provide ade-

quate matting so that he would not injure himself in such a fall. If the plaintiff accepted the physical risk, he did not accept the legal risk to give up any right of action which he had.[41]

However, in *Sholtes* v. *Stranaghan et al.*, the woodsman plaintiff failed in his claim against his guide because the courts believed he was old enough, and of sufficient intelligence and experience to assume the inherent risks wildlife present to travellers in the wilderness.[42]

Where the plaintiff is a mature adult, who willingly affects his or her mental and physical capacities through the excessive consumption of alcohol or other mind altering substances, contributory negligence may be found. In the recent Ontario case of *Crocker* v. *Sundance Northwest Resorts Ltd.*,[43] the inebriated plaintiff entered a "tubing race" sponsored by the defendant's commercial ski operation as part of its winter carnival activities. Some days prior to the event, the plaintiff and his co-contestants received videotapes of the previous year's event, which illustrated the risks involved quite graphically. He nevertheless registered for the event, paid his $15 entry fee, and signed the entry form and waiver.

The plaintiff drank heavily all during the day of the event and was visibly intoxicated. He ignored suggestions by race officials that he withdraw due to his intoxicated condition and continued to race even after sustaining a scratch over his eye on the first heat. On his second run, he and his partner lost control of their tube after hitting a particularly large mogul and Crocker either landed on his head or was hit by another tube from behind. The net result was that he was rendered a quadriplegic.

Crocker brought a suit against the defendant ski complex for failing to adequately warn him of the dangers of the ski hill and of tube racing and for negligently allowing him to participate when visibly intoxicated.[44] While winning at trial (25 percent contributorily negligent), he appealed for more damages. The plaintiffs cross-appealed regarding the question of liability.

The Ontario Court of Appeal allowed the cross-appeal and dismissed the action, saying that the plaintiff was the "sole author of his own tragic misfortune."[45] The judge cited as his rationale the fact that Crocker should have known that the competition was inherently dangerous, and that he not only voluntarily accepted the inherent risks, but compounded them by becoming drunk prior to participating. The defendant was not responsible for his inebriation, and "any responsibility they assumed was more than discharged by the warnings they gave."[46] A higher standard of care was not required.

The case was then appealed by Crocker to the Supreme Court of Canada.[47] This highest court reinstated the trial decision, apportioning liability at 75 percent Sundance and 25 percent contributory negligence on the part of Crocker. The Supreme Court decision was based, in large part, on the fact that Sundance had advertised and promoted the tubing race as a profit venture. It had contributed to Crocker's drunken condition by selling him alcohol and had facilitated his accident by providing him with the tube which he rode into the moguls where he was hurt. Sundance was not held to have taken any or all of the steps deemed within their power as reasonable under the circumstances (for example, disqualification, stronger identification of the risks and encouragement to withdraw, withholding of a tube).

> The fact that Crocker was an irresponsible individual and was voluntarily intoxicated during the tubing competition is the very reason why Sundance was legally obliged to take all reasonable steps to prevent him from competing.[48]

Sundance was found to have had a duty to care for an inebriated participant and to have failed in meeting the required standard of care expected in this light. Crocker's injuries were found to be proximally caused by his drunkenness, as a sober participant was held to be more capable of slowing and steering his tube using his feet.[49]

Crocker was found to have assumed the physical but not all of the legal risks involved in participating. The Supreme Court agreed with the trial judge's assertion that the waiver clause on the entry form had not been brought to Crocker's attention, "that he had not read it, nor in fact did he know of its existence." The court accepted Crocker's testimony that he believed that all he was signing was an entry form.[50]

While the defense of voluntary assumption of risk thereby failed, Crocker was found 25 percent contributorily negligent for his voluntary intoxication during the event. Nevertheless, clients who insist on imbibing while engaged in outdoor programs or special events should be informed of the increased physical and legal risks they must assume for themselves. This case should provide strong motivation to outdoor programming agencies to actively prevent individuals in such condition from participating in sponsored activities or programs.

In narrowing the scope of adult assumption of risk even further, previous experience has been shown, in at least one case, not to constitute a particularly important consideration when the plaintiff is a mature adult and therefore deemed of sufficient age and intelligence to appreciate the risk as a reasonable person would. In *Gilbert* v. *Lamont*,[51] the plaintiff sought damages from the defendant stable owner when she fell off a horse she rented from him. She claimed that the horse was of nervous temperament and that it veered off the trail, causing her to fall. The action was dismissed because it was believed that she had received adequate instruction, and that even if she had not, controlling and steering a horse with reins was presumed to be obvious to any mature adult. Here the adult plaintiff was held to be a novice horsewoman who voluntarily accepted the risk of the injury she sustained when she rented the horse to go riding.[52]

In all of the cases discussed to this point, the defendant has claimed that by mere pursuit of the activity in question, the plaintiff has implicitly agreed to accept all risks inherent in the activity, including the legal risks involved. However, as the success rate of the defendants in these cases has indicated, only when the accident is the direct result of the plaintiff assuming a physical risk which is completely inherent to the activity at the plaintiff's level of participation (for instance, falling while learning to ski), is there any possibility of winning such counterclaims. This implies that while a participant may accept some risks, they may reject others. In *Ainge* v. *Siemon*,[53] for example, the courts distinguished between those risks a snowmobile passenger normally assumes such as falling off the machine, from those which he does not usually lay claim to, in this case being run over by a second snowmobile.

A participant may willingly accept risks inherent to the activity, but not those related to the employment of defective or inadequate equipment. In *Piszel* v. *Board of Education of Etobicoke*,[54] a high school student was injured during a wrestling match when the wrestling mats separated just prior to his attempting to take down his opponent, with the result that he landed on his elbow on the hard gymnasium floor. The courts held the school board liable because the accident did not occur due to a risk inherent to the sport, but due to one over which they had control and, ultimately, responsibility.[55] Also, in *Delaney et al.* v. *Cascade River Holidays Ltd. et al.*,[56] the defendant whitewater rafting agency was found negligent in failing to provide lifejackets with sufficient buoyancy for use by passengers it took running whitewater rivers in British Columbia.[57]

Outdoor programmers who provide their participants with technical and safety equipment may be held liable if a participant is injured due to a malfunction of this equipment. When the problem can be traced to a fault in the manufacture of the piece of equipment which could not easily have been inspected and noted by the outdoor agency handing it out, the injured party may sue the manufacturer.[58] But, where the fault lies in poor maintenance or improper use (for example, using light touring ski equipment for heavy duty backcountry expeditioning), liability will remain with the outfitting agency.

The Reliance upon Waivers in a Defense

One way many outdoor education/recreation delivery agencies attempt to exclude themselves from liability and place this responsibility on the individual participant is through the use of "waivers," otherwise called "disclaimers," "responsibility releases" or "exemption clauses." Such waivers are an attempt to contract out liability to the participant and as such, are governed by the dictates of contract law.[59] It may be instructive to take a closer look at the Canadian outdoor education/recreation cases in which the employment and/or content of waivers has been raised as an issue in deciding the case, one way or the other.

Whether found in fine print on application or registration forms, on entry tickets or on warning signs, waivers all attempt to expressly transfer liability to the participant.[60] When it can be shown that the release was express in its terminology, that the risk involved was of the sort the waiver was intended to cover and that the disclaimer was drawn to the attention of the adult plaintiff prior to the accident, then regardless of whether the defendant was negligent or not, the waiver may protect him or her from legal action.

> A person who makes an agreement with another, either expressly or by implication, to run the risk of injury caused by that other, cannot recover for damage caused to him by any of the risks he agreed to run.[61]

However, in an effort to continue facilitating compensation of victims injured by another's negligence, the law honors exclusion clauses only when there can be no question as to their intent and parameters. That is, their wording must be very precise and specific, the plaintiff must have been aware of and understood the clause and must have made a free choice in participating in the activity.[62]

Signed documents, while certainly not universally successful,[63] have a much greater chance of forcing the courts to find the plaintiff volens than do releases on tickets and/or posted signs. In two recent Canadian cases involving downhill ski operators who placed liability disclaimers on all ski tow tickets, neither defendant was successful in stating that the injured plaintiff voluntarily assumed the risks. In *Wilson* v. *Blue Mountain Resorts Ltd.*,[64] it was held that the ticket waiver used was inadequate because it had not been drawn to the attention of the plaintiff skier. In *Lyster* v. *Fortress Mountain Resorts Ltd.*, the courts found the ticket disclaimer invalid because it did not explicitly address the issue of the defendant's negligence.

> ... there is nothing in its wording which expressly exempts [the defendant] from the consequences of the negligence of its employees, and any doubts as to its being wide enough to cover such negligence must be resolved against the resort.[65]

The exclusionary power of signage, like ticket disclaimers, depends on the language of the sign and the certainty with which it has been drawn to the attention of the plaintiff and others in his or her class. In *Sturdy et al.* v. *R.*,[66] the Crown successfully defended itself against a claim by the plaintiff who was mauled by a grizzly bear near a garbage dump in Jasper National Park. The plaintiff stated that the Parks department failed in its duty to protect him from or at least warn him of the danger of bears at the site. The Crown won the case on the grounds that there had been no previous attacks by bears in that area, that bears did not constitute an unusual hazard in this semi-wilderness area and that general warnings about bears were distributed in brochures at entranceways to the Park and on highway signs. However, despite the Crown's absence of liability in this case, the court held that this was not due to volenti on the part of the plaintiff. Even though Sturdy may have, by implication, agreed to accept the risk of physical injury by walking near the dump,

> ... there was no consent or agreement, implied or expressed, that he waived any right of action in case of injury by a bear.[67]

In *Saari* v. *Sunshine Riding Academy Ltd.*,[68] a sign posted at the academy stating, "Riders Ride at Their Own Risk" was not held to provide adequate warning to patrons. When the academy was taken to court for failing to provide competent riding guides, the court determined that the sign had not been properly drawn to the attention of the plaintiff, or to other riders for that matter. In addition:

> Even if such had been the evidence, it is doubtful whether the words used are wide enough in their ordinary meaning to cover negligence on the part of the... Academy.[69]

The use of written waivers has been illustrated in two recent cases brought before the British Columbia Supreme Court. In *Smith v. Horizon Aero Sports Ltd. et al.*,[70] the plaintiff read and signed a "hold-harmless" agreement, but it was later found invalid because it did not specifically exclude the agency of liability caused by its own negligence. However, in *Delaney et al. v. Cascade River Holidays Ltd. et al.*,[71] the drowned plaintiff's estate was barred from recovery solely because such a clause had been included in the disclaimer. The standard liability release form signed by all clients prior to departure read in part:

> **Disclaimer Clause:** Cascade River Holidays Ltd. is not responsible for any loss or damage suffered by any person either in travelling to the location of the trip, before, during or after the trip, for any reason whatsoever including negligence on the part of the company, its agents or servants.

> **Agreement:** I agree to assume all risks involved in taking the trip including travelling before and after, and agree to pay the cost of any emergency evacuation of my person and belongings that may become necessary. I agree to Cascade River Holidays Ltd. its agents and servants relieving themselves of all liability for losses and damages of all and every descriptions. I acknowledge having read this liability release and that I am of the full age and my acceptance of the above disclaimer clause by my signature and seal. (Parents or Guardians please sign for minors.)[72]

Even though the defendant rafting agency was found negligent and its negligence was shown to be a proximate cause of the plaintiff's death, he had effectively barred himself and/or his estate from any recovery in tort or contract law by signing the release clause.

The strongest support for waivers was recently realized in the Supreme Court of Canada decision in *Dyck v. Manitoba Snowmobile Association Inc. and Wood*.[73] In this case, the plaintiff signed a waiver form prior to competing in a snowmobile race. The defendant Wood was an official at this race, and it was his job to move onto the track as the winners came by to signal the end of the race. The plaintiff, driving the third place machine, struck the official Wood while he was still standing on the track. As a result of trying to avoid Wood, Dyck ran his snowmobile into the outside track wall and was seriously injured.

At both trial and appeal, the official was found negligent; 100 percent responsible according to the Manitoba Court of Appeal.[74] However, the expressly stated waiver was recognized at both previous trials prior to bringing his case to the Supreme Court of Canada. Here again, the waiver held up, and the appeal was dismissed with costs.

The entry form waiver Mr. Dyck signed:

> expressly set forth his agreement to save harmless and keep indemnified the association, its organizers, agents, officials, servants and representatives from all liability, howsoever caused, in connection with taking part in the race, "notwithstanding that the same may have been contributed to or occasioned by [their] negligence."[75]

In arguing against the reasonableness and validity of the disclaimer, Dyck claimed that Wood's negligent conduct in standing on the track was not foreseeable, and hence not excludable. The court countered that this was not particularly unusual conduct by race officials and that the waiver was designed to cover precisely this type of negligence should it occur.[76] Dyck also tried to state that the waiver constituted a fundamental breach; that it was so "manifestly unfair and unreasonable as to be unenforceable."[77] To this, the court replied that the appellant was expected to have known that snowmobile racing is an inherently risky sport, in which he voluntarily chose to participate. "It is in no way unreasonable for an organization like the association to protect itself against liability"[78] given the high level of inherent risk present in the sport. In this case, as the waiver successfully protected the association from liability, it also vicariously exonerated the race official from his negligence. However, such support is by no means universal. The recognition of a signed waiver in the *Dyck* case was called upon in the *Crocker* case, also recently tried at the Supreme Court of Canada.[79] Here, the waiver clause on the tubing event entry form was rejected. In distinguishing these two cases with regards to the application of the waivers used, Justice Wilson stated:

> In *Dyck*, the plaintiff had read the rules of the Association that purported to release the Association from liability for injuries suffered in the Association's races. The plaintiff D signed the waiver in full knowledge of the Association's intention to exempt itself from liability. Not so here... the waiver provision in the entry form was not drawn to the plaintiff's attention, he had not read it, and indeed did not know of its existence. He thought he was simply signing an entry form. In these circumstances, Sundance cannot rely upon the waiver clause in the entry form.[80]

Given the current difficulties many agencies and boards are facing in securing adequate insurance, and their subsequent increasing reliance on waivers, the limitations of this risk management avenue must be clearly understood and appreciated. Organizations operating programs and premises with total reliance on waiver forms, with no insurance back up, are *not* completely immune from potential lawsuits.

These cases will undoubtedly sound like good news to all of the agency/association directors and administrators employing waivers. Given the current difficulties many organizations are facing in securing adequate insurance and their subsequent increased reliance on responsibility release statements, this judicial support may be the only thing keeping many operators going. However, waivers are not the panacea of all outdoor program risk management problems. It is important to understand and appreciate the legal limitations and ethical implications of reliance upon this tool.

OTHER DEFENSES

A defendant may win his or her case based on the presentation of rebutting evidence which puts reasonable doubt in the judge's or jury's mind regarding the defendant's failure to meet the criteria for negligence. A variety of ways this may be accomplished have been presented using adjudicated cases as illustration. In addition to defending one's position within this context, a number of other defenses exist. Most of these can also be tied to the test for negligence in some fashion, but a few will stand independent of these criteria.

Contributory Negligence

Contributory negligence is "conduct on the part of the plaintiff, contributing as the legal cause to the harm suffered, which falls below the standard to which one is required to conform for his/her own protection."[81] The defendant who claims that a plaintiff was contributorily negligent retains the onus of proving that the plaintiff acted unreasonably in the circumstances and that this failure to take greater care was a proximate cause of the injury(ies) sustained.[82]

Although the term "negligence" normally implies a breach of some legal duty to care, in the case of contributory negligence it refers only to the plaintiff's failure to meet the standard of care required for his or her own safety. That contributory negligence cannot be construed as implying a breach of duty owed the negligent defendant by the plaintiff was best clarified by Lord Simon when he said:

> When contributory negligence is set up as a defense, its existence does not depend on any duty owed by the injured party to the party sued, and all that is necessary to establish such a defense is to prove... that the injured party did not in his own interest take reasonable care of himself and contributed by this want of care, to his own injury.[83]

A plaintiff will not be contributorily negligent "if the risk is one created by the negligence or breach of statutory duty of the defendant, and it is one which a reasonably prudent man in the plaintiff's position would take."[84]

Further, traditionally if one negligently placed another in a perilous position from which the latter was forced to react promptly to save himself or herself, it was not contributory negligence if that other failed to act in a way which was shown on reflection to have been the best way out of the difficulty.[85] The courts historically granted plaintiffs placed in emergency situations great latitude in the "presence of mind and degree of judgment" they were expected to demonstrate, allowing the actual standard of care they exhibited to be appreciably lower than that of their defendants. The rationale was of course closely tied to the promotion of unprejudiced recovery by injured plaintiffs, especially where the defendant was insured or an otherwise suitable channel for loss distribution.[86]

Today, with the institution of apportionment legislation, contributory negligence is no longer considered a complete bar to recovery. As a result, the courts have become somewhat less biased towards plaintiffs and are now more apt to allow the damages to be divided in relation to where the fault lies. As stated in the province of Ontario's statutes:

> In any action for damages which is founded upon the fault or negligence of the defendant if fault or negligence is found on the part of the plaintiff that contributed to the damages, the court shall apportion the damages in proportion to the degree of fault or negligence found against the parties respectively.
>
> If it is not practicable to determine the respective degree of fault or negligence as between any parties to an action; such parties shall be deemed to be equally at fault or negligent.[87]

Two rather recent Canadian Supreme Court decisions illustrate the employment of this type of legislation.

In *Henricks et al.* v. *R.*,[88] the plaintiff sued the defendant Crown for failing to replace signs on a navigation buoy indicating the presence of a weir downstream. An accident resulted when Henricks, his wife and another passenger drove their motorboat to within 15 meters of the weir before perceiving the waterfall it created and attempting to take evasive action. In their haste to turn or reverse the small craft, it overturned with the result that the plaintiff's wife was drowned.

The Crown was held liable, under the tenets of the *Crown Liability Act*,[89] for placing in the "navigable water a menace to navigation and in failing to replace the warning signs... to adequately warn of the menace."[90] However, the courts, under the *Tortfeasors and Contributory Negligence Act*,[91] held that the supplicant and his wife were contributorily negligent in their failure to keep a proper lookout and in their "failure to keep the boat in control during the progress forward from the point of turning to the moment when, all too late, they appreciated the danger."[92] As a result, negligence and subsequent damages were apportioned equally between the supplicant and the Crown.[93]

A similar 50-50 division of damages was again found by the Supreme Court of Canada in the case of *Holomis* v. *Dubuc*.[94] Here, the defendant was found negligent after the amphibious plane he was attempting to land on a wilderness lake in British Columbia struck an unseen object while taxiing along the surface. The collision tore a gaping hole in the passenger compartment and as the plane began to fill with water, three passengers leaped out of the aircraft into the icy lake. Although two of the three were subsequently rescued, one passenger, Holomis, drowned.

The court held that the defendant's negligence lay in his failure to warn his passengers of his plan to land and to instruct them in how to behave in the event of an emergency "arising when the aircraft became waterborne." The deceased plaintiff was held contributorily negligent, not for evacuating the aircraft, as this was perceived as certainly within the realm of reasonable conduct in the circumstances, but in his "failure to take with him one of the clearly available lifejackets."[95]

Although both of these cases have implications for outdoor leaders, the general issues of the *Holomis* case should strike especially close to home. The outdoor leader's duties to assess risk, warn participants and instruct them in emergency procedures closely parallel those responsibilities the court identified as belonging to the pilot.

Also, the standard of care mature participants are expected to exercise for their own protection is also clearly illustrated. The more knowledgeable and experienced the individual, the greater will be the duty to take reasonable care of oneself.[96] Adult participants are expected to appreciate the additional hazards precipitated by participating in outdoor activities while not in full control of their faculties. In the recent case of *Crocker v. Sundance Northwest Resorts Ltd.*, an inebriated tubing participant was found 25 percent contributorily negligent for the quadriplegia he incurred as a result of insisting on participating in a tubing race while he was voluntarily intoxicated.[97]

Although the test for contributory negligence is based upon the objective criteria of the reasonable sober person acting in similar circumstances, factors such as age and experience in the activity will be considered. For example, in the British Columbia case of *Pawlak et al. v. Doucette et al.*,[98] the plaintiff was held 15 percent contributorily negligent for injuries sustained as he tried to grab the moving water-ski tow rope. The judge believed that through his work, the plaintiff was very experienced with regard to mechanical objects and moving cable and ropes. His action in grabbing the moving tow rope fell below the standard of care expected of someone with his knowledge and experience.

Outdoor education/recreation thrives on placing people in unfamiliar situations in what is often an unfamiliar environment. The novice outdoorsperson cannot be expected to understand and appreciate risks with the same level of comprehension as a seasoned outdoor pursuitist.

The test meets its subjective limits when dealing with child plaintiffs whose conduct will be evaluated according to that expected of a youth of like age, intelligence and experience, acting in the same situation.[99] A number of cases have been reviewed involving youths who were found contributorily negligent for their injuries. One of the most notable of these was the *Meyers*[100] case, where a 15-year-old gymnastics student was held 20 percent contributorily negligent for injuries he sustained in a fall from the rings. Another was the case of *Ryan et al. v. Hickson et al.*,[101] where a 9-year-old boy fell off a snowmobile he was a passenger on while turning to wave at the driver of a second snowmobile. When he was run over by the second snowmobile the courts apportioned the damages in this manner: 33.3 percent to each of the two infant drivers and their respective fathers and 33.3 percent to the plaintiff for failing in his duty to hang on to his driver.[102] Yet another was the Ontario Court of Appeal's decision in the McErlean case[103] where a youthful trailbike rider was held 75 percent responsible for the serious injuries he sustained in a collision accident with another youth.

In sum, the introduction of apportionment legislation has resulted in a much greater tendency for courts to hold plaintiffs responsible for negligent conduct on their part which contributes to their injuries. In outdoor education/recreation situations the likelihood of contributory negligence being found against a plaintiff increases with the individual's age (to adulthood) and experience in the natural environment and in the activity being pursued at the time of accident.

Statutory Time Limitations

Each province has its own *Limitations of Actions Act*,[104] which serves to establish the time period within which most types of civil actions must be commenced. Generally, a plaintiff will have 2 years following an accident to initiate an action in tort, but there are a number of notable exceptions.

In Alberta, for example, the *Municipal Government Act*[105] serves to bar all actions against municipalities

> ...unless notice in writing of the accident and the cause of it has been served on the municipal secretary or municipal solicitor within six months of the happening of the accident.[106]

The following subsection further clarifies this citation and allows an action to be commenced past the limitation period if the plaintiff is dead or if the "court considers there is reasonable excuse for the want or insufficiency of notice. . . . "[107]

Actions against teachers and/or school boards must, according to most *School* and *Public Authorities Protection Acts*, also be commenced within 6 months of the accident. The *School Act* of Saskatchewan, for example, states that:

> No action shall be brought against a school district for the recovery of damages after the expiration of six months from the date upon which damages were sustained. . . . [108]

A case which employed similar legislation was *Levine et al.* v. *Board of Education of Toronto*,[109] where a boy injured during a school sponsored athletic meet failed to commence his action against the board until five years later. The Ontario Court of Appeal dismissed the case, holding that the school board was in this case protected by the six month time limitation stated in the *Public Authorities Protection Act*.[110]

In the extreme case, the federal *Crown Liability Act*[111] stipulates that for an action to proceed against the Crown, a written notice of the injury and claim must be presented to an administrator and employee of the department controlling the land or activity within *one week* of the accident. The Attorney-General of Canada must also be notified, usually by registered mail. Although a succeeding subsection mitigates the severity of this limitation (such as where the victim is deceased or where the Crown would not be prejudiced due to a lack of notice), it still serves to bar many potential claims against the federal government as most plaintiffs are not aware of this statute. Ignorance of the law is rarely viewed as a viable excuse for breaching it, even when the law is recorded in rather obscure legislation.

In brief, as a defendant, the outdoor leader and/or agency should be aware of the length of time following an accident in which they are open to litigation. This information will normally be contained in the province's *Limitations Act*, but may also be found in other acts specifically related to the agency.

Unauthorized Activity

This defense is available for use by employer agencies only, not by outdoor leaders working in the field. It would be relevant in the rare instance where an accident occurred when a leader had taken participants on an outing not sanctioned by the agency the individual was working for. The leader may have taken participants out during a time, to a place or to engage in an activity which was not within his or her scope of employment and which the agency had expressly prohibited. An employer will remain vicariously liable for his employees' unauthorized actions only where the latter "are so connected with the acts which he has authorized that they might rightly be regarded as modes, although improper modes of doing them.... "[112] In establishing whether a leader's conduct fell within this definition, the courts would review the decision-making autonomy normally granted the leader, the scope of employment of employees performing similar jobs in other agencies and the duties and decisions foreseeably incidental to performance of the duties expressly authorized by the employer.[113]

In the case of *Beauparlant* v. *Appleby Separate School Board of Trustees*,[114] an accident ensued after a group of teachers, unbeknownst to the principal, board or parents, granted their students a half-day holiday to attend a concert and attempted to transport them to it in an overloaded truck. In this particular case the action was completely defeated because the plaintiffs had dropped their action against all but the defendant school board, which was not found liable. Had the plaintiffs retained the teachers involved as defendants they would have won their suit against these individuals. As the teachers were acting beyond their authority and outside their scope of employment, they would have been personally liable for injuries resulting from their negligence.[115]

Outdoor agency directors may decide to protect themselves from vicarious liability by expressly delimiting their employees' scope of duties. Although this is a valid practice within limits, it must be well-tempered with opportunities for mature, experienced leaders to exercise some autonomy in the manner in which they perform their jobs. Staff morale will suffer greatly where leaders perceive they are not trusted to make any decisions for themselves.

Error in Judgment

While not technically a defense per se, an error of judgment may arise in relation to a deviation from the required standard of care. The issue to consider will be the relative placement of the error(s) (there are almost always more than one) on the continuum from reasonably prudent conduct to that constituting negligence. If the error(s) was (were) minor enough that it would not be unreasonable to predict that the reasonably prudent leader could have made the same error(s), then the existence of one or more errors may not necessarily imply negligence.

Where an outdoor leader and/or agency has, despite concerted efforts to provide an enjoyable, safe outdoor experience, made one or more mistakes which resulted in injury(ies), they may indeed plead that they made an error in judgment. Outdoor leaders are only human and hence subject to human error. The Témiscamingue, Cairngorm and Mount Hood tragedies discussed earlier all illustrate disasters which resulted from a number of leader errors in judgment. And although none have resulted in legal action, the outdoor leader who studies the causal links to these accidents will learn much from the inquest and enquiry findings and recommendations presented by the analysts.

Although a pleading of error in judgment may provide a leader with a judicially valid defense (or partial defense) in certain circumstances, it is certainly not one which outdoor leaders should rely upon in planning and executing their programs. In addition to the strong possibility of the courts finding negligence anyway, en route to attempting to compensate the innocent victim, it is certain that no outdoor leader would want to be forced to live with the realization that his or her "error" caused someone else to be seriously injured or killed.

In summary, once a case is taken to court, the plaintiff must demonstrate that the defendant leader and/or agency was negligent according to the 5 criteria contained in the test for negligence. The defendant in turn, will attempt to refute this evidence and/or show that the plaintiff did not meet the standard of care required for his or her own safety, that the action was brought outside the statutory time limitations, and/or that the alleged negligence did not consist of more than an error in judgment.

WHAT TO DO IN THE EVENT OF A POTENTIAL LAWSUIT

Despite the apparent plethora of defenses at the outdoor leader's disposal, one's chances of being successfully sued for some negligent act or omission are steadily growing. If and when a situation arises which has the potential to lead to litigation, there are a number of things the instructor/guide and/or agency/board can and should do to protect their interests before the incident goes to trial.

Care for the Victim

If, after an instructor/guide's best efforts to run a safe, enjoyable program fail and someone is injured, the first priority must always be the initial care and evacuation of the injured person(s). The need for suitable first aid equipment and the knowledge required to use it, as well as the necessity of adequate communications systems and/or quick evacuation routes, may all be essential to ensuring that a relatively minor accident occurring in the backcountry does not turn into a more complicated situation, with more serious consequences. An efficient, confident and sincere approach to the emergency situation will also reassure the victim and reduce the likelihood of that individual considering suing.

Employment of a Scribe

As the leader will undoubtedly be busy (doing first aid, planning and executing an evacuation, keeping other participants busy and so on), an assistant leader or other participant should be given the job of *scribe*. As the leader and/or first aider works, they dictate information to the scribe who records it on paper. All potentially relevant information should be recorded at the scene: what happened (where, when and how the accident occurred); the condition of the victim (including any changes in response to the first aid administered); all remedial steps taken (first aid, evacuation procedures) and a timeline of these steps, and the names and addresses of all witnesses.

After the situation is under control and the victim is stable, the leader should review this record and fill in any potentially important details (weather, water level, subjective impressions of the accident and the handling of it, etc.). What seems irrelevant at the time could be crucial information in court. Photographs taken during the rescue or as soon as possible afterwards may also provide vital information and evidence. This should all be done in addition to the completion of standard agency accident report forms.

Securement of Assistance/Contact of Employer

A good communications system or quick evacuation route which messengers may take is essential. A minimum of two capable people should be sent for help, complete with a written description of what happened, victim's names, suspected injuries, type of assistance needed and grid coordinates or a map of the victim's location. The director of the agency responsible for the program must be notified of any accidents as soon as possible.

Contact of Insurance Agent and Lawyer

The agency director will normally be responsible for contacting the agency's insurance agent and lawyer, in that order.[116] This will allow them to investigate the incident immediately and to preserve facts and evidence while they remain fresh. It will also help prevent the leader/instructor or agency director from pursuing any course of action that could prejudice their legal position at a later date.[117]

Avoiding Discussion of the Issue

Although sometimes difficult to do when emotions are running high, it is a wise defendant (or potential defendant) who avoids making any public statements, especially to the media, regarding the particulars of an incident which has not been settled. No verbal or written admission of guilt or responsibility should be made from the time of the accident until the agency's lawyer has suggested such be made.

In fact, in the section describing what the insured must do in the event of an accident, most liability insurance policies contain a condition prohibiting assumption of liability even where the amount of damages appears small. The policy stipulates that if the insured accepts any responsibility, "voluntarily makes any payment or incurs any expense other than for immediate medical and surgical relief as is necessary at the time of accident, it is at the insured's own expense."[118] As the costs related to a given injury or loss may run much higher than they initially appear, it is certainly in both the programming organization's and the injured victim's long term best interest for the leader and staff to remain reserved.

The area of communications in the event of an injury accident requires serious preplanning before and careful monitoring during and following an incident. For example, all printed or mailed material should be checked by legal counsel. All phone conversations with insurance representatives, lawyers, doctors or families of the injured individual(s) should be taped to protect against possible misrepresentation later.[119] In the event of a very serious injury or death, the program director will be responsible for deciding how to deal with sharing the news of the tragedy not only with the family of the injured/deceased person, but also with the program staff, program participants and perhaps even parents where the participants are children. Even here, the need to deal openly and honestly with a traumatic life experience must be balanced with the ever-looming legal considerations.[120]

Avoiding Operational Changes

Unless an obvious, unnecessary risk has been exposed through the accident (one likely to lead to additional foreseeable accidents) the agency would be legally wise not to change the manner in which it directs its staff or operates its programs until after the matter is settled. While not necessarily so,[121] any immediate changes may be construed by the courts as indicative of an admission of error, corrected in hindsight.

Trying to Settle Out of Court

If the injured party threatens to sue and the leader and/or agency do not have an iron-clad defense, it is best to meet with the agency's insurance agent (or an adjuster) and lawyer and make a concerted attempt to settle the matter fairly out of court. Litigation is often a "zero-sum" game; there is one winner and one loser (except where damages are apportioned).

Other potential benefits to the out-of-court settlement include:

faster issue resolution than that attained while waiting for trial; ensures plaintiff recovery of some damages; ensures civil defendants that they will not have to pay as much in damages as they would if they lost a court verdict; saves lawyer and clients the effort, time and expense required of trial preparation; allows preparation of greater control over case outcomes; and reduces the courts caseload enabling it to concentrate on the most difficult cases.[122]

Lawyers thrive on the financial return they accrue through fighting the issue aggressively for as long as it takes to settle satisfactorily. Although this is occasionally necessary, especially where damages are extensive and no legal precedents prevail, the agency may save time and legal costs if they and their insurance adjuster and lawyer work out a fair compromise based on the damages the plaintiff will claim in pleadings, and if the agency directs their lawyer to work toward this settlement. Most suits are settled before they end up in court, "but usually not until both sides have wearied of the escalating costs and the disruptive influence on operations."[123] In addition to the conservation of money, time and human resources, early out-of-court settlement will do much to prevent the unfavorable publicity a protracted litigation is likely to cost the agency, regardless of the outcome of the case.

Out-of-court settlements may on occasion also leave the plaintiff (or his estate) in a better position financially than an arbitrated court assessment. Ironically, the results of damage assessments are one of the prime reasons that few cases have been taken to court and hence, relatively few precedents exist in outdoor education/recreation. Unlike gymnastics or football injuries where the plaintiff is likely to have been seriously injured and perhaps rendered a paraplegic or quadriplegic, in outdoor pursuits the tendency is for accident victims to die by drowning, exposure, burial in an avalanche or from a serious fall off a mountain. More often than not, the deceased is under 18 years of age. The other very highly active population in outdoor pursuits is that of young adults (18-35), and most of these people have no dependants. Statute restricts the assessments for fatal accidents to children or adults with no dependants to such a low sum (presently in the order of 10,000 dollars), that the bereaved families normally avoid the additional trauma of a court case and settle out of court or do not attempt to make a claim at all.[124]

However, societal attitudes toward legal rights have continued to grow more individualistic. As the expected standard of care of professionals has concomitantly increased, the trend of nonlitigation has definitely ended and Canada is seeing a swing of the pendulum toward increased legally-enforced accountability in all areas, including outdoor education/recreation.

Comprehensive risk identification, evaluation and appropriate management are the outdoor agency's best defense against this trend. Where this process fails and someone is inadvertently injured, the organization and its leadership staff may have one or more valid defenses which will protect them from successful litigation. Where some possible liability is perceived, the agency should strive to settle the matter quickly, cleanly and fairly out of court.

APPENDIX

Sample Assumption of Risk Agreement and Indemnifying Release: for use by associations, member clubs and affiliates or by private companies.

Assumption of Risk Agreement and Indemnifying Release for the Canyou Canoe Association

WARNING:

Please *read* carefully before signing; activity waivers have held up in Canadian courts. Consider that you are assuming both *physical* and *legal* risks which have potential financial implications for yourself and/or your family should you be injured or killed while participating in an association activity.

AGREEMENT AND INDEMNIFYING RELEASE:

I, _____ (name) hereby acknowledge and agree that in consideration of being permitted to participate in canoesport activities or programs organized by the Canyou Canoe Association (herein called "the Association"):

  1. do hereby release the Association, its members, officers, directors, employees, independent contractors and agents from all liability, and do hereby waive as against the Association, its members, officers, directors, employees, independent contractors and agents all recourses, claims, causes of action of any kind whatsoever, in respect of all per-

207

sonal injuries or property losses which I may suffer arising out of or connected with my preparation for, or participation in, the aforesaid canoesport programs or activities, notwithstanding that such injuries or losses may have been caused solely or partly by the negligence of the Association or any of its members, officers, directors, employees, independent contractors or agents.

_____

Initial

2. And, I do hereby acknowledge and agree:
   a. that the sports of canoeing and kayaking are very dangerous, exposing participants to many inherent risks and hazards, including but not restricted to: loss or damage to personal property, immersion in cold water, hypothermia, drowning, inclement weather, slipping and falling, falling objects, or suffering any type of accident or illness in remote areas without easy access to medical facilities. While some of these risks are inherent in the very nature of the sport itself, others may result from human error and negligence on the part of persons involved in preparing, organizing and staging canoesport programs and activities;
   b. that, as a result of the aforesaid risks and hazards, I as a participant may suffer serious personal injury, even DEATH, as well as property loss;
   c. that some of the aforesaid risks and hazards are foreseeable, but others are not;
   d. that I nevertheless freely and voluntarily assume all the aforesaid risks and hazards, and that, accordingly, my preparation for and participation in the aforesaid canoesport programs and activities shall be entirely at my own risk;
   e. that I am personally responsible for my preparation prior to joining association activities. Such preparation will include, but not be limited to: (i) my health and physical fitness, (ii) securement of adequate prerequisite knowledge of lake/river hazards, and skills to meet program/trip/event requirements, (iii) the adequacy and condition of my paddling equipment;
   f. that while I recognize that association leaders and/or instructors will make every reasonable effort to minimize exposure to known risks, that I have a personal responsibility to learn and follow safety rules and procedures established by my leaders/instructors

and to make them aware at any point in which I question my
knowledge of these procedures or my ability to participate in any
activity;

g. that I will refrain from the consumption of alcohol or mind altering drugs while participating in association programs or activities;

h. that I consent to receive first aid and medical treatment by the
leader/instructor and medical personnel in the event of an accident, injury, and/or illness during an association activity or program;

i. that I understand that neither the Association nor any of its members, officers, directors, employees, independent contractors or
agents assume any responsibility whatsoever for my safety during
the course of my preparation for or participation in the aforesaid
canoesport programs and activities;

j. that I have carefully read this ASSUMPTION OF RISK AGREEMENT
AND INDEMNIFYING RELEASE agreement, that I fully understand
same, and that I am freely and voluntarily executing same;

k. that I understand clearly that by signing this release, I will be forever prevented from suing or otherwise claiming against the Association, its members, officers, directors, employees, independent
contractors and agents for any loss or damage connected with any
property loss or personal injury that I may sustain while participating in or preparing for any of the above mentioned canoesport
programs or activities, whether or not such loss or injury is caused
solely or partly by the NEGLIGENCE of the Association or any of
its members, officers, directors, employees, independent contractors and agents;

l. that I have been given the opportunity and have been encouraged
to seek independent legal advice prior to signing this agreement;

m. that I understand clearly that the Association would not permit
me to participate in any such canoesport programs or activities
unless I signed this ASSUMPTION OF RISK AGREEMENT AND IN-
DEMNIFYING RELEASE, that this agreement applies to all the
aforesaid canoesport programs and activities whether occurring
in the near or distant future, and that the terms of this Agreement
need not be brought to my attention each time I participate in
such canoesport program or activity in order to be effective;

n. that the term "canoesport programs or activities" as used in this

ASSUMPTION OF RISK AGREEMENT AND INDEMNIFYING RELEASE includes without limiting the generality of that term, the provincial, regional and local programs and activities as well as all other trips, outings, training sessions, clinics, races, programs and events that are in any way authorized, sanctioned, organized or operated by the Association;

o. that this ASSUMPTION OF RISK AGREEMENT AND INDEMNIFYING RELEASE is binding on myself, my heirs, my executors, administrators, personal representatives and assigns;

p. that I understand clearly that the Association is and shall be deemed to be acting for itself and as agent on behalf of and for the benefit of the members, officers, directors, employees, independent contractors and agents of the Association for the purposes set out in the above-stated clauses of this agreement; and

q. that I am of sufficient age and mental capacity to sign this ASSUMPTION OF RISK AND INDEMNIFYING RELEASE.

_____
Initial

_____
Signature of Participant

Dated at _____, this _____ day of _____, 19 _____

_____
Signature (Parent or Guardian if the participant is under 18 years of age.)

_____   _____
Witnessed by (Print name here)   Signature of Witness

_____
Date

NOTES

1 IS THE RISK WORTH TAKING?

1. Gina McLellan, "The Future of Outdoor Recreation: What the Trends Tell Us," *Parks and Recreation* 21, no. 5 (1986).

2. Robert Kraus, *Recreation and Leisure in Modern Society,* Third Edition (Glenview, Ill.: Foresman and Co., 1984).

3. William March, "Outdoor Pursuits—What are the Legal Implications?" *Canadian Intramural Recreation Association Bulletin* 6, no. 1, n.d., p. 1.

4. John Naisbitt, *Megatrends* (New York: Warner Books, 1984), p. 35.

5. David Hopkins, "Changes in Self Concept as the Result of Adventure Training," *CAHPER Journal* 48, no. 6 (July-August 1982); S. Thomas (Comp.), *Adventure Education: A Bibliography* (Amherst, N.Y.: Institute of Classroom Management and School Discipline, State University of New York at Buffalo, 1977); Alan N. Wright, "Youth Development through Adventure Programs," *Camping Magazine* (September-October 1983), pp. 24–30.

6. James Wiltens, "High Touch Wilderness and High Tech Campers," *Camping Magazine* (May 1986), pp. 22–29.

7. Betty van der Smissen, "Legal Aspects of Adventure Activities," *Journal of Outdoor Education* 10 (1975), p. 12.

8. Donald H. Rogers, "The Increasing Standard of Care for Teachers," *Education Canada* (Spring 1980), p. 26.

9. Betty van der Smissen, "Where is Legal Liability Heading?" *Parks and Recreation* 15, no. 5 (May 1980), p. 50.

10. Rogers, p. 27.

11. Paul W. Darst and G.P. Armstrong, *Outdoor Adventure Activities for School and Recreation Programs* (Minneapolis, Mn: Burgess Publishing Co., 1980).

12. Simon Priest, "Redefining Outdoor Education: A Matter of Many Rela-

tionships," *Journal of Environmental Education* 17, no. 3 (Spring 1986), pp. 13–15.

13. Seppo Iso Ahola, *The Social Psychology of Leisure and Recreation* (Dubuque, Iowa: W.M.C. Brown Pub. Co., 1980), p. 275. Citing Jensen, C.R., *Outdoor Recreation in America* (3rd Edition) (Minneapolis, Mn: Burgess Publishing Co., 1977).

14. Alan Ewert, "Outdoor Adventure Activity Programs: A New Dimension," *Journal of Physical Education, Recreation and Dance* (May/June 1986), pp. 56–60.

15. Heinz-Gunter Vester, "Adventure as a Form of Leisure," *Leisure Studies* 6 (1987), p. 246.

16. M.L. Backiel, "Comparative Study of Attitudes Toward the Meaning of the Term 'Outdoor Education' as Viewed by Selected Members of AAHPER's Council on Outdoor Education in 1968 and 1975" (unpublished Master of Science Thesis, George Williams College, 1976).

17. Glenda Hanna (nee Wuyda), Ambrose G. Gilmet and Harvey Scott, "Leadership Qualification Versus Certification in Outdoor Education in Canada," an attitudinal survey completed for the CAHPER Outdoor Committee, 1981; presented at the CAHPER Conference, Victoria, 11 June 1981.

18. The panel consisted of the following regional representatives: Stephen Cook (Atlantic Provinces), Alphonse Caissie (New Brunswick and Quebec), Patricia de St. Croix (Ontario), Andrew Power (Prairie Provinces) and James Boulding (Pacific Region).

19. William March, Byron Henderson, Eberhart Grav, Sandra Kalef and Brian Leroy, *Legal Liability in Outdoor Education/Recreation in Alberta* (Calgary: Alberta Law Foundation, 1981).

20. Eberhart Grav, in March et al., p. 13.

21. Ibid., p. 11.

2 AN OVERVIEW OF THE CANADIAN LEGAL SYSTEM

1. Ronald J. Walker and M.G. Walker, *The English Legal System*, Third Edition (London: Butterworths, 1972), p. 92.

2. Gerald Gall, *The Canadian Legal System*, Second Edition (Toronto: Carswell Co. Ltd., 1983), pp. 23–24.

3. Ibid., pp. 35–36.

4. Innis Christie, editor, *Legal Writing and Research Manual* (Toronto: Butterworths, 1970), p. 11.

5. Phillip S. James, *Introduction to English Law*, Tenth Edition (London: Butterworth, 1979), p. 9.

6. Gall, pp. 23–24.

7. Gall, p. 32.

8. Owen H. Phillips, *A First Book of English Law*, Seventh Edition (London: Sweet and Maxwell, 1977), p. 192.

9. James, *Introduction to English Law*, p. 17.

10. Gall, pp. 230–32.

11. Ibid., pp. 235–36.

12. Ronald J. Walker, *The English Legal System*, Fourth Edition, Walker & Walker (London: Butterworths, 1976), pp. 58–59.
13. Gall, p. 36, quoting Gray in *The Nature and Sources of the Law*, 1921, p. 302.
14. Ibid., p. 20.
15. James, *Introduction to English Law*, p. 173.
16. *British North America Act* (1867), 30 and 31 Victoria c. 3, s. 101.
17. Ibid., s. 92 (14).
18. Gall, pp. 117–25.
19. *Supreme Court Act*, R.S.C. 1970, c. 259, s. 3.
20. Ibid., s. 4.
21. Ibid., s. 25.
22. Gall, p. 120.
23. *Judicature Act*, R.S.A. 1970, c. 193, s. 3.
24. Ibid., s. 15 and 16.
25. Gall, p. 122.
26. *Surrogate Court Act*, R.S.A. 1970, c. 357, s. 13.
27. Phillips, p. 372.
28. M. McDonald, *Legal First Aid* (Toronto: Coles Publishing Co., 1978), p. 33.
29. James, *Introduction to English Law*, p. 65.
30. McDonald, p. 34.
31. R. Gerald Glassford, Richard Moriarty and Gerald Redmond, "Physical Activity and Legal Liability," CAHPER Research Council Monograph (1978), p. 8.
32. Phillips, p. 375.
33. Glassford et al., p. 9.
34. Ibid.
35. Phillip S. James with D.L. Brown, *General Principles of Torts* (London: Butterworths, 1978), p. 428.
36. Cecil A. Wright, Allen M. Linden and Lewis N. Klar, *Canadian Tort Law: Cases, Notes and Materials*, Ninth Edition (Toronto: Butterworths, 1990), p. 20–24.
37. Ibid.
38. James, *Introduction to English Law*, p. 406.
39. Walker et al., pp. 278–79.
40. Ibid.
41. *McKay v. Govan School Unit No. 29 of Saskatchewan* [1968] S.C.R. 589 (S.C.C.).
42. *Thornton v. Board of School Trustees (Prince George, British Columbia) et al.* [1978] 2 S.C.R. 275 (S.C.C.).
43. *McErlean v. Sarel and the City of Brampton* (1985), 32 C.C.L.T. 199 (Ont. S.C.).
44. *McErlean v. Sarel et al.* (1988) 42 C.C.L.T. 78 (Ont. C.A.).
45. *Smith v. Horizon Aero Sports Ltd. et al.* [1981] B.C.D. Civ. 3391-01.
46. *Lowry et al. v. Canadian Mountain Holidays Ltd. et al.* (1985), 33 C.C.L.T. 261; (1987) 40 C.C.L.T. 1 (B.C.C.A.).

3 THE BASIS OF TORT LIABILITY

1. Phillip S. James, *General Principles of the Law of Torts*, Fourth Edition (London: Butterworths, 1978), p. 3.
2. Wright, Linden and Klar, pp. 1–2, quoting from *Salmond on the Law of Torts*, Eighteenth Edition, 1981.
3. Ibid., pp. 1–7, quoting William L. Prosser in *Handbook of the Law of Torts*, Fourth Edition, 1971.
4. P.S. Atiyah, *Accidents, Compensation and The Law*, Fourth Edition (London: Weidenfeld and Nicolson, 1975), p. 34.
5. Ibid., p. 55.
6. John G. Fleming, *The Law of Torts*, Fifth Edition (Sydney: The Law Book Co., 1977), pp. 104–5.
7. *Blyth v. Birmingham Water Works Co.* (1856), 11 Ex. 781.
8. Fleming, pp. 113–14, quoted and accepted in *Dziwenka v. Mapplebeck* [1972] W.W.R. 350 (S.C.C.).
9. Ibid., p. 114.
10. *Boese v. Board of Education of St. Paul's Roman Catholic Separate School District No. 20 (Saskatoon)* (1976), Q.B.D. 607 (Q.B.D.).
11. Allen M. Linden, *Canadian Negligence Law*, Third Edition (Toronto: Butterworths, 1982), p. 102.
12. Ibid., p. 103.
13. *Bolton et al. v. Stone* [1951] 1 All E.R. 1078.
14. Ibid., p. 1086.
15. Fleming, p. 109.
16. *Gibbons et al. v. Harris* [1924] 1 W.W.R. 675, at p. 706.
17. Fleming, p. 110.
18. *Williams v. Eady* (1893), 10 T.L.R. 41.
19. *Thornton et al. v. Board of School Trustees of District 57 (Prince George) et al.* [1978] 2 S.C.R.; *Meyers et al. v. Peel County Board of Education* [1981] S.C.C.D. 3081.
20. James, *Introduction to English Law*, p. 383.
21. The Wagon Mound (No. 1) *Overseas Tankship (U.K. Ltd.) v. Morts Dock and Engineering Co. Ltd.* [1961] A.C. at pp. 422–23 (P.C.).
22. Ibid., p. 424.
23. *Hughes v. Lord Advocate* [1963] A.C. 837.
24. Ibid., at p. 845.
25. *School Division of Assiniboine South No. 3 v. Hoffer et al.* [1971] 1 W.W.R. 1.
26. *School Division of Assiniboine South and Hoffer et al. v. Great Winnipeg Gas Co. Ltd.* [1971] 4 W.W.R. 752.
27. *Smith v. Leech Brain Co.* [1962] 2 Q.B.D. 414 (Q.B.).
28. Ibid., p. 44, quoting Kennedy in *Dulieu v. White and Sons* [1901] 2 K.B. 669.
29. *School Division of Assiniboine South No. 3 v. Hoffer et al.* [1971] 4 W.N.E. 752.

30. *Wieland* v. *Cyril Lord Carpets Ltd.* [1969] 3 All E.R. 1006; *McKew* v. *Holland et al.* [1969] 3 All E.R. 1621 (H.L.).
31. McTague, J.A., in *Mercer* v. *Gray* [1941] 3 D.L.R. 564 (Ont. C.A.), quoting from *Beven on Negligence*, Fourth Edition, p. 104.
32. Ibid., p. 568.
33. Ibid., p. 567.
34. *R.* v. *Saskatchewan Wheat Pool* [1983] 1 S.C.R. 205.
35. Ibid., p. 205.
36. Ibid., pp. 227–28.
37. MacKay, J.A., in *Queensway Tank Lines Ltd.* v. *Moise* [1970] 1 O.R. 535 (C.A.).
38. William L. Prosser, *Handbook of the Law of Torts*, Fourth Edition (St. Paul, Minnesota: West's Publishing Co., 1971), pp. 416–17.
39. Ibid., p. 416.
40. Ibid., p. 417.
41. Wright et al., pp. 13–15.
42. *Nance* v. *British Columbia Electric Railway Company Ltd.* [1951] A.C. 601, p. 611.
43. *Butterfield* v. *Forrester* (1809), 103 E.R. 926 (K.B.D.).
44. *The Contributory Negligence Act*, R.S.A. 1970, c. 65; *The Negligence Act*, R.S.O. 1980, c. 315.
45. *Restatement of the Law of Torts*, Second Edition, 1964. s. 464 (2).
46. *Myers et al.* v. *Peel County Board of Education* (1977), 2 C.C.L.T. 269, at p. 290.
47. There are a number of other Canadian cases dealing with contributory negligence of child and adult plaintiffs; for example, see *Ryan et al.* v. *R. Hickson et al.* (1974), 55 D.L.R. (3d) 196 (Ont H. Ct.); *Henricks et al.* v. *R* (1970), 9 D.L.R. (3d) 454 (S.C.C.).
48. J.B. Saunders, *Mozley and Whitley's Law Dictionary*, Ninth Edition (London: Butterworths, 1977), p. 353.
49. Sandra Kalef, "Volenti Non Fit Injuria," in March et al., *Legal Liability in Outdoor Education in Alberta* (Calgary: Alberta Law Foundation, 1981), p. 1.
50. *Harrison* v. *Toronto Motor Car et al.* [1945] 1 O.R. 9.
51. Wright et al., pp. 13–21.
52. *Ainge* v. *Siemon* (1972), 19 D.L.R. (3d) 531 (Ont. H. Ct.).
53. *Rootes* v. *Skelton* (1967), 116 C.L.R. 383.
54. *Restatement of Torts*, s. 496 (B).
55. *Hedley Byrne and Co. Ltd.* v. *Heller and Partners Ltd.* [1964] A.C. 465.
56. *Toromont Industrial Holdings Ltd.* v. *Thorne, Gunn, Helliwell and Christenson* (1976), 14 O.R. (2d) 87 (Ont. C.A.).

4 THE CHILD PLAINTIFF

1. G.O. Jewers, "Damages Suffered by Children—The Standard of Care Owed Children," in *Isaac Pitblado Lectures on Continuing Legal Education, The*

Law and the Minor (Manitoba Bar Association, 1970), p. 49.
2. *Seamone* v. *Fancy* [1924] 1 D.L.R. 650, p. 652.
3. *McEllistrum* v. *Etches* [1956] S.C.R., p. 787. The facts of this case involve a 6-year-old girl who ran out on the road and was struck by a car.
4. *Williams* v. *Eady* (1893), 10 T.L.R. 41. In this case a teacher was found negligent for leaving a container of phosphorus lying about. An explosion resulted when some boys played with the phosphorus.
5. Ibid., 9 T.L.R., p. 637.
6. *Smerkinich* v. *Newport Corporation* (1912), L.C.T. 265, p. 265.
7. R.A. Percy, *Charlesworth on Negligence*, Sixth Edition (London: Sweet and Maxwell, 1977), p. 594.
8. *Public Trustee Act*, R.S.A. 1970, c. 301, s. 4.
9. James, *Introduction to English Law*, p. 18.
10. P.S. Morse, "Infant Settlements," in *Isaac Pitblado Lectures*, p. 54.
11. Ibid.
12. Fleming, p. 669.
13. *Deziel et al.* v. *Deziel* [1953] 1 D.L.R. 651 (Ont. H. Ct.), p. 653.
14. Ibid., pp. 653–54.
15. *School Act*, R.S.A. 1970, c. 329, s. 133.
16. Fleming, p. 151.
17. *Hatfield* v. *Pearson* (1956), 209 W.W.R. 580 (B.C.C.A.).
18. *Streifel* v. *S.B. and G.* [1957] 25 W.W.R. 182 (B.C.S.C.).
19. *Sullivan* v. *Creed* [1904] 2 I.R. 560.
20. *Starr and McNulty* v. *Crone* [1950] 2 W.W.R. 560.
21. *School Division of Assiniboine South No. 3* v. *Hoffer et al.* [1971] 4 W.W.R. 746.
22. *Ryan et al.* v. *Hickson et al.* (1974), 55 D.L.R. (3d) 196.
23. Ibid., p. 196.
24. *Williams* v. *Eady* (1893), 10 T.L.R. 41.
25. *Meyers et al.* v. *Peel County Board of Education* [1981] S.C.C.D. 3081-01.
26. *Beaumont* v. *Surrey C.C.* (1968), 112 S.J. 704.
27. *Nicholson* v. *Westmorland County Council, The Times*, 25 October 1962.
28. Geoffrey R. Barrell, *Teachers and the Law*, Fifth Edition (London: Methuen and Co. Ltd., 1978), p. 293.
29. *Meyers et al.* v. *Peel County Board of Education* [1981] S.C.C.D. 3081-01.
30. *Thornton et al.* v. *Board of School Trustees of District No. 57 (Prince George) et al.* [1976] 5 W.W.R. 240 (B.C.C.A.).
31. Ibid., p. 265.
32. *Meyers et al.* v. *Peel County Board of Education* (1981), unreported Supreme Court of Canada case notes, p. 10.
33. Ellen I. Picard and Steve W. Mendryk, "Legal Liability in Physical Education and Athletics," paper presented at the Conference on Curriculum Development and Teaching in Sports Medicine, Edmonton, 19–21 June 1981, pp. 3–8.
34. *Marston* v. *St. George Hospital* (1956), 1 All E.R. 384.

35. H. Shulman, "The Standard of Care Required For Children" (1927–28), 37 *Yale L.J.* 618.
36. *McEllistrum* v. *Etches*, p. 787.
37. Ibid., p. 793.
38. J.F. O'Sullivan, "Infants and Contributory Negligence," in *Isaac Pitblado Lectures*, pp. 38–39.
39. *Messenger et al.* v. *Sears and Murray Knowles Ltd.* (1960), 23 D.L.R. (2d) 297.
40. Kerwin, C.J.C., in *McEllistrum* v. *Etches*, criticizing Trueman J. in *Eyers* v. *Gillis and Warren* [1940] 4 D.L.R. 747.
41. Rand, J., dissenting in *The King* v. *Laperriere* [1946] S.C.R. 415, p. 446.
42. Ibid., p. 445.
43. *Flett* v. *Coulter* (1903), 5 D.L.R. 375, p. 378.
44. *McHale* v. *Watson* [1966] 39 A.L.J.R. 459 (Aust. H. Ct.), p. 464.
45. *Sheasgreen et al.* v. *Morgan et al.* [1952] 1 D.L.R. 48 (B.C.S.C.), p. 61.
46. *Hatfield* v. *Pearson*, p. 581.
47. *Schade and Schade* v. *Winnipeg School District No. 1 et al.* (1959), 28 W.W.R. 577 (Man. C.A.), p. 580.
48. *Messenger et al.* v. *Sears and Murray Knowles Ltd.*
49. Ibid., p. 300.
50. *Ryan et al.* v. *Hickson et al.*
51. Ibid., p. 196.
52. *Meyers et al.* v. *Peel County Board of Education* [1981] S.C.C.D. 3081-01.
53. Ibid. (1981), unreported Supreme Court of Canada case notes, p. 4.
54. Ibid., pp. 2–3.
55. *Meyers et al.* v. *Peel County Board of Education* (1977), 2 C.C.L.T. 269.
56. *The King* v. *Laperriere*, p. 445.
57. *Holmes* v. *Goldenberg* [1953] 1 D.L.R. 92 (N.S.C.A.).
58. *Grieco et al.* v. *L'Externat Classique St. Croix* [1962] S.C.R. 519 (Que. S.C.).
59. Linden, *Canadian Negligence Law*, p. 126; *McErlean* v. *Sarel and the City of Brampton* (1988) 42 C.C.L.T. (Ont. C.A.) 78.
60. *Highway Traffic Act*, R.S.O. 1970, c. 202, s. 18.

5 STATUTE LAW AND THE OUTDOOR LEADER

1. Although the statutes reviewed are intended for all teachers, they will have special relevance to those working in the disciplines of physical education and in general outdoor education. They were written in each case for certified teachers (and in some cases student-teachers), working for a recognized school board in a particular province. They will not apply as law to individuals working for other public or private agencies or ventures.
2. *Alberta School Trustees Act*, R.S.A. 1970, c. 330.
3. *Municipal School Administration Act*, R.S.A. 1970, c. 249.
4. *Teaching Profession Act*, R.S.A. 1970, c. 362.
5. *Public School Act*, R.S.B.C. 1974, c. 74, s. 10 (a).

6. *Education Act*, R.S.O. 1974, c. 129, s. 235 (1).
7. *Education Act*, R.S.N.S. 1967, c. 81, s. 74 (b).
8. *Education Act*, R.S.S. 1978, c. 17, s. 227 (b).
9. Ibid., (c).
10. Ibid., (g).
11. Ibid., (j).
12. Ibid., (h).
13. *School Act*, R.S.N.S. 1970, c. 346, s. 81 (e).
14. *Secondary School Act*, R.S.M. 1970, c. 250, s. 183 (9).
15. *Public School Act*, R.S.M. 1970, c. 215, s. 259.
16. Ibid. See the next section, "The Statutory Duties of Occupiers" for further discussion of this concept.
17. Ibid., s. 260.
18. E.g., *Occupiers' Liability Act*, R.S.A. 1973, c. 79; *Occupiers' Liability Act*, R.S.B.C. 1974, c. 60; *Occupiers' Liability Act*, R.S.O. 1980, c. 14.
19. Fleming, p. 432.
20. *Occupiers' Liability Act*, R.S.O. 1980, c. 14, s. 2 (n).
21. Linden, (1988) pp. 599–600.
22. *Haynes* v. *C.P.R.* (1972), 31 D.L.R. (3d) 62 (B.C.C.A.).
23. *Addie* v. *Pumbreck* [1929] A.C. 358.
24. E.C. Harris, "Some Trends in the Law of Occupiers' Liability" (1963), 41 *Canadian Bar Review* 401.
25. *Indermaur* v. *Dames* (1867), L.R. 2 C.P. 311 (Ex. Ct.), p. 388.
26. *Phillips* v. *Regina Public Schools District No. 4 Board of Education* (1976), 1 C.C.L.T. 197 (Sask. Q.B.).
27. *Nickell* v. *City of Windsor* (1927), 59 O.L.R. 618.
28. *Occupiers' Liability Act*, R.S.A. 1973, c. 79, s. 5.
29. Ibid., c. 79, s. 1.
30. Ibid., s. 6.
31. *Occupiers' Liability Act*, R.S.O. 1980, c. 14, s. 3.
32. *Occupiers' Liability Act*, S.M. 1982–84, c. 29, s. 4.
33. *Occupiers' Liability Act*, R.S.O. 1980, c. 14, s. 4.
34. Ibid.
35. Ibid.
36. *Occupiers' Liability Act*, R.S.A. 1973, c. 79, s. 9.
37. *Walker* v. *Sheffield Bronze* (1977), 2 C.C.L.T. 97.
38. *Occupiers' Liability Act*, R.S.A. 1973, c. 79, s. 9.
39. James, *General Principles of the Law of Torts*, p. 98.
40. *Occupiers' Liability Act*, R.S.A. 1973, c. 79, s. 13 (2a and b).
41. *Glasgow Corporation* v. *Taylor* (1922), 1 A.C. 44.
42. Ibid., p. 44.
43. *Liddle* v. *Yorks North Riding* (1944), 2 K.B. 101, p. 112.
44. *Moddejonge* v. *Huron County Board of Education* (1972), 2 O.R. 437 (Ont. H. Ct.).
45. *Latham* v. *R. Johnson and Nephew Ltd.* [1913] K.B. 398, p. 407.
46. Ibid., p. 416.

47. *Occupiers' Liability Act*, R.S.A. 1973, c. 79, s. 13 (2c).
48. *Ware's Taxi Ltd.* v. *Gilliham* [1949] S.C.R. 637.
49. Ibid., p. 640.
50. *McErlean* v. *Sarel and the City of Brampton* (1985), 32 C.C.L.T. 199.
51. Ibid., pp. 201–2.
52. Ibid.
53. Ibid., p. 205.
54. *McErlean* v. *Sarel and the City of Brampton* (1988), 42 C.C.L.T. 78 (O.C.A.).
55. Ibid., p. 80.
56. *Bisson* v. *Corporation of Powell River* (1967), 62 W.W.R. 707.
57. Ibid., p. 714.
58. *Bundas* v. *Oyma Regional Park Authority* (1980), 4 Sask. R. 124 (Sask. Q.B.).
59. *Petty Trespass Act*, R.S.A. 1970, c. 273.
60. Ibid., s. (2a) and (2b).
61. Ibid., s. 2 (1).
62. *Public Lands Act*, R.S.A. 1970, c. 297.
63. Ibid., s. 38 (1a).
64. *Forests Act*, R.S.A. 1971, c. 37.
65. Ibid.
66. *Environment Council Act*, R.S.A. 1970, c. 125, s. 3.
67. *National Parks Act*, R.S.C. 1970, c. 189.
68. Ibid., s. 4.
69. Ibid., s. 7 (1).
70. *Crown Liability Act*, R.S.C. 1970, c. C-38.
71. Ibid., s. 3 (1a).
72. Ibid., s. 3 (1b).
73. Dwight Gibson, "The Federal Enclave Fallacy in Canadian Constitutional Law," *Alberta Law Review*, 14, n.d., p. 167.
74. *Crown Liability Act*, R.S.C. 1970, c. C-38 s. 4 (4).
75. *Diversified Holdings* v. *The Queen in Right of B.C.* [1982] 133 D.C.R. (3) 712.
76. *Wildlife Act*, R.S.B.C. 1979, c. 433; *Wildlife Act*, R.S.N.S. 1987, c. 13, s. 4 (3).; *Wildlife Act*, S.M. 1980, c. 73, s. 85.; *Wildlife Act*, R.S.A. 1987, C. W9-1, s. 14(a).
77. *Indermaur* v. *Dames* (1866), L.R. 1 C.P., p. 274.
78. *Sturdy et al.* v. *The Queen* (1974), 47 D.L.R. (3d) 71.
79. Ibid., p. 96.
80. Ibid., p. 98.
81. *Rudko et al.* v. *R.* (1983), 1 W.W.R. 741.
82. Ibid., p. 742.
83. Ibid., p. 743.
84. Ibid., p. 756.
85. Ibid., p. 745.
86. Ibid., p. 760.

87. Ibid., p. 761.
88. Ibid.
89. *Ashdown* v. *Williams* (1957), 1 Q.B. 409.
90. *Wilson* v. *Blue Mountain Resorts Ltd.* (1974), 4 O.R. (2d) 713.
91. *Crown Liability Act*, R.S.C. 1970.
92. *Judicature Act*, R.S.A. 1974, c. 65.
93. *Proceedings Against the Crown Act*, R.S.A. 1970, c. 285, s. 5.
94. Ibid., s. 5 (1).
95. *Provincial Parks Act*, R.S.A. 1980, c. P-22, s. 3.
96. Ibid., s. 4.
97. Ibid., s. 11.
98. *Municipal Government Act*, R.S.A. 1970, c. 246.
99. For example, City of Edmonton By-law No. 5769.
100. *Edmonton Parks and Recreation Department*, City of Edmonton By-law No. 2202 (as amended by By-laws No. 2281, 2750, 2874, 2929, 2977 and 3015).
101. Ibid., 3 (6) (9) and (11), pp. 1–2.
102. Ibid.
103. City of Edmonton By-law No. 2202, s. 5.

6 THE LEGAL LIABILITY OF THE OUTDOOR LEADER

1. See Donna L. Hawley, "The Legal Liability of Canadian Physical Education Teachers," unpublished Master of Arts Thesis, University of Alberta, 1974.
2. Linden, p. 106.
3. P.S. Atiyah, *Accidents, Compensation and the Law*, Fourth Edition (1987), p. 51.
4. *Michalak* v. *Dalhousie College and University, Governors of* (1983), 61 N.S.R. (2d) 374.
5. Ibid., p. 375.
6. Ibid., pp. 376–77.
7. Ibid., p. 381.
8. Ibid., p. 378.
9. Fleming, p. 107.
10. *Ware's Taxi Ltd.* v. *Gilliham* [1949] S.C.R. 635.
11. *Sturdy et al.* v. *R.*
12. *Williams* v. *Eady* (1893), 10 T.L.R. 41.
13. *Moddejonge* v. *Huron County Board of Education.*
14. Ibid., p. 443.
15. *Taylor* v. *R.* (1978), 95 D.L.R. (3d) 82 (B.C.S.C.).
16. Ibid., p. 82.
17. *Meyers et al.* v. *Peel County Board of Education* (1981), unreported S.C.C. notes, p. 10.
18. *McKay* v. *Board of Govan School Unit No. 29.*
19. *Thornton et al.* v. *Board of School Trustees of School Division No. 57 (Prince George) et al.* [1976] 5 W.W.R. 240 (B.C.C.A.).

20. *Myers et al.* v. *Peel County Board of Education* (1981), unreported S.C.C. notes, p. 10.
21. Donald H. Rogers, "The Increasing Standard of Care for Teachers," *Education Canada* (Spring 1981), p. 27.
22. *Walton* v. *Vancouver* [1924] 2 D.L.R. 387.
23. *Moddejonge* v. *Huron County Board of Education.*
24. "The Cairngorm Tragedy: A Report on the Fatal Accidents Enquiry," *Mountain*, No. 20, 1972.
25. *Ross* v. *Colorado Outward Bound* (1977), unreported case, December 1978.
26. Ibid.
27. William March, "Outdoor Pursuits: What are the Legal Implications?" *Canadian Intramural Recreation Association Bulletin* 6, no. 1, n.d, p. 3.
28. Fleming, pp. 104–5.
29. Tom Morganthan, "Trapped in a Blizzard at 8,300': Nine Die in Oregon Climb," *Newsweek*, 26 May 1986, p. 20.
30. Ibid.
31. William Plumber, "Step by Step a Routine Hike up Mount Hood Turns Into a Nightmare," *People* (June 1986), pp. 14–16.
32. Robert Sullivan, "The Search, Then Soul Searching," *Sports Illustrated* (26 May 1986), p. 16.
33. Plumber, p. 52.
34. David Roberts, "Reflections on Mount Hood," *Outside* (September 1986), p. 40.
35. *Morehouse College* v. *Russel* (1964), 136 S.E. (2d) 179.
36. *Dziwenka* v. *Mapplebeck.*
37. Ibid., p. 189.
38. David Godfrey-Smith, "Hiking Accidents," *Explore Alberta,* no. 2 (July, 1981).
39. *Weston* v. *London* [1941] 1 All E.R. 555.
40. *Brost* v. *Board of Trustees of Eastern Irrigation* [1955] 3 D.L.R. 159 (Alta. C.A.).
41. *McWilliam* v. *Thunder Bay Flying Club* [1950] O.W.N. 696 (Ont. H.C.).
42. *Boese* v. *Board of Education of St. Paul's Roman Catholic Separate School District No. 20* (Saskatoon).
43. *Thornton et al.* v. *Board of School Trustees of District No. 57 (Prince George)* [1976] 5 W.W.R. 240 (B.C.C.A.), pp. 265–66.
44. *Taylor* v. *R.*
45. *Smith* v. *Horizon Aero Sports Ltd. et al.* (1980), 130 D.L.R. (3d) 91 (B.C.S.C).
46. *Hedley Byrne Co. Ltd.* v. *Heller and Partners Ltd.*
47. "The Cairngorm Tragedy: A Report on the Fatal Accidents Enquiry," *Mountain*, no. 20, 1972.
48. Ibid., p. 2.
49. Ibid.

50. Ibid., p. 4.
51. *Lowry et al.* v. *Canadian Mountain Holidays Ltd. et al.* (1985), 33 C.C.L.T. 261 (B.C.S.C.).
52. *Lowry et al.* v. *Canadian Mountain Holidays Ltd. et al.* (1987), 40 C.C.L.T., (B.C.C.A.).
53. Canadian Mountain Holidays, *Heli-Skiing Handbook*, n.d., p. 5.
54. Ibid., pp. 265–66.
55. *Family Compensation Act*, R.S.B.C. 1969, c. 120.
56. *Lowry et al.* v. *Canadian Mountain Holidays Ltd. et al.* (1987), 40 C.C.L.T. 1 (B.C.C.A.), p. 261.
57. Ibid., p. 270.
58. Ibid., pp. 272–73.
59. Ibid.
60. Hans Gmoser, *Operators Manual,* produced by the Association of British Columbia Heli-Ski Operators in co-operation with the Government of B.C., Minister of Lands, Parks and Housing, Parks and Outdoor Recreation Division, n.d.
61. Ibid.
62. Ibid., p. 276.
63. Ibid., pp. 277–78.
64. Ibid.
65. Edward LaChapelle, *The ABC of Avalanche Safety* (North Vancouver: Douglas and McIntyre Ltd., 1978).
66. Ibid., Rule #2, p. 23.
67. Ibid., Rule #3.
68. Ibid., Rule #7.
69. *Lowry* v. *Canadian Mountain Holidays Ltd. et al.* (1985), p. 281.
70. *Sholtes* v. *Stranaghan* (1981), 8 A.C.W.S. (2d) 219 (B.C.S.C.).
71. Ibid., p. 219.
72. Ibid., p. 219.
73. Barrel, p. 274.
74. *Jeffery* v. *London County Council* (1954), 119 J.P. 43, p. 43.
75. *Carmarthenshire County Council* v. *Lewis* [1955] A.C. 559 (H.L.).
76. *Dziwenka* v. *Mapplebeck.*
77. Ibid., p. 36.
78. *Moddejonge* v. *Huron County Board of Education*, p. 437.
79. Percy, p. 594.
80. Megan Rosenfeld, "Outward Bound: Life and Death in the Wild, Lawsuits and Sorrow in the Aftermath," *The Washington Post* (23 November 1979), p. E1.
81. Ibid., p. E3.
82. *Gard* v. *Board of School Trustees of Duncan* (1946), 1 W.W.R. 305 (B.C.C.A.).
83. *Butt* v. *Cambridgeshire and Isle of Ely C.C.* (1969), 119 New L.J. 118.
84. *James* v. *River East School* (1975), 64 D.L.R. (3d) 338 (Man. C.A.).
85. *Dukes* v. *Vancouver* (4 December 1973), unreported case (B.C.S.C.).

86. *Michalak* v. *Dalhousie College and University, Governors of*, p. 381.
87. *Olsen* v. *Corry* [1936] 3 All E.R. 241 (K.B.D.).
88. Ibid., p. 438.
89. *Starr and McNulty* v. *Crone* [1950] 4 D.L.R. 433; 2 W.W.R. 560.
90. Ibid., p. 438.
91. *School Division of Assiniboine South No. 3* v. *Hoffer et al.* (1971), 21 D.L.R. (3d) 608.
92. Also stated in *Murray et al.* v. *Board of Education of the City of Belleville* [1943] 1 D.L.R. 494 (Ont. H. Ct.).
93. *School Division of Assiniboine South No. 3* v. *Hoffer et al.* (1971).
94. *Ryan et al.* v. *Hickson et al.*
95. Ibid., p. 196.
96. *McKay* v. *Board of Govan School et al.*, p. 592.
97. *Murray et al.* v. *Board of Education of the City of Belleville.*
98. Ibid., p. 495.
99. *McKay* v. *Board of Govan School et al.*, p. 589.
100. *Meyers et al.* v. *Peel County Board of Education* [1981] S.C.C.D. 3081-01.
101. *Meyers et al.* v. *Peel County Board of Education* (1981), unreported S.C.C. notes, p. 14.
102. *Smith* v. *Horizon Aero Sport Ltd. et al.* (1980), 130 D.L.R. (3a) 91 (B.C.S.C.).
103. Ibid., p. 102.
104. Ibid., p. 103.
105. Ibid., p. 102.
106. Ibid.
107. *Durham et al.* v. *Public School Board of Township School Area of North Oxford* (1960), 23 D.L.R. (2d) 719 (Ont. C.A.).
108. *Starr and McNulty* v. *Crone*, p. 563.
109. *Delaney et al.* v. *Cascade River Holidays Ltd. et al.* (1982), 34 B.C.L.R. 62 (B.C.S.C.); (1983) 24 C.C.L.T. 8.
110. Ibid., p. 67.
111. Ibid.
112. *Thornton et al.* v. *Board of School Trustees of District No. 57 (Prince George) et al.* [1976].
113. *Meyers et al.* v. *Peel County Board of Education* (1981), unreported S.C.C. case notes, p. 7.
114. *Michalak* v. *Dalhousie College and University, Governors of.*
115. Ibid., p. 381.
116. Ibid.
117. *Moddejonge* v. *Huron County Board of Education*, p. 437.
118. *Meyers et al.* v. *Peel County Board of Education* [1981] S.C.C.D. 3081-01.
119. Stanislas Dery, "Coroner's Report of Lake Temiscamingue Drownings," inquest held by the Province of Quebec, 28–29 June 1978.
120. Ibid., p. 12.
121. Ibid., pp. 12–14.
122. Ibid., p. 15.

123. H. Frazer and F. Wenger, "Report on the Twenty-two Foot Selkirk," sent to Quebec coroner; also in Canadian Recreation Canoe Association files, 30 September 1978.
124. Dery.
125. Terry Miller, "New Rafting Regulations Offer No Guarantees," *Action* 1, no. 4, p. 14.
126. Ralph Aldridge, "Certification: Is It the Answer," presented at the Calgary Area Outdoor Council Water Conference, 5 June 1988, Calgary, Alberta.
127. See Glenda Hanna, *Safety Oriented Guidelines for Outdoor Leadership and Programming* (Ottawa: CAPHER, 1986).

7 VICARIOUS LIABILITY

1. Brian Leroy, "The Legal Responsibilities of Individuals and Agencies Delivering Outdoor Education/Recreation Programs," in March et al., *The Legal Liability of Outdoor Educators in Alberta* (Calgary: Alberta Law Foundation, 1981), p. 30.
2. Atiyah, *Vicarious Liability*, p. 3.
3. *School Act*, R.S.A. 1970, c. 329, s. 65; *Education Act*, R.S.O. 1974, c. 109, s. 146.
4. *Occupiers' Liability Act*, R.S.A. 1973, c. 79; *Pook v. Ernesttown Public School Trustees* [1974] 4 D.L.R. 268.
5. *Meyers et al. v. Peel County Board of Education* [1981] S.C.C.D. 3081-01.
6. *Walton v. Vancouver*; *McKay v. Board of Govan School District No. 29*, 589, p. 592.
7. Atiyah, *Vicarious Liability*, p. 5.
8. *Smith v. Horizon Aero Sports Ltd. et al.* (1980), 130 D.L.R. (3d) 91.
9. Ibid., pp. 108–9.
10. Ibid., p. 110.
11. William March, "Assessing Outdoor Leaders," *Foothills Wilderness Journal*, n.d., pp. 16–17.
12. Wright et al., pp. 12–34.
13. *Rose v. Plenty* [1976] 1 W.W.R. 141, p. 147.
14. Fleming, p. 355.
15. Atiyah, *Vicarious Liability*.
16. Fleming.
17. Glanville Williams, "Vicarious Liability and the Master's Indemnity" (1957), 20 *Mod.L.Rev.* 220, p. 232.
18. Fleming.
19. Atiyah, *Vicarious Liability*.
20. James, *General Principles of Tort Law*, p. 357.
21. *Rheaume v. Gowland* (1978), 91 D.L.R. (3d) 223 (B.C.S.C.), p. 225.
22. Ibid.
23. James, *General Principles of Tort Law*.
24. *Morren v. Swinton and Pendlebury Council* [1965] 2 All E.R. 349, p. 351.
25. James, *General Principles of Tort Law*, p. 358.
26. *Market Investigations Ltd. v. Minister of Social Security* [1969] 2 Q.B.D. 173, p. 184.

27. *Mersey Dock and Harbour Board* v. *Coggins and Griffiths Ltd.* [1946] 2 All E.R. 345; [1947] A.C. 1.
28. Leroy, p. 34.
29. Ibid.
30. James, *General Principles of Tort Law*, p. 361.
31. *Poland* v. *John Parr and Sons* [1927] 1 K.B. 236, p. 240.
32. Leroy, p. 36.
33. Atiyah, *Vicarious Liability*, pp. 51–69.
34. Fleming, footnote 5, p. 365.
35. *C.P.R.* v. *Lockhart* [1942] A.C. 591 (P.C.).
36. Ibid.
37. *Beauparlant* v. *Appleby Separate School Board of Trustees* [1955] 4 D.L.R. 558 (Ont. H. Ct.).
38. Ibid., p. 444.
39. *Moddejonge* v. *Huron County Board of Education*.
40. Ibid., p. 444.
41. *Societies Act*, R.S.N.S 1967, c. 286; R.S.S. 1965, c. 142; R.S.B.C. 1979, c. 390.
42. Richard Moriarty et al., *Sport Activity and the Law* (Windsor: University of Windsor (SIR/CAR), 1982), p. 110.
43. Ibid., p. 111.
44. *Pawlak and Pawlak* v. *Doucette and Reinks* (1985), 2 W.W.R., p. 588.
45. Ibid., pp. 591–93.
46. Ibid., p. 594.
47. Ibid., p. 595.
48. Ibid.
49. Ibid., p. 596.
50. Ibid., p. 597.
51. Ibid.
52. Ibid., p. 603.

8 RISK MANAGEMENT

1. Emmett J. Vaughan and Curtis Elliot, *Fundamentals of Risk and Insurance,* Second Edition (Toronto: John Wiley and Sons, 1978), p. 7.
2. Ibid., p. 9.
3. Dan Meyer, "The Management of Risk," *Journal of Experimental Education* (Fall 1979), p. 10.
4. Ibid., p. 10.
5. Alan Hale, Director of the National Safety Network. Personal contact, Columbus, Ohio, 5 February 1987.
6. *National Safety Network Annual Review* (Belfontaine, Ohio: National Safety Network, 1987).
7. Ibid., p. 11.
8. Ibid., p. 4.
9. Ibid., p. 22.
10. Canadian Red Cross Society, Water Safety Branch, Alberta and North West Territories, *Drowning Statistics* (1985).

11. Canadian Red Cross, Water Safety Branch, Alberta and Northwest Territories, "Drowning Statistics Summary: 1985–1987," 1988.
12. Meyer, p. 10.
13. *National Safety Network Annual Review*, p. 13.
14. Dery.
15. Meyer, p. 10.
16. Paul Anhorn, N.R.C. in lecture in BCIT/NRC Avalanche Course, Mt. Assiniboine Lodge, 19 January 1986.
17. Ibid.
18. Godfrey-Smith.
19. *National Safety Network Annual Review*, p. 15.
20. Meyers.
21. *National Safety Network Annual Review*, p. 21.
22. Ibid., p. 19.
23. Ibid., pp. 23–24.
24. Meyers, p. 14.
25. Vaughan, pp. 10–11.
26. Ibid.
27. Ibid., p. 11.
28. Ibid., pp. 11–12.
29. Betty van der Smissen, "Releases, Waivers and Agreements to Participate," *National Safety Network* (March 1985), p. 1.
30. Alan Wood, "Insurance and Outdoor Programming: The Insurers Perspective," presented at the Calgary Area Outdoor Council Symposium on Legal Liability and Risk Management, Calgary, Alberta, October, 1986.
31. *Dyck* v. *Manitoba Snowmobile Association Inc. and Wood* [1985] 32 C.C.L.T. 153 (S.C.C.)
32. Jewers, p. 54; *Butterfield* v. *Sibbit and Nipissing Electric Co.* [1950] 4 D.L.R. 302 (Ont. H. Ct.).
33. R. Kaiser, "Personal Liability Waivers: Do They Protect the Agency and Staff?" *JOPERD* (August 1984), pp. 55A-C.
34. Fitness and Amateur Sport, Final Report of the Commission on the Insurance Crisis Facing Canada's National Sport and Recreation Associations, Ottawa (October, 1986), p. 67.
35. Ibid., p. 74.
36. Janna Rankin, "Waivers," *Camping Magazine* (January 1986), p. 25.
37. Ibid.
38. Fitness and Amateur Sport, p. 66.
39. *Wilson* v. *Blue Mountain Resorts Ltd.* (1974), 48 D.L.R. (3d) 161 (Ont. H. Ct.).
40. *Saari* v. *Sunshine Riding Academy Ltd.* (1967), 65 D.L.R. (2d) 92 (Man. Q.B.)
41. *Crocker* v. *Sundance Northwest Resorts Ltd.*, June 1988, Supreme Court of Canada case report.
42. Fitness and Amateur Sport, p. 71.

43. Alan Ewert and Timothy Boone, "Risk Management Planning: Defusing the Dragon," *Journal of Experiential Education* (Winter 1987).
44. Fitness and Amateur Sport, p. 71.
45. *Dyck v. Manitoba Snowmobile Association et al.*
46. van der Smissen, "Releases, Waivers and Agreements," p. 32 and p. 1.
47. Fitness and Amateur Sport, p. 71.
48. *Delaney et al. v. Cascade River Holidays Ltd. et al.* (1982), 34 B.C.L.R. 62 (B.C.S.C.); (1983), 24 C.C.L.T. 8 (B.C.C.A.); *Dyck v. Manitoba Snowmobile Association Inc. and Wood.*
49. *Lowry et al. v. Canadian Mountain Holidays et al.* (1987), 40 C.C.L.T. 1 (B.C.C.A.); *Smith v. Horizon Aero Sports Ltd. et al.* (1981), 130 D.L.R. (3d) 91 (B.C.S.C.).
50. Fitness and Amateur Sport, p. 73.
51. Ibid., p. 44.
52. *Dyck v. Manitoba Snowmobile Association Inc. and Wood.*

9 INSURANCE

1. Ron Payment, Exec. Director CSA, in correspondence to CSA Board of Directors, 27 January 1986.
2. Barbara Henkar, "The Fear of Chute Suits," *Alberta Report* (24 February 1986), p. 54.
3. Paul Conrad, Alberta Sport Council, personal interview, Edmonton, Alberta, 27 April 1988.
4. Fay Orr, "The Insurance Crisis," *Alberta Report* (2 December 1985), p. 15.
5. Ibid.
6. J. Lyndon, "The Courts and the Insurance Crisis: How the judicial bubble burst in Canada," *Canadian Insurance* (February 1986), p. 22.
7. Phillip Kane, "1986 Forecast: results improving but liability problems still loom," *Canadian Insurance* (February 1986), p. 20.
8. *McErlean v. Sarel and the City of Brampton* (1985), 32 C.C.L.T. (Ont. S.C.) 199; (1988), 42 C.C.L.T. (Ont. C.A.) 78.
9. Belton, "1986 Forecast," *Canadian Insurance*, p. 20.
10. Fitness and Amateur Sport, p. 22.
11. Ibid., pp. 24–26.
12. Ibid., pp. 27–29.
13. Conrad.
14. *Smith v. Horizon Aero Sports Ltd. et al.* (1981), 130 D.L.R. (3d) 91 (B.C.S.C.).
15. Fitness and Amateur Sport, p. 37.
16. Ibid., p. 44.
17. Ibid., p. 32 and pp. 42–43.
18. Lyndon, p. 23.
19. George J. Church, "Sorry, Your Policy Is Cancelled," *Time* (24 March 1986), p. 30.
20. Fitness and Amateur Sport, p. 48.

21. Ibid., p. 49.
22. Ibid., p. 50.
23. Ibid.
24. Ibid., pp. 51–52.
25. Conrad.
26. Fitness and Amateur Sport, p. 52.
27. Fleming, p. 340.
28. Vaughan, pp. 427–28.
29. Ed Schirick, "Buying Insurance Wisely: Some Tips on How to Obtain the Best Results for Your Camp," *Camping Magazine* (January 1986), p. 15.
30. Fitness and Amateur Sport, p. 34.
31. *Canadian and British Insurance Companies Act,* R.S.C. 1970, c. 1–15.
32. Robert Riegel, J. Miller, and C.A. Williams, Jr., *Insurance Principles and Practices: Property and Liability,* Sixth Edition (Englewood Cliffs: Prentice Hall Inc., 1976), pp. 9–11.
33. Francis Tierney and Paul Braithwaite, *Effective Insurance: A Guide for Buyer and Seller* (Toronto: Butterworths, 1984), p. 294.
34. Mark R. Greene, *Risk and Insurance* (Cincinnati: Southwestern Publishing Co., 1977), pp. 52–83.
35. Tierney, pp. 168–73.
36. Henkar, p. 54.
37. Greene, p. 319.
38. Christopher Morgan and T. B. Anderson, "The New Commercial General Liability Policy: Not just a rose by any other name," *Canadian Insurance* (February 1986), p. 25.
39. Ibid.
40. Tierney.
41. Ibid., pp. 212–18.
42. Ibid., pp. 221–22.
43. Ibid., pp. 241–42.

10 MOTOR VEHICLE LIABILITY

1. *Baldwin* v. *Lyons et al.* [1963] 36 D.L.R. 244 (S.C.C.).
2. *Tyler* v. *Board of Ardath* [1935] 2 D.L.R. 814.
3. Ibid., pp. 814–15.
4. John Barnes, "Tort Liability of School Boards to Pupils," in Klar, *Studies in Canadian Tort Law* (Toronto: Butterworths, 1977), p. 206.
5. Richard Whitehouse, Manager of Risk Management of the Government of Alberta, personal interview, Edmonton, 14 September 1982.
6. Donald E. Arnold, "Legal Aspects of Off-Campus Physical Education Programs," *Journal of Physical Education and Recreation* (April 1979), p. 22.
7. Patricia McNulty, "Legal Liability in Physical Education and Recreation," *Canadian Coach* 6, no. 3 (1975), p. 8.
8. Tierney and Braithwaite, pp. 232–33.
9. Ibid., p. 232.

10. Ibid.
11. Dwight Daigneault, "Teachers and Liability," *The Forum*, Ontario Secondary School Teachers' Federation (May-June 1978).
12. *Highway Traffic Act*, R.S.A. 1975, (2) c. 56, s. 160.
13. Fleming, p. 439.
14. Linden, *Canadian Negligence Law*, p. 574.
15. *Oulette v. Johnson* [1963] S.C.R. 96.
16. Ibid., p. 100.
17. *Teasdale v. MacIntyre* [1968] S.C.R. 735.
18. Ibid., pp. 740–41.

II RESCUE AND EMERGENCY SITUATIONS

1. Allen M. Linden, "Rescuers and Good Samaritans," *Alta. Law Review* 10 (1971), p. 90.
2. *Canada Shipping Act*, R.S.C. 1952, c. 29.
3. Ibid., s. 526 (1).
4. Fleming, p. 146; adopted in *Matthews et al. v. MacLaren et al.* and *Horsley et al. v. MacLaren et al.* (1969), 2 O.R. 137, p. 143.
5. Linden, "Rescuers and Good Samaritans," p. 90, from Bohen, "The Moral Duty to Aid Others as a Basis of Tort Liability" (1908), 56 *U. Pa. Law Rev.*, p. 217.
6. Wright et al., pp. 8–26.
7. Ibid.
8. Linden, *Canadian Negligence Law*, p. 301.
9. *Matthews et al. v. MacLaren et al.* and *Horsley et al. v. MacLaren et al.* (1969), 2 O.R., 137, p. 144.
10. Ibid., p. 137.
11. Ibid., p. 146.
12. Ibid., pp. 145–46.
13. *Horsley et al. v. MacLaren et al.* (1972), 22 D.L.R. (3d) 545 (S.C.C.), p. 545.
14. Proceedings from the Public Inquiry into the death of M.L. Williams, held 14 April 1975, Edmonton, Alberta.
15. Ibid., per Ronald Kirstein, pp. 61–64.
16. Ibid., p. 70.
17. Linden, "Rescuers and Good Samaritans," p. 89.
18. Fleming, p. 135.
19. *Smith v. Rae* (1919), 46 O.L.R. 518.
20. *Gautret v. Egerton* (1867), L.R. C.P. 371.
21. Fleming, footnote 61, p. 135.
22. *Emergency Medical Aid Act*, R.S.A. 1970, c. 122, s. 3; 1975 (2), c. 26, s. 82 (2b).
23. *An Act Respecting Emergency Medical Aid*, R.S.S. 1976, c. 17, s. 3.
24. *Volunteer Services Act*, S.N.S. 1977, c. 20, s. 3.
25. *Emergency Medical Aid Act*, s. 31.

26. *East Suffolk Rivers Catchment Board* v. *Kent et al.* [1941] A.C. 74.
27. Ibid., p. 102.
28. Fleming, pp. 135–36.
29. *Horsley et al.* v. *MacLaren et al.* (1972).
30. *Horsley et al.* v. *MacLaren et al.* [1970] 2 O.R. 487, p. 500.
31. Ibid., p. 502.
32. *Horsley et al.* v. *MacLaren et al.* (1972).
33. Linden, *Canadian Tort Law*, p. 344.
34. *Seymour* v. *Winnipeg Electric Railway* (1910), 13 W.L.R. 566.
35. Ibid., p. 568.
36. Linden, p. 99.
37. *Wagner* v. *International Railway Co.* (1921), 133 N.E. 437.
38. *Moddejonge* v. *Huron County Board of Education* (1972).
39. Ibid., p. 444.
40. Linden, "Rescuers and Good Samaritans," p. 101.
41. Barry J. in *Baker* v. *Hopkins* [1958] 3 All E.R. 147, p. 153.
42. Linden, *Canadian Tort Law*, p. 339.
43. Ibid., p. 293.
44. *Wagner* v. *International Railway Co.*
45. *Ould* v. *Butler's Wharf* [1953] 2 L.R. 44.
46. Ibid., p. 46.
47. Fleming, pp. 156–57.
48. *Brandon et al.* v. *Osborne, Garrett and Co.* [1924] 1 K.B. 548.
49. Ibid., p. 552.
50. *Horsley et al.* v. *MacLaren et al.* (1972), p. 548.
51. Ibid.
52. *Horsley et al.* v. *MacLaren et al.* [1970].
53. Linden, *Canadian Negligence Law*, p. 378.
54. Ibid., p. 296.
55. *Moddejonge* v. *Huron County Board of Education.*
56. Ibid., p. 444.

12 DEFENDING AGAINST CLAIMS OF NEGLIGENCE

1. Fleming, p. 95.
2. *Scoffield et al.* v. *Public School Board No. 20 North York* [1942] O.W.N. 458 (Ont. C.A.).
3. Ibid., p. 458.
4. *Pearson* v. *Vancouver Board of School Trustees et al.* [1941] 3 W.W.R. 874 (B.C.S.C.), p. 876.
5. Barbara Brown, "Risk Recreation—A Challenge for Municipal Departments," *Recreation Canada* 5, no. 36 (1978), p. 67.
6. *Sholtes* v. *Stranaghan et al.* (1981), 8 A.C.W.S. (2d) 219 (B.C.C.A.).
7. Ibid., p. 219.
8. Ibid., p. 220.
9. Betty van der Smissen, "Minimizing Legal Liability Risks," *Journal of Experiential Education* 2, no. 1 (1979).

10. *Lowry et al.* v. *Canadian Mountain Holidays Ltd. et al.* (1987), 40 C.C.L.T. 1 (B.C.C.A).
11. *Michalak* v. *Dalhousie College and University, Governors of.*
12. Ibid.
13. Wright et al., pp. 10–19.
14. Linden, *Canadian Tort Law*, p. 367.
15. Mors Kochanski, Freelance Outdoor Educator, personal interview, 6 May 1984, Edmonton, Alberta.
16. Kalef, p. 1.
17. *Pawlak and Pawlak* v. *Doucette and Reinks*, p. 603.
18. *Harrison* v. *Toronto Motor Car et al.*, p. 9.
19. Kalef, p. 8.
20. *Dodd et al.* v. *Cook et al.* (1956), 4 D.L.R. (2d) 43 (Ont. H. Ct.).
21. Ibid., p. 57.
22. *Siddal* v. *Corporation of District of Oak Bay* [1980] B.C.D. Civ. 3374-09.
23. Kalef, footnote 50, p. 14.
24. *Fink* v. *Greeniaus* (1973), 43 D.L.R. (3d) 485.
25. Ibid., p. 496.
26. Ibid.
27. *Lowry et al.* v. *Canadian Mountain Holidays Ltd. et al.* (1987).
28. *Turanec* v. *Ross* (1980), 21 B.C.L.R. 198 (B.C.S.C.).
29. Ibid., pp. 201–2.
30. Ibid., pp. 202–3.
31. Kalef, p. 15.
32. Betty van der Smissen, "Legal Liability," *Coaching Women's Athletics* 5, no. 1 (January–February 1979), p. 50.
33. *Sholtes* v. *Stranaghan et al.*, p. 219.
34. van der Smissen, "Minimizing Legal Liability Risks."
35. *Tomlinson* v. *Manchester Corporation* (1947), 111 J.P. 503.
36. Ibid.
37. *Butterworth* v. *Collegiate Institute Board of Etobicoke* (1940), D.L.R. 466 (Ont. C.A.).
38. Ibid., p. 472.
39. Ibid., pp. 472–73.
40. *Meyers et al.* v. *Peel County Board of Education* [1981] S.C.C.D. 3081.
41. *Meyers et al.* v. *Peel County Board of Education* [1977] 2 C.C.L.T. 269 (Ont. H. Ct.), p. 289.
42. *Sholtes* v. *Stranaghan et al.*
43. *Crocker* v. *Sundance Northwest Resorts Ltd.* (1985), 33 C.C.L.T. 73 (Ont. S.C.).
44. Ibid., p. 74.
45. Ibid., p. 75.
46. Ibid., p. 90.
47. Ibid., June 1988; Supreme Court of Canada case report, p. 15.
48. Ibid., p. 15.
49. Ibid., p. 16.

50. Ibid., p. 19.
51. *Gilbert v. Lamont* (1981), 29 Nfld. and P.E.I. R. 258 (P.E.I.S.C.).
52. Ibid., p. 258.
53. *Ainge v. Siemon* [1971] 3 O.R. 119 (Ont. H. Ct.).
54. *Piszel v. Board of Education of Etobicoke* (1977), 16 O.R. (2d) 22 (Ont. H. Ct.).
55. Ibid.
56. *Delaney et al. v. Cascade River Holidays Ltd. et al.* (1982), 34 B.C.L.R. 62.
57. Ibid., p. 67.
58. *M'Alister (or Donoghue) v. Stevenson* [1932] A.C. 532 (H.L.).
59. Rankin, "Waivers," p. 24.
60. Kalef.
61. Percy, p. 745.
62. Fleming, p. 266.
63. *Crocker v. Sundance Northwest Resorts Ltd.* (June 1988).
64. *Wilson v. Blue Mountain Resorts Ltd.* (1975), 49 D.L.R. (3d) 161 (Ont. H. Ct.).
65. Ibid., p. 350.
66. *Sturdy et al. v. R.* (1974), 47 D.L.R. (3d) 71.
67. Ibid., p. 98.
68. *Saari v. Sunshine Riding Academy Ltd.*
69. Ibid., p. 100.
70. *Smith v. Horizon Aero Sport Ltd. et al.* (1981), 130 D.L.R. (3d) 91.
71. *Delaney et al. v. Cascade River Holidays Ltd. et al.* (1982).
72. Ibid., p. 65.
73. *Dyck v. Manitoba Snowmobile Association Inc. and Wood.*
74. Ibid.
75. *Dyck v. Manitoba Snowmobile Association Inc. and Wood*, p. 321.
76. Ibid., p. 322.
77. Ibid.
78. Ibid., p. 320.
79. *Crocker v. Sundance Northwest Resorts Ltd.* (June 1988).
80. Ibid., p. 20.
81. Prosser, p. 417.
82. *Nance v. British Columbia Electric Railway*, p. 611.
83. Charlesworth, p. 718.
84. Ibid., p. 719.
85. Fleming, p. 258.
86. Ibid., p. 259.
87. *Negligence Act*, R.S.O. 1970, c. 296, s. 4–5.
88. *Henricks et al. v. R.* [1969] 9 D.L.R. (3d) 454.
89. *Crown Liability Act* 1952–53, (Can.) c. 30.
90. *Henricks et al. v. R.*, p. 454.
91. *Tortfeasors and Contributory Negligence Act*, R.S.M. 1954, c. 266.
92. *Henricks et al. v. R.*, p. 472.
93. Ibid., p. 473.

94. *Holomis* v. *Dubuc* [1975] 56 D.L.R. (3rd) 351.
95. Ibid., p. 351.
96. Charlesworth, p. 723. See also *Hicks* v. *British Transport Commission* [1958] 1 W.L.R. 493.
97. *Crocker* v. *Sundance Northwest Resorts Ltd.* (June 1988).
98. *Pawlak and Pawlak* v. *Doucette and Reinks.*
99. *McEllistrum* v. *Etches* (1956), 6 D.L.R. (2d) 1, pp. 6–7.
100. *Meyer et al.* v. *Peel County Board of Education* [1981].
101. *Ryan et al.* v. *Hickson et al.*
102. Ibid., p. 196.
103. *McErlean* v. *Sarel and the City of Brampton* (1988), 42 C.C.L.T. 78 (Ont. C.A.).
104. *Limitations of Actions Act*, R.S.N.S. 1967, c. 168; R.S.A. 1970, c. 209.
105. *Municipal Government Act*, R.S.A. 1970, c. 246, s. 385.
106. Ibid., s. 385 (1).
107. Ibid., s. 385 (2).
108. *School Act*, R.S.S. 1965, c. 184.
109. *Levine et al.* v. *Board of Education of Toronto* [1933] O.W.N. 238.
110. *Public Authorities Protection Act*, R.S.O. 1970, c. 374.
111. *Crown Liability Act*, R.S.C. 1970, c. C38.
112. *Poland* v. *John Parr and Sons*, p. 240.
113. Atiyah, *Vicarious Liability*, pp. 51–69.
114. *Beauparlant* v. *Appleby Separate School Board of Trustees.*
115. Ibid., p. 240.
116. Glassford et al.
117. Ibid., p. 6.
118. Tierney and Braithwaite, p. 256.
119. Jean Davies, "Crisis Management: Case Studies Suggest Ways to Deal with Serious Problems," *Camping Magazine* (May 1984), pp. 28–29.
120. Jean Davies, "Handling a Camping Death," *Camping Magazine* (January 1986), pp. 32–35.
121. *Rudko et al.* v. *R.*
122. Donald E. Vinson, "Making a Rational Decision to Settle Out of Court," *Risk Management* 31, no. 5 (May 1984), p. 40.
123. Ibid., p. 5.
124. David Manning, "Damages: Canadian Eh?," *Recreation Alberta* 6, no. 6 (November/December 1987), p. 16.

ABBREVIATIONS OF COURT TITLES

C.A.—Court of Appeal (England)
H.L.—House of Lords (England)
Ex. Ct.—Exchequer Court (England)
K.B.D.—King's Bench Division
Q.B.D.—Queen's Bench Division
S.C.C.—Supreme Court of Canada
Alta. C.A.—Alberta Court of Appeal
B.C.C.A.—British Columbia Court of Appeal
B.C.S.C.—British Columbia Supreme Court
Man. C.A.—Manitoba Court of Appeal
Man. Q.B.—Manitoba Queen's Bench
N.S.C.A.—Nova Scotia Court of Appeal
Ont. C.A.—Ontario Court of Appeal
Ont. S.C.—Ontario Supreme Court
Ont. H. Ct.—Ontario High Court
P.E.I.S.C.—Prince Edward Island Supreme Court
Sask. Q.B.—Saskatchewan Queen's Bench
H. Ct. Aust.—High Court of Australia

BIBLIOGRAPHY

Books

Ahola, S.I. *The Social Psychology of Leisure and Recreation*. Dubuque, Iowa: W.M.C. Brown Publishing Co., 1980.

American Law Institute. *Restatement of the Law of Torts*. Second Edition. St. Paul: American Law Institute Publishers, 1964.

Atiyah, P.S. *Vicarious Liability*. London: Butterworth, 1967.

———. *Accidents Compensation and the Law*. London: Weidenfeld and Nicolson, 1987.

Barnes, J., R. Brown, J. Dewer and R. Moriarty. *Canadian-American Sports, Torts and Courts*. Ottawa: Canadian Association For Health, Physical Education and Recreation, 1982.

Barrell, G.R. *Teachers and the Law*. Fifth Edition. London: Methuen and Co. Ltd., 1978.

Black, H.C. *Black's Law Dictionary*. Fifth Edition. St. Paul: West's Publishing Co., 1979.

Christie, I., editor. *Legal Writing and Research Manual*. Toronto: Butterworth, 1970.

Darst, P.W., and G.P. Armstrong. *Outdoor Adventure Activities for School and Recreation Programs*. Minneapolis: Burgess Publishing Co., 1980.

Fleming, J.G. *The Law of Torts*. Seventh Edition. Sydney: The Law Book Co., 1987.

Gall, G. *The Canadian Legal System*. Second Edition. Toronto: Carswell Co., Ltd., 1983.

Greene, M. *Risk and Insurance*. Cincinnati: Southwestern Publishing Co., 1977.

James, P.S. with P.L. Brown. *General Principles of the Law of Torts*. Fourth Edition. London: Butterworths, 1978.

James, P.S. *Introduction to English Law*. Tenth Edition. London: Butterworth, 1979.

Klar, L., editor. *Studies in Canadian Tort Law*. Toronto: Butterworths, 1979.

237

Kraus, R. *Recreation and Leisure in Modern Society*. Third Edition. Glenview, Ill.: Foresman and Co., 1984.

LaChapelle, E.R. *The ABC of Avalanche Safety*. North Vancouver: Douglas and McIntyre, Ltd., 1978.

Linden, A.M. *Canadian Tort Law*. Fourth Edition. Toronto: Butterworths, 1988.

———. *Canadian Negligence Law*. Third Edition. Toronto: Butterworths, 1982.

McDonald, M. *Legal First Aid*. Toronto: Coles Publishing Co., 1978.

Moriarty, R. et al. *Sport Activity and the Law*. Windsor: University of Windsor (SIR/CAR), 1982.

Naisbitt, J. *Megatrends*. New York: Warner Books, 1984.

National Coaching Development Program, Alberta Plan. *Level One Theory Coaches Manual*. Alberta Recreation, Parks and Wildlife, n.d.

Percy, R.A. *Charlesworth on Negligence*. Sixth Edition. London: Sweet and Maxwell, 1977.

Phillips, O.H. *A First Book of English Law*. Seventh Edition. London: Sweet and Maxwell, 1977.

Prosser, W.L. *Handbook of the Law of Torts*. Fourth Edition. St. Paul: West's Publishing Co., 1971.

Riegel, R., J. S. Miller and C.A. Williams, Jr. *Insurance Principles and Practices: Property and Liability*. Sixth Edition. Englewood Cliffs: Prentice Hall Inc., 1976.

Roose, N. *Government Risk Management Manual*. Tucson: Risk Management Publishing Co., n.d.

Saunders, J.B. *Mozley and Whiteley's Law Dictionary*. Ninth Edition. London: Butterworth, 1977.

Spetz, S. *Can I Sue? An Introduction to Canadian Tort Law*. Toronto: Pitman Publishing Co., 1974.

Thomas, S. Compiler. *Adventure Education: A Bibliography*. Amherst, N.Y.: Institute on Classroom Management and School Discipline, State University of New York at Buffalo, 1977.

Tierney, F. and P. Braithwaite. *Effective Insurance: A Guide for Buyer and Seller*. Toronto: Butterworths, 1984.

Vasan, R.S. Editor. *Canadian Law Dictionary*. Toronto: Law and Business Publications of Canada Ltd., 1980.

Vaughan, J. and C. Elliot. *Fundamentals of Risk and Insurance*. Second Edition. Toronto: John Wiley and Sons, 1978.

Walker, R.J. and M.G. Walker. *The English Legal System*. Third Edition. London: Butterworth, 1972.

Walker, R.J. *The English Legal System*. Fourth Edition. London: Butterworth, 1976.

Wright, C.A., A.M. Linden and L. Klar. *Canadian Tort Law Cases, Notes and Materials*. Nineth Edition. Toronto: Butterworths, 1990.

Articles

Arnold, D. "Legal Aspects of Off-Campus Physical Education Programs." *Journal of Physical Education and Recreation* (April 1979), p. 22.

Barnes, J. "Tort Liability of School Boards to Pupils." In Klar, *Studies in Canadian Tort Law* (Toronto: Butterworths, 1977), pp. 21–34.

Belton, E. "1986 Forecast." *Canadian Insurance*, p. 20.

Bernstein, C. "Legal-Ease." *The Calgary Herald*, 14 July 1980, p. A-20.

Bird, S. "Park Managers Beware." *Recreation Canada* (June 1980), pp. 32–33.

Bohlen, F. "The Moral Duty to Aid Others As a Basis of Tort Liability." (1908) 56 *U.Pa.L.Rev.* 217.

Booth, B.F. and J. Barnes. "Legal Constraints and Innovative Sports Programs For Children." *Recreation Research Review* 7, no. 1 (June 1979), pp. 49–56.

Brown, B. "Risk Recreation—A Challenge For Municipal Departments." *Recreation Canada* 5, no. 36 (1978), pp. 64–68.

Budd, M. "The Risk Factor in Outdoor Pursuits." *Canadian Camping* 33, no. 6 (Winter 1982), pp. 11–12.

Caden, C. "Risk Management Insurance." *Camping Magazine* (May 1980), pp. 15–19.

"The Cairngorm Tragedy: A Report on the Fatal Accidents Enquiry." *Mountain*, no. 20 (1972).

Church, G.J. "Sorry, Your Policy Is Cancelled." *Time* (24 March 1986), pp. 16–30.

Daigneault, D. "Teachers and Liability." *The Forum*, Ontario Secondary School Teachers' Federation (May-June 1978).

Davies, J. "Crisis Management: Case Studies Suggest Ways to Deal with Serious Problems." *Camping Magazine* (May 1984), pp. 28–32.

———. "Handling a Camp Death." *Camping Magazine* (January 1986), pp. 32–35.

Dunn, D. and J. Gulbis. "The Risk Revolution." *Parks and Recreation* (August 1976), p. 16.

Ewert, A. "Outdoor Adventure Activity Programs: A New Dimension." *JOPERD* (May/June 1986), pp. 56–60.

Ewert, A. and T. Boone. "Risk Management Planning: Defusing the Dragon." *Journal of Experiential Education* (Winter 1987).

Frakt, A.N. "Adventure Programming and Legal Liability." *Journal of Physical Education and Recreation* 49, no. 4 (April 1978), pp. 25–27.

Gest, T. and C.P. Work. "Sky High Damage Suits: the impact on consumers, businessmen, and professionals." *U.S. News and World Report* (27 January 1986), pp. 35–43.

Gibson, D. "The Federal Enclave Fallacy in Canadian Constitutional Law." *Alberta Law Review* 14, n.d., p. 167.

Godfrey-Smith, D. "Hiking Accidents." *Explore Alberta*, no. 2 (July 1981).

Harris, E.C. "Some Trends in the Law of Occupiers' Liability." (1963), 41 *Can. Bar Rev.* 401.

Henkar, B. "The Fear of Chute Suits." *Alberta Report* (24 February 1986), p. 54.

Hopkins, D. "Changes in Self Concept as the Result of Adventure Training." *Canadian Association of Health, Physical Education, and Recreation Journal* 48, no. 6 (July-August 1982), pp. 8–10.

Jewers, G.O. "Damages Suffered by Children—The Standard of Care Owed Children." In *Isaac Pitblado Lectures on Continuing Legal Education, The Law and the Minor*. Manitoba Bar Association, 1970.

Kaiser, R. "Personal Liability Waivers: Do They Protect the Agency and Staff?" *JOPERD* (August, 1984), pp. 55A-C.

Kane, P. "1986 Forecast: results improving but liability problems still loom." *Canadian Insurance* (February 1986), pp. 20–21.

Koehler, R.W. "Legal Aspects of Activity, Especially Physical Education and Athletics." In *Proceedings From International Congress of Physical Activity Sciences*, Quebec, July 1976, Book 9.

Linden, A.M. "Rescuers and Good Samaritans." *Alberta Law Review* 10 (1971), p. 90.

Loft, B.J. "Legal Liability." In C.P. Yost (Editor), *Accident Prevention and Injury Control in Physical Education, Athletics and Recreation*, AAHPER, n.d., pp. 73–75.

Lyndon, J. "The Courts and the Insurance Crisis: How the judicial bubble burst in Canada." *Canadian Insurance* (February 1986), pp. 22–24.

Manning, D. "Damages: Canadian Eh?" *Recreation Alberta* 6, no. 6 (November/December 1987), p. 16.

March, W. "Assessing Outdoor Leaders." *Foothills Wilderness Journal*, n.d., pp. 17–19.

_____. "Outdoor Pursuits: What Are the Legal Implications?" *Canadian Intramural Recreation Association Bulletin* 6, no. 1, p. 1.

McLellan, "The Future of Outdoor Recreation: What the Trends Tell Us." *Parks and Recreation* 21, no. 5 (1986).

McNulty, P. "Legal Liability in Physical Education and Recreation." *Canadian Coach* 6, no. 3 (1975), p. 8.

Meier, J.F. "Is the Risk Worth Taking?" *Journal of Physical Education and Recreation* 49, no. 4 (April 1978).

Meyer, D. "The Management of Risk." *Journal of Experimental Education* (Fall 1979), pp. 10–12.

Miller, T. "New Rafting Regulations Offer No Guarantees." *Action* 1, no. 4 (1987), p. 14.

Morgan, C. and T.B. Anderson. "The New Commercial General Library Policy: not just a rose by any other name." *Canadian Insurance* (February 1986), pp. 25–26.

Morganthan, T. "Trapped in a Blizzard at 8,300': Nine Die in Oregon Climb." *Newsweek* (26 May 1986), p. 20.

Morse, P.S. "Infant Settlements." In *Isaac Pitblado Lectures on Continuing Legal Education, 1970, The Law and the Minor*, Manitoba Bar Association.

Orr, F. "The Insurance Crisis." *Alberta Report* (2 December 1985), pp. 14–20.

O'Sullivan, J.F. "Infants and Contributory Negligence." In *Isaac Pitblado Lectures on Continuing Legal Education, 1970, The Law and the Minor*, pp. 38–39.

Plumber, W. "Step by Step a Routine Hike up Mount Hood Turns into a Nightmare." *People* (June 1986), pp. 14–16.

Priest, S. "Redefining Outdoor Education: A Matter of Many Relationships." *Journal of Environmental Education* 17, no. 3 (Spring 1986), pp. 13–15.

Rankin, J.S. "Legal Risks and Bold Programming." *Parks and Recreation* 12 (July 1977), pp. 47–48 and 67–68.

———. "The Legal System as a Proponent of Bold Programming." *Journal of Physical Education and Recreation* 49, no. 4 (April 1978), pp. 28–29.

———. "Waivers." *Camping Magazine* (January 1986), pp. 24–26.

Robbins, M.P. "Duty of Care." *Ontario Education* (March 1976), pp. 8–13.

Roberts, D. "Reflections on Mount Hood." *Outside* (September 1986), pp. 39–41.

Rogers, D.H. "The Increasing Standard of Care For Teachers." *Education Canada* (Spring 1980), pp. 26–27.

Rosenfeld, M. "Outward Bound: Life and Death in the Wild, Lawsuits and Sorrow in the Aftermath." *The Washington Post* (23 November 1979), p. E1.

Schirick, E. "Buying Insurance Wisely: Some Tips on How to Obtain the Best Results for Your Camp." *Camping Magazine* (January 1986), pp. 14–15.

Shulman, H. "The Standard of Care Required For Children." (1927–28) 37 *Yale Law Journal* 618.

Smith, M.L., R. Gabriel, J. Schott and W.L. Padua. "Evaluation of the Effects of Outward Bound." *Evaluation Studies Annual Review* 1 (1976).

Sullivan, R. "The Search, Then Soul Searching." *Sports Illustrated* (26 May 1986), p. 16.

Toft, M. "Where is Leadership Certification Going?" *Foothills Wilderness Journal* (January-March 1979), p. 13.

van der Smissen, B. "Legal Aspects of Adventure Activities." *Journal of Outdoor Education* 10 (1975), p. 12.

———. "Legal Liability." *Coaching Women's Athletics* 5, no. 1 (January-February 1979), p. 50.

———. "Minimizing Legal Liability Risks." *Journal of Experiential Education* 2, no. 1 (1979).

———. "Releases, Waivers and Agreements to Participate." *National Safety Network* (March 1985), pp. 1–3.

———. "Where is Legal Liability Heading?" *Parks and Recreation* 15, no. 5 (May 1980), pp. 51–52.

Vester, H-G. "Adventure as a Form of Leisure." *Leisure Studies* 6 (1987), pp. 237–49.

Vinson, D.E. "Making a Rational Decision to Settle Out of Court." *Risk Management* 31, no. 5 (May 1984), pp. 40–42.

Williams, G. "Vicarious Liability and the Master's Indemnity." (1957) 20 *Modern Law Review*, pp. 220–33.

Wiltens, James. "High Touch Wilderness and High Tech Campers." *Camping Magazine* (May 1986), pp. 22–29.

Wright, A.N. "Youth Development through Adventure Programs." *Camping Magazine* (September-October 1983), pp. 24–30.

Unpublished Materials

Aldridge, R. "Certification: Is It the Answer?" Presented at the Calgary Area Outdoor Council Water Conference, 5 June 1988, Calgary, Alberta.

Backiel, M.L. "Comparative Study of Attitudes Toward the Meaning of the Term Outdoor Education as Viewed by Selected Members of AAHPER's Council on Outdoor Education in 1968 and 1975." Master of Science Thesis, Sir George Williams College, 1976.

Bell, R. and Associates Ltd. "Insurance Report for Members of the Alberta Camping Association." 12 January 1981.

Bird, S. "Tort Liability of Recreation Activities in Canada." Master of Arts Thesis, University of Waterloo, 1979.

Bresnehan, B. "Legal Liability and Protection in the Junior Forest Warden Program." Script from Slide-Tape Presentation.

Canadian Red Cross Society, Water Safety Branch, Alberta and Northwest Territories, "Drowning Statistics Summary: 1985–87," 1988.

Dery, S. "Coroner's Report of Lake Témiscamingue Drownings." Inquest held by the Province of Quebec, 28–29 June 1978.

Frazer, H. and F. Wenger. "Report on the Twenty-two Foot Selkirk." Sent to Quebec coroner; also in CRCA files, 30 September 1978.

Gibson, W.G. "Evaluation of Outdoor Education Using Guttman Scales and Sociometric Analysis." Master of Arts Thesis, University of Alberta, 1966.

Grant, R. "A Juvenile Wilderness Corrections Program Assessment." Master of Arts Thesis, University of Alberta, 1979.

Hanna (nee Wuyda), G.M. "The Legal Liability of Outdoor Educators in Canada." Paper presented at the CAHPER Conference, Victoria, 12 June 1981.

Hanna (nee Wuyda), G.M., A.G. Gilmet and H.A. Scott. "Leadership Qualification Versus Certification in Outdoor Education in Canada." An attitudinal survey completed for the CAHPER Outdoor Committee and presented at the CAHPER Conference, Victoria, 11 June 1981.

Hawley, D.L. "The Legal Liability of Physical Education Teachers in Canada." Master of Arts Thesis, University of Alberta, 1974.

McNulty, P.M. "Legal Liability of the Physical Education Teacher." Master of Arts Thesis, University of British Columbia, 1975.

Neil, R. and J. Blimkie. "Legal Liability." Ottawa: Coaching Association of Canada, Item No. 4, circa 76.

Palm, J. "Adventure Versus Risk." Paper presented to the National Outdoor and Environmental Education Conference, 4 October 1975.

Picard, E.I. and S.W. Mendryk. "Legal Liability in Physical Education and Athletics." Paper presented at the Conference on Curriculum Development and Teaching in Sports Medicine, Edmonton, 19–21 June 1981.

Power, M. "Recreation and the Law." Paper presented to the Recreation Board Members' Provincial Workshop, Alberta, 19 March 1978.

Proceedings from the Public Inquiry held into the death of M.L. Williams, 14 April 1975, Edmonton, Alberta.

Thompson, S. "Self and Groups in Outdoor Education." Master of Arts Thesis, University of Alberta, 1974.

Wood, A. "Insurance and Outdoor Programming: The Insurer's Perspective." Presented at the Calgary Area Outdoor Council Symposium on Legal Liability and Risk Management, Calgary, Alberta, October 1986.

Wuyda-Hanna, G. "The Legal Liability of Outdoor Education in Canada." Master of Arts Thesis, University of Alberta, 1983.

Monographs/Reports

Canadian Mountain Holidays. *Heliskiing Handbook.* n.d.

Fitness and Amateur Sport. Final Report of the Commission on the Insurance Crisis Facing Canada's National Sport and Recreation Associations, Ottawa, October 1986.

Glassford, R.G., R. Moriarty and G. Redmond. "Physical Activity and Legal Liability." CAHPER Research Council Monograph, 1978.

Gmoser, H. "Operators Manual." Association of British Columbia Heli-ski Operators in co-operation with the Government of B.C., Ministry of Lands, Parks and Housing, Parks and Outdoor Recreation Division, n.d.

Hanna, G. "Safety Oriented Guidelines for Outdoor Leadership and Programming." Ottawa: CAHPER. 1986.

March, B., B. Henderson, E. Grav, S. Kalef, and B. Leroy. "Legal Liability in Outdoor Education/Recreation in Alberta." Calgary: Alberta Law Foundation, 1981.

National Safety Network. *Annual Review.* Belfontaine, Ohio: National Safety Network, 1987 and 1988.

Robertson, B.W. Selected Cases on Negligence Liability in Parks, Recreation and Sport. Wolfville, N.S.: Recreation Resource Centre of Nova Scotia, 1987.

Personal Contacts

Anhorn, P. National Research Council, BCIT/NRC Avalanche Course, Mount Assiniboine Lodge, 19 January 1986.

Conrad, P. Alberta Sport Council, Edmonton, Alberta, 27 April, 1988.

Hale, A. Director of the National Safety Network, Columbus, Ohio, 5 February 1987.

Kochanski, M. Freelance Outdoor Instructor, Edmonton, Alberta, 6 May 1984.

Payment, R. Executive Director, Canadian Ski Association. Correspondence to CSA Board of Directors, 27 January 1986.

Whitehouse, R. Manager of Risk Management of the Government of Alberta, Edmonton, Alberta, 14 September 1982.

Canadian Cases

Ainge v. *Siemon et al.* (1971), 19 D.L.R. (3d) 531 (Ont. H. Ct.); [1971] 30.R.119.

Baldwin v. *Lyons et al.* [1963] 36 D.L.R. 244 (S.C.C.).

Beauparlant v. *Appleby Separate School Board of Trustees* [1955] 4 D.L.R. 558 (Ont. H. Ct.).

Bisson v. *Corporation of Powell River* (1967), 62 W.W.R. 707 (B.C.C.A.).

Boese v. *Board of Education of St. Paul's Roman Catholic Separate School District No. 20 (Saskatoon)* (1976), Q.B.D. 607 (Sask. Q.B.).

Brost v. *Board of Trustees of Eastern Irrigation* [1955] 3 D.L.R. 159 (Alta. C.A.).

Bundas v. *Oyma Regional Park Authority* (1980), 4 Sask. R. 124 (Sask. Q.B.).
Butterfield v. *Sibbit and Nipissing Electric Co.* [1950] 4 D.L.R. 302 (Ont. H. Ct.).
Butterworth v. *Collegiate Institute Board of Etobicoke* (1940), D.L.R. 446 (Ont. C.A.).
Crocker v. *Sundance Northwest Resorts Ltd.* (1985), 33 C.C.L.T. 73 (Ont. S.C.).; June 1988, Supreme Court of Canada case report.
Delaney et al. v. *Cascade River Holidays Ltd. et al.* (1982), 34 B.C.L.R. 62 (B.C.S.C.); (1983), 24 C.C.L.T. 8 (B.C.C.A.).
Deziel et al. v. *Deziel* [1953] 1 D.L.R. 651 (Ont. H. Ct.).
Diversified Holdings v. *R. in Right of B.C.* [1982] 133 D.L.R. (3) 712.
Dodd et al. v. *Cook et al.* (1956), 4 D.L.R. (2d) 43 (Ont. H. Ct.).
Dukes v. *Vancouver* (4 December 1973), unreported case (B.C.S.C.).
Durham et al. v. *Public School Board of Township School Area of North Oxford* (1960), 23 D.L.R. (2d) 719 (Ont. C.A.).
Dyck v. *Manitoba Snowmobile Association Inc. and Wood* [1985] 4 W.W.R. 318; 32 C.C.L.T. 153.
Dziwenka v. *Mapplebeck* [1972] 1 W.W.R. 350 (S.C.C.).
Eyers v. *Gillis and Warren* [1940] 4 D.L.R. 747.
Fink v. *Greeniaus* (1973), 43 D.L.R. (3d) 485.
Flett v. *Coulter* (1903), 5 D.L.R. 375.
Gard v. *Board of School Trustees of Duncan* (1946), 1 W.W.R. 305 (B.C.C.A.).
Gibbons et al. v. *Harris* [1924] 1 W.W.R. 675 (Alta. S.C.).
Gilbert v. *Lamont* (1981), 29 Nfld. and P.E.I. R. 258 (P.E.I.S.C.).
Grieco et al. v. *L'Externat Classique St. Croix* [1962] S.C.R. 519 (Que. S.C.).
Harrison v. *Toronto Motor Car et al.* [1945] 1 O.R. 9.
Hatfield v. *Pearson* (1956), 20 W.W.R. 580 (B.C.C.A.); 17 W.W.R. 575 (B.C.S.C.).
Haynes v. *C.P.R.* (1972), 31 D.L.R. (3d) 62 (B.C.C.A.).
Henricks et al. v. *R.* [1969] 9 D.L.R. (3d) 454 (S.C.C.).
Hicks v. *British Transport Commission* [1958] 1 W.L.R. 493.
Holmes v. *Goldenberg* [1953] 1 D.L.R. 92 (N.S.C.A.).
Holomis v. *Dubuc* [1975] 56 D.L.R. (3d) 351.
Horsley et al. v. *MacLaren et al.* [1970] 2 O.R. 487; (1972), 22 D.L.R. (3d) 545 (S.C.C.).; (1969), 2 O.R. 137.
James v. *River East School* (1975), 64 D.L.R. (3d) 338 (Man. C.A.).
The King v. *Laperriere* [1946] S.C.R. 415.
Levine et al. v. *Board of Education of the City of Toronto* [1933] O.W.N. 238.
Lowry et al. v. *Canadian Mountain Holidays Ltd. et al.* (1985), 33 C.C.L.T. 261 (B.C.S.C.); (1987), 40 C.C.L.T. 1 (B.C.C.A.).
Lyster v. *Fortress Mountain Resorts Ltd.* (1978), 6 Alta. L.R. (2d) 338.
Matthews et al. v. *MacLaren et al. Horsley et al.* v. *MacLaren et al.* (1969), 2 O.R. 144.
McEllistrum v. *Etches* [1956] S.C.R. 787; 6 D.L.R. (2d) 1.
McErlean v. *Sarel and the City of Brampton* (1985), 32 C.C.L.T. 199; (1988), 42 C.C.L.T. (Ont. C.A.) 78.

McKay v. *Board of Govan School Unit No. 29 of Saskatchewan* [1968] S.C.R. 589 (S.C.C.).

McWilliam v. *Thunder Bay Flying Club* [1950] O.W.N. 696 (Ont. H. Ct.).

Mercer v. *Gray* [1941] 3 D.L.R. 564 (Ont. C.A.).

Messenger et al. v. *Sears and Murray Knowles Ltd.* (1960), 23 D.L.R. (2d) 297.

Meyers et al. v. *Peel County Board of Education* (1977), 2 C.C.L.T. 269; (1981) unreported S.C.C. case notes; [1981] S.C.C.D. 3081–01.

Michalak v. *Dalhousie College and University, Governers of* (1983), 61 N.S.R (2d) 374.

Moddejonge v. *Huron County Board of Education* (1972), 2 O.R. 437 (Ont. H. Ct.).

Murray et al. v. *Board of Education of the City of Belleville* [1943] 1 D.L.R. 494 (Ont. H. Ct.).

Nickell v. *City of Windsor* (1927), 59 O.L.R. 618.

Oke v. *Weide Transport Ltd.* (1964), 46 D.L.R. (2d) 53 (Man. C.A.).

Oulette v. *Johnson* [1963] S.C.R. 96.

Pawlak and Pawlak v. *Doucette and Reinks* (1985), 2 W.W.R. 588 (B.C.S.C.).

Pearson v. *Vancouver Board of School Trustees et al.* [1941] 3 W.W.R. 874 (B.C.S.C.).

Piszel v. *Board of Education of Etobicoke* (1977), 16 O.R. (2d) 22 (Ont. C.A.).

Phillips v. *Regina Public Schools District No. 4 Board of Education* (1976), 1 C.C.L.T. 197 (Sask. Q.B.).

Pook v. *Ernesttown Public School Trustees* [1944] 4 D.L.R. 268.

Queensway Tank Lines Ltd. v. *Moise* [1970] 1 O.R. 535.

R. v. *Saskatchewan Wheat Pool* [1983] 1 S.C.R. 205.

Rheaume v. *Gowland* (1978), 91 D.L.R. (3d) 223 (B.C.S.C.).

Rootes v. *Skelton* (1967), 116 C.L.R. 383.

Rose v. *Plenty* [1976] 1 W.L.R. 141.

Rudko et al. v. *R.* (1983), 1 W.W.R. 741.

Ryan et al. v. *Hickson et al.* (1974), 55 D.L.R. (3d) 196.

Saari v. *Sunshine Riding Academy Ltd.* (1967), 65 D.L.R. (2d) 92 (Man. Q.B.).

Schade and Schade v. *Winnipeg School District No. 1 et al.* (1959), 28 W.W.R. 577 (Man. C.A.).

Scoffield et al. v. *Public School Board No. 20 North York* [1942] O.W.N. 458 (Ont. C.A.).

School Division of Assiniboine South No. 3 v. *Hoffer et al.* (1971), 21 D.L.R. (3d) 608; [1971] 1 W.W.R. 1; 4 W.W.R. 746.

School Division of Assiniboine South No. 3 and Hoffer et al. v. *Great Winnipeg Gas Company Ltd.* [1971] 4 W.W.R. 752.

Schwab v. *R.* (1984), Alta D. 3388-03.

Seamone v. *Fancy* [1924] 1 D.L.R. 650.

Seymour v. *Winnipeg Electric Railway* 13 (1910), W.L.R. 566 (Man. C.A.).

Sheasgreen et al. v. *Morgan et al.* [1952] 1 D.L.R. 48 (B.C.S.C.).

Sholtes v. *Stranaghan et al.* (1981), 8 A.C.W.S. (2d) 219 (B.C.S.C.).

Siddal v. *Corporation of District of Oak Bay* [1980] B.C.D. Civ. 3374-09.

Smith v. *Horizon Aero Sports Ltd. et al.* (1981), 130 D.L.R. (3d) 91; [1982]

B.C.D. Civ. 3391-01 (B.C.S.C.).

Smith v. Rae (1919), O.L.R. 518.

Starr and McNulty v. Crone [1950] 4 D.L.R. 433; 2 W.W.R. 560.

Sturdy et al. v. R. (1974), 47 D.L.R. (3d) 71.

Striefel v. S., B. and G. [1957] 25 W.W.R. 182 (B.C.S.C.).

Taylor v. R. (1978), 95 D.L.R. (3d) 82 (B.C.S.C.).

Teasdale v. MacIntyre [1968] S.C.R. 735.

Thornton et al. v. Board of School Trustees of District No. 57 (Prince George) et al. [1976] 5 W.W.R. 240 (B.C.C.A.); [1978] 2 S.C.R.

Toromont Industrial Holdings Ltd. v. Thorne, Gunn, Helliwell and Christenson (1976), 14 O.R. (2d) 87 (Ont. C.A.).

Turanec v. Ross (1980), 21 B.C.L.R. 198 (B.C.S.C.).

Tyler v. Board of Ardath [1935] 2 D.L.R. 814.

Walker v. Sheffield Bronze (1977), 2 C.C.L.T. 97.

Walton v. Vancouver [1924] 2 D.L.R. 387 (B.C.C.A.).

Ware's Taxi Ltd. v. Gilliham [1949] S.C.R. 637.

Wilson v. Blue Mountain Resorts Ltd. (1974), 4 O.R. (2d) 713; (1975), 49 D.L.R. (3d) 161 (Ont. H. Ct.).

British Cases

Addie v. Pumbreck [1929] A.C. 358.

Ashdown v. Williams (1957), 1 Q.B. 409.

Baker v. Hopkins [1958] 3 All E.R. 147 (Q.B.D.).

Blyth v. Birmingham Water Works Co. (1856), 11 Ex. 781.

Bolton et al. v. Stone [1951] 1 All E.R. 1078.

Brandon v. Osborne, Garrett and Co. [1924] 1 K.B. 548.

Butt v. Cambridgeshire and Isle of Ely C.C. (1969), 119 New L.J. 1118.

Butterfield v. Forrester (1809), 103 E.R. 926 (K.B.D.).

Carmarthenshire County Council v. Lewis [1955] A.C. 559 (H.L.).

Chipchase v. British Titan Products Co. [1956] 1 Q.B. 545; [1956] 1 All E.R. 613.

C.P.R. v. Lockhart [1942] A.C. 591.

Dulieu v. White and Sons [1901] 2 K.B. 669.

East Suffolk Rivers Catchment Board v. Kent et al. [1941] A.C. 74.

Gautret v. Egerton (1867), L.R. C.P. 371.

Glasgow Corporation v. Taylor (1922), 1 A.C. 44.

Gorris v. Scott (1874), L.R. 9 Ex. 125; 43 L.J. Ex. 92; 30 L.J. 431.

Hedley Byrne and Co. Ltd. v. Heller and Partners Ltd. [1964] A.C. 465 (H.L.).

Hughes v. Lord Advocate [1963] A.C. 837.

Indermaur v. Dames (1866), L.R. 1 C.P. 274.; (1867), L.R. 2 C.P. 311.

Jeffery v. London County Council (1954), 119 J.P. 43.

Latham v. R. Johnson and Nephew Ltd. [1913] K.B. 398.

Liddle v. Yorks North Riding (1944), 2 K.B. 101.

Market Investigations Ltd. v. Minister of Social Security [1969] 2 Q.B.D. 173.

Marston v. St. George Hospital (1956), 1 All E.R. 384.

M'Alister (or Donoghue) v. *Stevenson* [1932] A.C. 532 (H.L.).
McKew v. *Holland et al.* [1969] 3 All E.R. 1621 (H.L.).
Mersey Dock and Harbour Board v. *Coggins and Griffiths Ltd.* [1946] 2 All E.R. 345; [1947] A.C. 1.
Morren v. *Swinton and Pendlebury Council* [1965] 2 All E.R. 349.
Nance v. *British Columbia Electric Railway Company Ltd.* [1951] A.C. 601.
Nicholson v. *Westmorland County Council, The Times,* 25 October 1962.
Olsen v. *Corry* [1936] 3 All E.R. 241 (K.B.D.).
Ould v. *Butler's Wharf* [1953] 2 L.R. 44.
Overseas Tankship (U.K. Ltd.) (The Wagon Mound (No. 1)). v. *Morts Dock and Engineering Co. Ltd.* [1961] A.C. 422.
Phillips v. *Britannia Hygienic Laundry Co. Ltd.* [1923] 2 K.B. 862; 129 L.T. 177; 93 L.J. K.B.S.
Poland v. *John Parr and Sons* [1927] 1 K.B. 236.
Smerkinich v. *Newport Corporation* (1912), L.C.T. 265.
Smith v. *Leech Brain and Co.* [1962] 2 Q.B.D. 414 (Q.B).
Tomlinson v. *Manchester Corporation* (1947), 111 J.P. 503.
Weston v. *London* [1941] 1 All E.R. 555.
Wieland v. *Cyril Lord Carpets Ltd.* [1969] 3 All E.R. 1006.
Williams v. *Eady* (1893), 9 T.L.R. 637; 10 T.L.R 41.

American Cases

Beaumont v. *Surrey County Council* (1968), 112 S.J. 704.
Morehouse College v. *Russel* (1964), 136 S.E. (2d) 179.
Ross v. *Colorado Outward Bound* (1977), unreported case (December, 1978).
Wagner v. *International Railway Co.* (1921), 133 N.E. 437; 232 N.Y.S. 176.

Other Cases

McHale v. *Watson* [1966] 39 A.L.J.R. 459 (H. Ct. Aust.).
Sullivan v. *Creed* [1904] 2 I.R. 317.

Statutes

An Act Respecting Emergency Medical Aid, R.S.S. 1976, c. 17.
Alberta School Trustee Act, R.S.A. 1970, c. 330.
British North America Act (1867), 30 and 31 Victoria, c. 3.
Canada Shipping Act, R.S.C. 1952, c. 29.
Canadian and British Insurance Companies Act, R.S.C. 1970, c. 1–15.
Contributory Negligence Act, R.S.A. 1970, c. 65.
Courts of Justice Act, R.S.O. 1980, c. 223.
Crown Liability Act, 1952–53 (Can.), c. 30, R.S.C. 1970, c. C-38.
Education Act, R.S.N.S. 1967, c. 81.
Education Act, R.S.O. 1974, c. 109.
Education Act, R.S.S. 1978, c. 17.
Emergency Medical Aid Act, R.S.A. 1970, c. 122, 1975 (2), c. 26.
Environment Council Act, R.S.A. 1970, c. 125.

Family Compensation Act, R.S.B.C. 1969, c. 120.
Family Reform Act, R.S.O. 1980, c. 2, s. 60.
Forests Act, R.S.A. 1971, c. 37.
Highway Traffic Act, R.S.A. 1975 (2), c. 56.
Highway Traffic Act, R.S.O. 1970, c. 202.
Judicature Act, R.S.A. 1970, c. 193; 1974, c. 65.
Limitations Act, R.S.O. 1970, c. 246.
Limitations of Actions Act, R.S.A. 1970, c. 209.
Limitations of Actions Act, R.S.N.S. 1967, c. 168.
Municipal Government Act, R.S.A. 1970, c. 246.
Municipal School Administration Act, 1970, c. 249.
National Parks Act, R.S.C. 1970, c. 189.
Negligence Act, R.S.O. 1970, c. 296.
Occupiers' Liability Act, R.S.A. 1973, c. 79.
Occupiers' Liability Act, R.S.B.C. 1974, c. 60.
Occupier's Liability Act, R.S.O. 1980, c. 14.
Occupier's Liability Act, S.M. 1982–84, c. 29.
Petty Trespass Act, R.S.A. 1970, c. 273.
Proceedings Against the Crown Act, R.S.A. 1970, c. 285.
Provincial Parks Act, R.S.A. 1980, CP-22.
Public Authorities Protection Act, R.S.O. 1970, c. 374.
Public Lands Act, R.S.A. 1970, c. 297.
Public Schools Act, R.S.B.C. 1960, c. 319.
Public School Act, R.S.B.C. 1974, c. 74.
Public Schools Act, R.S.M. 1970, c. 215.
Public Trustee Act, R.S.A. 1970, c. 301.
School Act, R.S.A. 1970, c. 329.
School Act, R.S.N.S. 1970, c. 346.
School Act, R.S.S. 1965, c. 184.
Secondary School Act, R.S.M. 1970, c. 250.
Societies Act, R.S.S. 1965, c. 142.
Societies Act, R.S.N.S. 1967, c. 286.
Societies Act, R.S.B.C. 1979, c. 390.
Supreme Court Act, R.S.C. 1970, c. 259.
Surrogate Court Act, R.S.A. 1970, c. 357.
Teaching Profession Act, R.S.A. 1970, c. 362.
Tortfeasors and Contributory Negligence Act, R.S.M. 1954, c. 266.
Volunteer Services Act, S.N.S. 1977, c. 20.
Wildlife Act, R.S.B.C. 1979, c. 433.
Wildlife Act, R.S.N.S. 1987, c. 13.
Wildlife Act, S.M. 1980, c. 73.
Wildlife Act, R.S.A. 1987, c. W9-1.

BY-LAWS

Edmonton Parks and Recreation Department, City of Edmonton By-law No. 2202 (as amended by By-laws No. 2281, 2750, 2874, 2929, 2977 and 3015).
Parks/School Joint Use Agreement, City of Edmonton By-law No. 5769.

INDEX